Thinking
Like a
TERRORIST

Potomac Titles of Related Interest

Al Qaeda's Great Escape: The Military and the Media on Terror's Trail
by Philip Smucker

Counterterrorism Strategies: Successes and Failures of Six Nations edited
by Yonah Alexander

*Hide and Seek: Intelligence, Law Enforcement, and the Stalled War
on Terrorist Finance*
by John A. Cassara

Imperial Hubris: Why the West Is Losing the War on Terror
by Michael Scheuer

Insurgency and Terrorism: From Revolution to Apocalypse
by Bard E. O'Neill

*Through Our Enemies' Eyes: Osama bin Laden, Radical Islam,
and the Future of America*
by Michael Scheuer

War of the Flea: The Classic Study of Guerrilla Warfare
by Robert Taber

Why Secret Intelligence Fails
by Michael A. Turner

Winning the Un-War: A New Strategy for the War on Terrorism
by Charles Peña

Thinking
Like a
TERRORIST

Insights of a Former FBI Undercover Agent

Mike German

Potomac Books, Inc.
Washington, D.C.

Published in the United States by Potomac Books, Inc. All rights reserved. No part of
this book may be reproduced in any manner whatsoever without written permission
from the publisher, except in the case of brief quotations embodied in critical articles
and reviews.

Stephen Band's and Steve Salmieri's endorsements of *Thinking Like a Terrorist* do not
necessarily represent the views of the FBI.

Library of Congress Cataloging-in-Publication Data
German, Mike, 1963–
 Thinking like a terrorist : insights of a former FBI undercover agent / Mike German.
  p. cm.
 Includes bibliographical references and index.
 ISBN-13: 978-1-59797-025-9 (alk. paper)
 ISBN-10: 1-59797-025-5 (alk. paper)
 1. Terrorism—United States. 2. Terrorism—United States—Prevention. 3. Terrorists—
United States. 4. War on Terrorism, 2001- 5. Radicalism—United States. I. Title.
 HV6432.G48 2006
 363.325—dc22

                           2006019251

Printed in the United States of America on acid-free paper that meets the American
National Standards Institute Z39-48 Standard.

Potomac Books, Inc.
22841 Quicksilver Drive
Dulles, Virginia 20166

First Edition

10 9 8 7 6 5 4 3 2 1

Contents

Preface   vii

1. Prologue: An Unusual Education in Terrorism   1

Part I: The Trouble With Terrorism
2. The Difficult Definition   29
3. Getting Beyond Good and Evil   37
4. Compounding Confusion   55

Part II: Mind-set and Methods
5. Understanding Political Violence   75
6. Grading the Government   83
7. Methods and Motives   95
8. Case Study #1: A Successful Terror Campaign   111
9. Ranking the Resistance   123
10. Terrorism Types   133

Part III: How to Win
11. Case Study #2: The Ku Klux Klan   139
12. A Winning Strategy Against Extremist Terrorists   149
13. Case Study #3: Lessons of the IRA   159
14. A Winning Strategy Against Legitimately Motivated Terrorists   173
15. Analysis of the Global War on Terrorism   179
16. Our Constitutional Shield Against Terrorism   191

Notes   201
Bibliography   219
Index   231
About the Author   239

Preface

As the fifth full year of America's "Global War on Terrorism" wound down, U.S. National Counterterrorism Center statistics revealed the number of international terrorist attacks in 2005 more than tripled those in 2004.[1] A year earlier the same agency reported a similar tripling of attacks in 2004 as compared to 2003, which had seen the highest number of terrorist incidents recorded in the previous twenty-one years.[2]

U.S. defense secretary Donald Rumsfeld once complained that he lacked the "metrics" necessary to measure success in the Global War on Terrorism,[3] but this data reflects a disturbing trend. And as the number of terrorist attacks continues to increase, so does the number of terrorists. Porter Goss, then the Central Intelligence Agency's director, told Congress in early 2005 that Islamic extremist groups were exploiting the war in Iraq to recruit and train a new generation of terrorists.[4] At this writing, the primary leaders of al Qaeda and the Taliban remain at large, deadly insurgencies rage in Iraq and Afghanistan, and representatives of U.S.–designated terrorist organizations won parliamentary elections in the Palestinian territories and Lebanon. A 2006 Department of Defense counterterrorism study reportedly identified thirty new al Qaeda–affiliated terrorist groups that have been created since September 11, 2001.[5] We may not have metrics to measure our success, but these realities certainly illuminate our failures. If the Global War on Terrorism's goal is to stop terrorism we are clearly losing. But why?

It is certainly not from a lack of effort. The U.S. military, the most skilled and equipped force in history, is engaged in Afghanistan, Iraq, and other untold places around the globe, demonstrating a national will to go on the offensive against terrorists and the states that sponsor them. U.S. intelligence and law enforcement agencies are now focused on counterterrorism as their top priority, and they are strengthening the country's defenses as never before. Congress has provided ample funding and has given the administration unprecedented powers to act against threats to national security. The American public has become more vigilant and has generously sacrificed civil liberties in exchange for greater security. The U.S. government has "taken the gloves off" and adopted aggressive techniques that once might never have been considered: extrajudicial arrests and detentions, renditions, secret prisons, and torture. Yet the number of terrorists and the number of attacks keeps growing. What more can we do?

The overarching problem, I believe, is a fundamental failure to understand terrorists—who they are, how they operate, and most important, why they think using indiscriminate violence will get them what they want. Our failure to understand them is peculiar, because terrorism is all about the message and terrorists are vocal about who they are, what they want, and how they intend to get it. They are prolific writers and enthusiastic public speakers, but we rarely pay enough attention to what they write or to what they say. Their words are dismissed as propaganda, hate speech, or the rantings of madmen.

In remarks criticizing leaks from the U.S. intelligence community, White House spokesman Trent Duffy once said, "The fact is al Qaeda's playbook is not printed on Page One,"[6] but he was wrong. The al Qaeda playbook was published years ago in fact, and updates appear regularly on the Internet and in audio and video recordings. These messages clearly delineate the group's operational goals and forecast the expected results. Incredibly, the U.S. government's responses often fulfill their predictions.

Since September 11, 2001, U.S. politicians often refer to the Global War on Terrorism as a "new kind of war," but it isn't new. Modern-day terrorists follow strategies pioneered centuries ago by Zealots, Thugs, and Assassins, ancient groups of varying ethnic, religious, and national origin who used bloody murder as a tool of political intimidation and earned permanent places of infamy in our lexicon. Those al Qaeda hijackers who used small knives to take over four planes on 9/11 were throwbacks to the Zealots Sicarii, known literally as "dagger-men"—and to the Assassins, who, as their ideological descendants, were never expected to survive their attacks. Today when U.S. political and military leaders speak of "our enemies" they often refer to them as "zealots," "thugs," and "assassins" without even a hint of irony. While al Qaeda follows an ancient game plan, American leaders pretend it's all brand new. This failure to look at the past is our mistake.

International terrorism experts marvel at al Qaeda's post–9/11 evolution from a hierarchal organization into independent groups of loosely associated, autonomous cells, but white supremacist groups in the United States pioneered this "leaderless resistance" strategy decades ago and published papers on it. Don't these experts think al Qaeda can read? The sophisticated terrorists of al Qaeda might appear to have little in common with neo-Nazi skinheads living in the United States, but that assumption again ignores history. Hitler's Third Reich had a Muslim Division in Croatia, organized by the Grand Mufti of Jerusalem, and the Nazis had strong ties to the Muslim Brotherhood in Egypt, Palestine, and Iraq. These ideologies are not as different as they might have seemed, and the newly minted term *Islamo-fascism* is not such a modern concept. A study of these groups' methods would reveal more similarities, yet the U.S. government treats domestic and international terrorism as completely different phenomena.

Perhaps it sees al Qaeda as different from the white supremacist movement because it represents a threat from abroad, and perhaps foreign threats justify a different, more vigorous response, such as curtailing traditional protections of civil liberties and due process to ensure that distant enemies cannot establish a foothold in the United States. Try to imagine what would happen to U.S. civil liberties if foreign-born terrorists infiltrated the country and instigated the president's assassination. Imagine if they staged riots, strikes, and bombings in major U.S. cities, including dozens of letter bombs sent to prominent government officials and business leaders, a suicide bomber blowing himself up on the attorney general's front lawn, and finally, a truck bombing in the heart of New York's financial district. Would Americans still care about civil liberties and the niceties of their justice system, or would they expect the government to err on the side of security, to make mass arrests, and to intern or deport people based on any evidence connecting them to the ideas these terrorists espouse? Would the government allow this movement's ideological leaders to continue to organize and agitate their followers at public rallies, or would it arrest and deport them for just talking?

We don't have to imagine this scenario. We just have to pick up a history book or type "Red Scare" into an Internet search engine and see how it all played out almost a hundred years ago. Red scares also occurred in the 1950s and the 1970s, and the reactionary 1919 Palmer raids were repeated in the form of the House Un-American Activities Hearings of the 1950s and the Federal Bureau of Investigation (FBI) Counter-intelligence Program (COINTELPRO) the 1960s and 1970s.

Our history and that of other nations' struggles with terrorism over the years provide a treasure trove of intelligence, a virtual guidebook for objectively analyzing which counterterrorism measures work and which do not. History shows us what our enemies might do next and what effect our policies could have on their ability to recruit new members, organize new attacks, and achieve their ultimate political goals. But this intelligence is also all but ignored.

We focus almost exclusively on what we don't know in formulating counterterrorism policies—the who, the where, and the when of the next attack—instead of focusing on what we do know. We spend our resources setting up protective security, hardening targets, and limiting public access to places we think terrorists might strike. We demand more intelligence, we scrutinize everyone a little more carefully, and we collect vast amounts of data like stacks of hay in the hope that the needle we're looking for will somehow be found among the chaff. But putting our energies into these misguided efforts is exactly what the terrorists want us to do, and if we read what they wrote we would know this fact. Ignoring their writings and our own history is the true failure of U.S. counterterrorism policies.

Unfortunately, attempting to understand terrorists is too often mistaken for sympathizing with terrorists. In June 2005 while defending the Global War on Terror, presidential adviser Karl Rove said, "Conservatives saw the savagery of 9/11 and the attacks and prepared for war; liberals saw the savagery of the 9/11 attacks and wanted to prepare indictments and offer therapy and understanding for our attackers."[7] But understanding does not connote sympathy. An anti-intellectual, antiliberal government response that favors using violence and the force of will over moral standards and the rule of law is exactly the response terrorist groups need to prosper. If we better understood what terrorists wanted, and what terrorists feared, we would see a better outcome.

When a misunderstanding of the enemy and his goals drives U.S. counterterrorism policies, we shouldn't be surprised at the results. A small, stateless band of organized criminals spent years calling for an international "holy war," and we responded with the Global War on Terrorism. Does this make sense?

I didn't know much about terrorism in 1992 when I was selected to go undercover and penetrate neo-Nazi skinhead groups conspiring to start a race war in Los Angeles. But I spent the next dozen years learning about it from the most knowledgeable instructors on earth. They weren't from the FBI, some university, or a government think tank. Everything I know about terrorism I learned from terrorists.

To become a terrorist I needed to learn things other students of terrorism usually don't. To successfully infiltrate the white supremacists' world, I needed to know not just their ideology, their motivations, and their methods, but even what they ate for breakfast and, more important, what they didn't eat. As I immersed myself in their world, they challenged all of my preconceptions. I didn't find crazed, hate-filled lunatics, but instead thoughtful, committed true believers and idealists who felt their use of violence was morally justified and necessary to secure their community's survival. This idealism separates them from ordinary criminals, and it is what makes them so dangerous. As Brian Flanagan, a former member of the Weather Underground Organization, once put it: "If you think that you have the moral high-ground that's a very dangerous position and you can do some really dreadful things."[8]

When I went undercover I discovered enigmatic underground communities living right here in the United States that were actively, but surreptitiously, at war with mainstream society. I met middle-class suburban families, teenage honor students, educated professionals, and businessmen—people you pass in the supermarket everyday without a second glance. But I know they were part of a secret war because I bought their bombs, stored their weapons, and listened in as they planned horrific terrorist attacks.

I spent months at a time working directly with people who conceived, planned, and committed terrorist acts of violence. All the while they considered themselves the good guys, soldiers in a just cause making personal sacrifices for their community's benefit. I learned their secrets because they spoke to me and trained me as if I was one of them. I learned that despite my abhorrence for their ideologies, I had far more in common with these terrorists than I ever would have imagined. This insight allowed me to quickly infiltrate their ranks and gain their trust, only to betray them before they could accomplish their awful goals.

By living among terrorists I got to know them as rational, thinking human beings whose violence, though cruel, was chillingly calculated to help them reach specific, articulated goals. I learned how terrorist groups recruit, indoctrinate, organize, and operate. As I prepared for assignments against right-wing, left-wing, and Islamic fundamentalist terrorists, I learned how to see the world through their eyes. I learned how to think like a terrorist. I learned despite differing, even conflicting ideologies, their motives and methods were the same. Most important, I learned if I wanted to stop them I had to understand them, and if I wanted to understand them I needed to pay attention to what they wrote and listen to what they said.

The bad news is the terrorists have a real plan, a blueprint that has brought them victory in the past, and they are executing that plan perfectly today. The good news is their plan is published and available to anyone who bothers to read it. Once the terrorists' plan is understood, developing a counterstrategy is easy.

In this book I will use my unusual education as a terrorist to explore why terrorism is such a persistent and difficult problem. I will show how and why terrorism works and, in turn, why our current approach to counterterrorism isn't working. I will expose inherent biases in the language we use to discuss terrorism, biases that blind us to the true nature of the problem we face and prevent us from developing effective policies to stop the violence. I will expose the terrorists' true goal, and I will reveal what terrorists fear most.

1

Prologue: An Unusual Education in Terrorism

As I have said, only a very credulous soul could think of binding himself to observe the rules of the game when he has to face a player for whom those rules are nothing but a mere bluff or a means of serving his own interests, which means he will discard them when they prove no longer useful for his purpose.

—ADOLF HITLER, *MEIN KAMPF*

I made a good terrorist. I was intelligent, conscientious, and capable. Once my eyes were open to the truth I was fully committed to the cause. I didn't know much about weapons or tactics, but I was willing to learn and, more important, willing to take the risks necessary to move from talk to revolution.

These qualities aren't what most government officials or terrorism experts use to describe terrorists. They use words like *evil, diabolical, fanatical, pathological,* and *insane.* But terrorists know they can't rely on psychopaths. They need someone like me. I had the humility to take orders without question, the guts to put their words into action, and the competence to do it without getting caught. The only thing I lacked was loyalty.

This small but fatal flaw meant the Fourth Reich skinheads would never fulfill their plan to storm Sunday services at the Los Angeles First African Methodist Episcopal Church with blazing machine guns and homemade pipe bombs. It meant dozens of automatic weapons, silencers, and improvised explosive devices manufactured for a war of resistance against the federal government would never be used, and it meant more than a score of extremists would go to jail rather than commit acts of terrorism. Because while I was a good terrorist, I was a better FBI agent.

I joined the FBI in 1988, directly after graduating from Northwestern University Law School. I can't say I was at the top of my class, but with a law degree in hand I had plenty of options. I could easily have started a comfortable and financially lucrative career in private practice. But as the son of a U.S. Army officer I was raised with a strong sense of duty to country, and I felt committed to finding a career in public service. I didn't see this obligation as a chore but rather as an opportunity, a chance to contribute to society in a meaningful way. I loved the law and believed that the government should defend justice and protect civil liberties. I wanted to be part of that effort, and I truly felt I could make a difference.

The government is riddled with lawyers, of course, so I could have applied for any number of jobs to satisfy my self-imposed obligation. I could have been a prosecutor or a civil attorney representing one of a dozen government agencies. But all these jobs had one major drawback: they were painfully boring. I barely managed to sit through three years of law school without losing my mind, and I dreaded the idea of taking a desk job in some drab government office. A thrill seeker by nature, I needed far more stimulation than even the best *Perry Mason* courtroom drama could muster. I needed to be active, physically engaged. I wanted to work with the law at the tip of the spear. I wanted to be in the FBI.

The FBI offered everything I was looking for. As a special agent I could use my legal education, enforcing federal law and defending constitutional rights, but I could also be out in the street, working on the front lines against crime. There were risks associated with a career in law enforcement, but I saw these risks as a challenge, as both a test of my commitment to my ideals and an opportunity for adventure. That the FBI was universally regarded as one of the elite law enforcement agencies in the world only added to the attraction. I wanted to be a G-man.

Fortunately for me, I was exactly what the FBI was looking for, too. In addition to my Army brat heritage and my legal education, my Irish-Catholic upbringing presumed a stable moral foundation and a sense of respect for authority. My background was free of any serious blemishes but showed enough scuffs to demonstrate a willingness to take risks. My record of accomplishment displayed independence, competence, and self-motivation. I was the quintessential all-American boy.

The FBI offered me the opportunity I wanted and a chance to use my talents to pursue worthy goals for an agency that represented the purest ideals: fidelity, bravery, and integrity. The job could be dangerous—FBI agents wear guns to work everyday for a reason—but the intense training, careful planning, and meticulous attention to detail mitigate the risks. FBI agents willingly put their lives on the line, but they aren't suicidal.

Still, few FBI agents ever join a terrorist group. In fact, only a small percentage of agents do any kind of undercover work at all. It wasn't part of my career plan when I received my first assignment to a bank fraud squad in Orange County, California, in 1988. I investigated white-collar criminals and made good use of my legal education. It wasn't as exciting as I had hoped for, but it was challenging work and a great opportunity to learn how to manage complex investigations.

But my career took a sharp turn in 1992, when an agent assigned to the Los Angeles Joint Terrorism Task Force (JTTF) asked me to go undercover for him. For more than a year the JTTF had been investigating violent neo-Nazi skinhead groups operating in the L.A. area during a period of pronounced racial unease. A cooperating witness, or CW in FBI parlance, had infiltrated one of the groups and was recording their meetings, but the JTTF needed an agent to go in and gather the evidence required to secure criminal convictions. In some ways I was an obvious choice. I had classic Aryan features—blonde hair and blue eyes—and although I was in my late twenties, I looked young enough to pass for a recent high school graduate.

I was not trained as an undercover agent, however, and I had no experience with terrorism investigations. In the four years I'd been an FBI agent, I'd never worked any violent crimes. I had a general knowledge of white supremacist groups from history books and news articles, and I certainly had met a few racists in my day, but I never interacted with anyone who claimed membership in a white hate organization. I expected I'd find a bunch of ignorant, belligerent, beer-fueled rednecks prone to spontaneous, mindless violence, and I was more than a little concerned about how I'd fit in. Their hateful ideology went against every value I was raised to respect, and with choirboy looks and a formal education I didn't seem to fit the profile of a white supremacist. Added to my concern was the knowledge that neo-Nazi groups were hyperconscious of law enforcement's interest in their activities. They'd been stung in undercover operations in the past, and they were always alert to "the Feds" trying to infiltrate their ranks. They had a record of being unforgiving to those they considered "race traitors." Everyone recognized this assignment was going to be dangerous.

There's no real incentive for FBI agents to accept an undercover assignment. In addition to the risk to their personal safety, the hours are terrible, mostly nights and weekends; they endure lengthy separations from friends and family; and they face a heavy administrative burden to boot. Every hour spent with the bad guys means at least an hour of preparation and two hours of administrative work afterward, debriefing the case agents, writing reports, and processing evidence. Working undercover does not pay extra and does not enhance their career. In fact, it does quite the opposite.

Many people advised me to pass on this assignment, and if I had looked at it logically I probably would have. But the case agent and the supervisor had confidence in me, and in the end, I saw it as an important investigation at a critical time. Los Angeles had been wracked by race riots after the 1991 Rodney King police beating, and everyone expected more violence. While the law enforcement community dreaded this possibility, the white supremacist community looked forward to it. They wanted to exploit the situation to instigate an all-out race war. If there was ever a case worth taking a big risk for, this one was it. I volunteered for the job.

The FBI did not give me any specialized terrorism training. Eventually I did take an undercover certification course, but the FBI didn't even offer a course that could teach me how white supremacist groups operated. I was just expected to jump in and figure a way to make it work without getting myself killed: sink or swim.

I wasn't completely naive about organized racism in America. When I lived in North Carolina as a kid I heard about Ku Klux Klan (KKK) cross burnings. White supremacists once came to my college campus to hand out something called *The White Man's Bible,* but no one took them seriously. They were dismissed as anachronistic remnants of a bygone era, a peek into the area's racist past. I figured I knew enough about white supremacist groups to get by. I couldn't have been more wrong.

I started preparing for the assignment by reviewing tape recordings the CW had made of his meetings with the various skinhead groups, but I had a hard time understanding what anyone was talking about. They were speaking English, but it seemed as if they were from an alien culture. They made almost no small talk. They didn't discuss the latest sporting events, recently released movies or popular television shows, or even what they'd seen on the evening news the night before. They were completely focused on their movement. They talked about the Zionist Occupied Government (ZOG), the Illuminati, the Trilateral Commission, the Bilderbergers, the Protocols of the Elders of Zion, and other shadowy conspiracies against the white race. They peppered their conversations with references to people and events I didn't recognize. Certain words seemed to carry significance beyond their normal meaning, as if they were speaking in code.

Imagine booking a well-educated person from New Zealand, who spoke perfect English but was unfamiliar with American culture, on a Sunday morning political talk show where the discussion topic was the Senate confirmation hearings of a Supreme Court justice nominee. The

New Zealander would have to try and absorb big concepts: the differences between Democrats and Republicans, the competing roles played by the separate branches of government under our Constitution, and how this nomination would affect the ideological balance on the Supreme Court. But subtle cultural references would be harder to pick up: how quoting from an article in the *New York Times* is different than quoting from an article in the *National Enquirer,* why the panelist from the American Civil Liberties Union (ACLU) always seems to disagree with the panelist from the Heritage Foundation, and what being "Borked" means. None of this language is intentionally coded, of course; the discussion just assumes a certain familiarity with American politics and culture. To the New Zealander, however, it would be gibberish. A smart New Zealander would keep his mouth shut to avoid looking like an idiot, and when I went undercover, that's exactly what I tried to do.

Meanwhile I read everything about these groups I could get my hands on. I was amazed at how much material white supremacist groups publish. During the course of the investigation, the CW had been given books, newspapers, pamphlets, magazines, and videotapes—literally bookcases full of material—and more arrived each week. At almost every white supremacist meeting, someone brought a new article or leaflet they wanted us to read. There were philosophical works, religious texts, military manuals, and news reports of significant events in the movement. Other papers read like celebrity gossip rags, with blow-by-blow coverage of all the internecine battles in the movement, providing not just a who's who but information about who was on the way up and who was going down at any given time. They also included articles of social interest, cartoons, children's books, and even racially themed works of fiction. These groups even had their own music and professional bands that toured the country singing racist rock songs. I discovered a complete underground community with its own values and traditions, its own heroes and villains, and its own successes and failures. This community wanted nothing to do with mainstream society, and for the most part they stayed separate and apart from it. I started reading as much of their material as I could to figure out what these people were talking about so I could participate in their conversation.

The quality and complexity of the material surprised me. They weren't just racist rants (though there were plenty of those). A philosophy major in college, I found much of their work as carefully written, well sourced, and logically argued as books I had read in college. In fact they often referred to philosophical works I had once studied.

One of the first things I discovered by reading this material was that white supremacist ideology was not monolithic. Several different religious, social, and political subgroups make up the white racialist movement. They all agree on the fundamental issues: race is the primary attribute of identity, the white race is pure and therefore superior to others, and finally this pure white race's survival is in peril from outside forces conspiring to destroy it. But each group comes to these conclusions following very different ideological paths.

The idea of white racial superiority is not new, of course. The United States only outlawed slavery 150 years ago, and Europeans justified their colonization of the new world with the common belief that white people had a moral obligation to rule over and "civilize" the darker-skinned peoples of the world. Anti-Semitism predates the Bible, and Jews suffered enslavement, forced exile, and murderous pogroms long before the Nazis' Holocaust. The idea of white racial superiority was rooted in various religious, philosophical, and even scientific belief systems that gradually lost popularity over time but never died out completely. These beliefs were no longer discussed in polite company, at least not directly, but they were passed down through the generations and kept circulating just under the surface of a more enlightened mainstream society.

The white supremacist movement has its own separate history that runs parallel to that of mainstream society, and it often views the same events through a very different lens. For instance, most people remember Henry Ford as the enterprising industrialist who founded the Ford Motor Company. White supermacists remember him as one of the twentieth century's leading anti-Semites and author of *The International Jew: The World's Foremost Problem.* In their version of history, World War II was not a victory of democratic values over the forces of fascism, but rather it was a disastrous "fratricidal war" in which white Americans were tricked into killing white Germans for the benefit of Jewish financiers who profited from the war. They maintain the Holocaust was a hoax designed to create white guilt.

Some white supremacist groups formed around a religious ideology. The infamous Aryan Nations, formerly of Hayden Lake, Idaho, was actually a church, whose formal name was the Church of Jesus Christ Christian, Aryan Nations. The leader of the Aryan Nations, a retired aeronautical engineer known as "Pastor" Richard Butler, preached a racist form of Christianity known as Christian Identity. Butler learned from the giants of the movement—Wesley Swift and William Potter Gale, a former aide to Gen. Douglas MacArthur during World War II and a recognized expert in guerrilla warfare.

Christian Identity followers believe that white people are the true Israelites of the Bible, the children of God from a lost tribe who fled the Middle East and settled in Europe. They believe Jesus Christ was not a

Jew, but a white man. In their interpretation of the Bible, Jews are descendants of Cain, a child born from a sexual liaison between Eve and the serpent in the Garden of Eden, literally Satan's offspring. Cain murdered his brother Abel in the first blow of a holy war that pits the children of God against the children of Satan. They believe the Jews' sole purpose on earth is to destroy God's children— the white race—and that the world is locked in a diabolical struggle between the forces of good and evil. They read a normal, King James version of the Christian Bible, with both the Old and the New Testaments, which any Christian would recognize, but they emphasize certain stories and specific passages they feel support their peculiar interpretation. They are a devout group for whom Bible study and prayer are important aspects of daily life, but these people are not lambs. Their reading of scriptures reveals the existence of a holy war, and they consider themselves God's warriors.

Other white supremacist groups organized around ideologies that are primarily political in nature. The White Aryan Resistance (WAR), the National Alliance, and the National Socialist Movement, for instance, are all neo-Nazi organizations that promote white unity and white nationalism under the concept "our race is our nation." They rely heavily on the political philosophy of Adolf Hitler's National Socialism as articulated in *Mein Kampf.*

Some groups, such as WAR, are openly antagonistic toward religion, particularly Christianity, which they consider to be a Jewish plot to subdue white nationalism by encouraging pacifism, tolerance, and forgiveness. Although their ideology is political, their devotion to their cause is as fervent as that of any religious fanatic.

As in mainstream society, these individuals can have both political and religious affiliations simultaneously. Outside their circles, for example, folks can be both Catholics and Republicans. Likewise, the white supremacists can be Identity Christians and National Socialists. In addition to being an Identity minister, Pastor Butler was an avowed Nazi, and swastikas adorned his church. Other groups mixed their political and religious philosophies into one ideology. The Ku Klux Klan members have long billed themselves as "white Christian patriots," but while they use the burning cross as a symbol of their Christian purity, their rhetoric is more oriented to social issues and is far less reliant on scripture than that of the Christian Identity devotees.

The different groups sometimes have common origins, with subgroups splintering off from a larger organization after ideological, strategic, or even personal differences between the leaders of the various factions. New groups spring up independently once in a while, typically under the charm of some charismatic self-appointed leader with a fresh twist on old themes. "New" religions based in ancient Norse mythology have become popular, arising out of a search for a historically authentic religion for white people. Neo-pagan religions, such as Asatru and Odinism (which is sometimes called "Wodenism" or "Wotanism"), have become fashionable among white supremacists in prison. These faiths are somewhat controversial, as any new religion can be, in part because many prison officials fear they might just be ruses designed to enable white supremacist prison gang members to congregate by exploiting laws protecting religious freedom.

But whether a particular group's ideology is primarily religious or political in nature doesn't change the level of commitment white supremacists feel toward their cause. In his manifesto *Mein Kampf,* Adolf Hitler referred to National Socialism as his "political faith," which perfectly describes the devotion I witnessed among modern-day Nazis. You simply can't be a part-time white supremacist.

Once in a while these different groups cooperate with one another, but more often their separate ideologies conflict, and despite their agreement on the fundamental issues they mostly hate each other. Sometimes the conflict is purely personal; maybe the leader of one group just can't stand the leader of another. Other times it's political. To share power one group's leaders would have to cede some authority to another group's leaders. Few politicians of any kind voluntarily surrender power to their competitors.

But most often, these groups' inability to cooperate is a product of the inherent incompatibility of their different ideologies. Imagine a devout Bible-quoting Identity Christian sitting down with a WAR skinhead who thinks Christ was a Jew and Christianity a Jewish plot to destroy the white race. It wouldn't take long for a fistfight—or worse—to break out. White supremacists putting their specific ideologies ahead of their shared goals may seem odd, but their ideology is everything to them. It's their reason for being, and it's all or nothing. Any compromise on any aspect of their ideology would risk undermining their belief system's entire foundation.

The FBI's cooperating witness had aligned himself with a group that was then known as the World Church of the Creator but has more recently become known as the Creativity Movement.[1] Creativity is a religion with a simple creed—"Our race is our religion"—and a simple golden rule: "What is good for the White Race is the highest virtue; what is bad for the White Race is the ultimate sin."[2] It was founded by Ben Klassen, the inventor of an early electric can opener, a one-time elected Florida legislator, and author of *The White Man's Bible,* which was handed to me in college so many years before. This religion does not foster a belief in a deity or in an afterlife, an idea it mocks as "pie in the sky when you die." Instead, it centers on an observable natural law, on logic, and on reason, which they feel demonstrate the white race's natural superiority. They believe the race's survival depends on "achieving a Sound Mind in a Sound Body in a Sound Society in a Sound Environment."[3]

I was about to enter a strange new world.

Luckily, being unfamiliar with their culture was not nearly as big an obstacle as I had feared. I was exactly the type of young Aryan they were looking for, and they eagerly recruited me. At this level they were surprisingly indiscriminate. The movement is so factious that each group has to compete mightily for new recruits, and much of this recruiting is brazenly public. Leafleting is probably the most popular technique. Members paper an entire neighborhood with racist flyers that include a phone number, a post office box, or an e-mail address. From this contact, like-minded people can learn more about the movement or establish fellowship with people who share their beliefs. Groups will put out hundreds of these flyers in the hopes of receiving just a handful of responses. But a handful is all they need.

If they're lucky the local press will pick up on the leafleting and write a story about the ugly racist literature that was spread around town. A few outraged citizens will make statements denouncing racism, and the local police chief will reassure the community that no crime has been committed and the flyers should just be ignored. All this attention just provides more publicity for the cause and extends the recruiting campaign. As the adage goes, bad press is better than no press.

Part of this recruiting effort is simply to build the groups' numbers. Numbers generate a greater revenue stream of dues, donations, and subscriptions, and they increase a group's influence within the larger movement, where, as in all political movements, numbers mean power. But a larger part of this recruiting effort comes from a genuine evangelical zeal to convert others. These people sincerely believe they are right, and as true believers, they want to convince others they are right. Proselytizing is necessary because they believe the racial revolution is imminent, and they need more people in the movement for greater strength when the war begins. They see the entire world at a tipping point, and a palpable urgency is in their recruiting, as in everything else they do.

They believe deep down inside everyone else knows they are right, too. They believe the Jews, blacks, and other minorities—whom they refer to as "mud people" as a slur against their supposed impurity—are, of course, part of the conspiracy and actively working against them. They view those white people who do not participate in the movement as too afraid, too corrupt, or too lazy. They call these whites "Sheeple," or half sheep, half people.

The Sheeple, they maintain, allow Jewish conspirators to seduce them into compliance with the vices of a decadent society. The white supremacists feel if the Sheeple would recognize the Jews' true goal —the white race's systematic destruction—they would get off their couches, into the movement, and take the war to the enemy. Educating and influencing the Sheeple are the primary struggles. The white supremacists try to inspire them with calls of "Wake up, white man!" They try to intimidate them with threats of an accounting after the race war, when they will remember who fought with them and who did not. They speak of "trials, piles, and smiles." Finally they try to force the Sheeple into the movement by committing terrorist acts designed to ignite the race war. Once the war starts they believe the Sheeple will have no choice but to join the fight out of self-preservation. Once the war starts, they expect the natural superiority of the white race will ensure victory.

As complex as the different white supremacist ideologies are, in the end they all hinge on the same simple concept: a secretive, diabolical, all-powerful "them" is conspiring against "us." If this enemy can somehow be defeated, all the world's other problems will evaporate. A conclusive cleansing war will be necessary to purify the decadent world, but a peaceful, just, and perfect society waits on the other side.

Imagine how coming to such a realization would simplify your life. All your problems would have one root cause that has nothing to do with who you are but simply with what you are. You didn't flunk out of college because you partied too much and didn't study; it was part of the conspiracy. You didn't get fired because you were ineffective at your job; it was part of the conspiracy. Your wife didn't leave you because you're an insufferable bore; it was just part of the conspiracy. The conspiracy is the source of all your problems.

All the logic these groups use to build their complex philosophical arguments rests on the foundation of this single premise, the big lie. Once someone accepts the premise that the conspiracy exists, everything else falls easily and logically into place. It's very empowering. Not only are you absolved of any personal responsibility for your failings, you're also one of the few people wise enough to see through the conspiracy. You are now part of an elite cadre, one of the few that knows.

This realization also creates a clarity of purpose, because with knowledge comes responsibility. There are no longer a million different things to do; there is only one—to save the white race from extermination. The enlightened ones' primary responsibility is to spread the word, to expose the conspiracy, and to educate other white people so they can resist. This sense of responsibility drives their recruiting efforts.

Their first step is to teach white people that race transcends all other characteristics of identity. They argue that nationality, religion, and political affiliation are all false constructs Jews created to confuse and divide the white race: We are not Americans and Germans and Russians, they say; we're white people. We're not Baptists and Catholics and Presbyterians; we're white people. Not Republicans or Democrats, liberals or conservatives; we're white people. They believe white people of the world make up one kindred people, or "Folk." For them, race is the only true, lasting attribute of identity.

The intense anti-Americanism of the white supremacist movement surprised me. I had always thought white supremacist groups, particularly the Klan, considered themselves representatives of "American" values, however twisted their perception of these values might have been. But the first time they burned an American flag in front of me I had a visceral, physical reaction that was impossible to stifle. A ritualistic destruction of the American flag—the primary symbol of my identity—was something I did not expect to see in middle America. I was just lucky no one noticed my reaction. These groups completely reject any notion of the America I recognize, which values truth, justice, and tolerance. Their only loyalty is to their race. Their race is their religion. Their race is their nation.

Once identification with the Folk community is established, the next step in the recruitment process is separation from mainstream society. Recruits undergo a purification process to cleanse them of society's corrupting influences. Each ideological group has its own peculiar cleansing rites. Skinheads, for example, shave their heads to symbolize their separation from society. They adorn themselves with symbols of Nazi Germany, not just to indicate their political beliefs, but to demonstrate their complete rejection of mainstream values. How better to communicate the rejection of societal values than to display universally abhorrent symbols on one's body? Each part of the skinhead "uniform" has symbolic meaning. The work boots and jeans represent the movement's working-class roots, the white T-shirt symbolizes purity, and the red suspenders, the blood of martyrs. White bootlaces display white pride, and red laces indicate the wearer has shed blood on the race's behalf. The bomber jacket symbolizes the movement's militancy. Just getting dressed is a purification ritual for a skinhead.

The Creativity Movement has perhaps the most complex purification rituals, which are outlined in another of Klassen's books, *Salubrious*

Living. Klassen advocated fasting and encouraged followers to limit their diet to uncooked organic foods, such as fruits, nuts, and vegetables. Creators are admonished to study, get proper rest and exercise, and to avoid all drugs, even for medicinal purposes. These practices are meant to cleanse the self by purifying the body and disciplining the mind.

All white supremacist groups honor labor and eschew materialism. They feel the quest for financial gain beyond what is necessary to support the family distracts from the movement and creates a quiet form of slavery that uses false promises of future wealth to keep white people toiling in a rat race instead of working with the resistance. They seek to end dependence on any sort of government services or reliance on anyone outside the movement. If recruits' employment requires them to interact with other races, they are encouraged to quit and find other work. They are taught it is better to be poor than to compromise their beliefs.

An Odinist, former member of the Order, and current federal prisoner, David Lane, argues materialism "leads men to seek artificial status through wealth or property. True social status comes from service to Family, Race and Nation."[4]

Part of this antimaterialism comes from the crass stereotypical notion that Jews rule the world by controlling financial institutions and currency markets. White supremacist recruiters will often show recruits a small, somewhat disguised Star of David on the back of a U.S. dollar bill as proof of this hidden control Jews have over the U.S. Treasury. They consider participating in financial markets as trading with the enemy. They believe wealth should only be earned through honest labor. Lane argued that "usury," or collecting interest on a debt, is a "high crime which cannot be tolerated." The white supremacist movement suffers financially because of these attitudes, and this fundamental weakness impedes its effectiveness.

Racial purity is emphasized as the highest goal. Miscegenation, or "mongrelization" in their terminology, is the greatest sin.

Separating group members from mainstream society serves two purposes. It reinforces solidarity within the group and isolates recruits from any outside influences. Once the individual is indoctrinated in the group's ideology, the group becomes the sole source of trusted information. Dissent within the group is not tolerated, conformity is key, and the beliefs become self-reinforcing.

The movement's next step is to begin purifying their community, and this stage is where things get dicey. Some community cleansing is entirely benign. Because they respect purity in all forms, most white supremacist groups revere nature and have an environmental platform as part of their program. But other community cleansing practices are potentially dangerous. Here is where their right to believe what they want, to say what they want, and to associate with whomever they choose begins to conflict with the rights of others and attracts the attention of law enforcement.

Running an organization whose stated purpose is to overthrow the existing government is bound to bring the group into conflict with the authorities and creates a formidable organizational challenge for any revolutionary group. The white supremacists' solution was to create a division of labor.

Foremost the movement needed charismatic leaders to develop its ideology and articulate its mission. It needed to produce and distribute its propaganda to spread the message among the masses and to recruit and indoctrinate new members. But leading an organization that declares war against the government is a tough job. The leaders can be quickly identified, arrested, or killed, dealing crippling blows to the organization. Forcing the leadership underground would accomplish the same result.

To solve this problem the white supremacist movement designed a strategy they call "leaderless resistance." Former Klansman and Aryan Nations ambassador-at-large Louis Beam published an article on the subject in 1988: "Utilizing the **Leaderless Resistance** concept, all individuals and groups operate independently of each other, and never report to a central headquarters or single leader for direction or instruction." Using this method operational units known as "phantom cells" would act on their own initiative based on the generalized group goals articulated by the leadership:

> Organs of information distribution such as newspapers, leaflets, computers, etc., which are widely available to all, keep each person informed of events, allowing for a planned response that will take many variations. No one need issue an order to anyone. Those idealist [sic] truly committed to the cause of freedom will act when they feel the time is ripe, or will take their cue from others who precede them.[5]

No operational orders would ever be communicated from the leaders to the cells or between the cells themselves. This arrangement allows the leadership to remain intact as an organizational and ideological driving force behind the violence, while insulating the leaders from criminal liability. The leadership's mission is simply to spread the ideology. It is up to the phantom cells to do the revolution's dirty work.

Forming effective phantom cells is a challenge under this system, which Beam acknowledges:

> It goes almost without saying that Leaderless Resistance leads to very small or even one man cells of resistance. Those who join organizations to play "let's pretend" or who are "groupies" will quickly be weeded out. While for those who are serious about their opposition to federal despotism, this is exactly what is desired.[6]

As I said, the white supremacist movement casts a wide net in its recruiting effort. The stereotypical white racists—ignorant, unemployed social misfits—show up in abundance. They account for a large percentage of the aboveground movement's population, which is why most observers identify the movement by this stereotype. They exist in a sort of soup. These groups usually don't require membership applications so no one can really say for sure who is part of the movement and who is not. The indoctrination process is designed to educate these loosely affiliated members, to eliminate or weed out the negative behaviors that impede the movement's progress, and to groom them for more important duties. The phantom cells look for the small bits of meat within this soup that they hope to turn into real nourishment for the movement.

Not all recruits take to this training, and that's also where some trouble lies. What Beam called groupies can be dangerous in that they often get drunk, act out indiscriminately and without proper planning, and get arrested. For a clandestine organization like a white supremacist group, such people pose a big problem. First, they aren't the perfect role models for the master race, yet their appearance in the local police blotter often makes them the movement's most public representatives. As the movement tries to appeal to a broader white audience, these delinquents weigh it down. Moreover, even though they can't be relied on for anything important and rarely progress beyond the movement's fringes, their irresponsible conduct creates risk for the entire group. If a fringe member gets in trouble, law enforcement is likely to take an interest in the entire group's activities. Recruits like these pose high risks with low rewards.

Every resistance movement assumes a certain amount of risk by its mere existence, but when someone who is not otherwise contributing to the group's mission adds to that risk, the solution seems obvious. But the leaders know they can't afford to be selective in their recruiting. They can't close the door to any whites who want to be part of the movement, so these troublemakers stay. And they can create big problems.

A fringe member in trouble with the law is the perfect subject for a law enforcement officer to turn into an informant. The group leaders know this tactic so they become suspicious of anyone who has contact with the authorities, and then anyone who has contact with anyone who has contact with the authorities. This fear of informants ratchets up the tension within the group. Members face threats from the government, from possible informants, and from the internal security apparatus that exists to weed informants out. Every person's behavior is examined, every word dissected, every unexplained absence questioned. Paranoia runs rampant, and members deal with any perceived disloyalty quickly and harshly. These groups' internal politics are intensely cutthroat, and accusations of disloyalty trade like currency as individuals jockey for positions of status. Successfully spotting an infiltrator not only knocks a potential rival out of the way, it demonstrates the accuser's loyalty and raises his standing in the group. Of course there's usually no way to know whether the accused was actually an informant. This uncertainty creates a high level of violence and distrust within the group.

The intra-group violence is an underreported phenomenon, because victims are unlikely to go to the police. Even when the police do become involved, a white-on-white crime is rarely reported as a hate crime and much less as an act of domestic terrorism. (Police often consider this type of violence a "victimless" crime anyway.) But it has an enormous impact on the behavior of these groups' members. The level of fear and suspicion within these groups is palpable, especially when they're engaged in criminal activity. Many times this paranoia prevents operations from moving forward to completion because the cells abort their operations whenever they feel their security has been compromised. But sometimes an intragroup rivalry triggers a violent spree.

The resistance movement's final goal is to purify the community at large. They see society as corrupt, unclean, immoral, and illegitimate. They believe evil Zionist forces, in violation of the Constitution, in violation of natural law, and in violation of God's law, have illegally occupied the U.S. government.

They assert that this Zionist Occupied Government is actively trying to destroy the white race:

◆   by creating an illegitimate education system that promotes multiculturalism and encourages race mixing, which destroys the white race by diluting its genetic purity

◆   by failing to enforce immigration laws, which allows nonwhites to infiltrate the homeland and threaten white electoral majorities

◆   by promoting homosexuality and legalizing abortion (which they believe is disproportionately performed on white women), which both impede white population growth

♦ by sapping the wealth of the white working class with high interest rates and high taxes

♦ by creating a welfare state that redistributes wealth from white workers to unemployed minorities

♦ by enacting and enforcing gun-control laws to reduce the threat of armed resistance and leave whites vulnerable to criminals

♦ by passing hate crime laws that put white people in jail just for speaking out in defense of their race

And the white supremacists say this treachery is just what is done out in the open. They believe a thousand other sneakier Zionist plots are afoot.

One recruiting pamphlet I received was directed at white people who might never have had contact with or even seen a Jew before. There are still communities in the United States where a white person can grow up with little or no direct contact with people from other racial groups. These communities are fertile recruiting grounds for racist groups who exploit people's natural fear of the unfamiliar, but to succeed they must convince these people that the Jewish conspiracy does affect them, even if they don't have contact with Jews.

The pamphlet purported to reveal a secret "Jew tax" on processed food products sold in the United States. It showed a symbol—a small circle with the letter *U* inside—which is often printed inconspicuously on the labels of many of the foods we buy. The pamphlet explained that it was the mark of the Union of Orthodox Rabbis, which indicated a "Jew tax" was paid on this product. It went on to claim that this "Jew tax" goes directly to Israel to finance the conspiracy against white people.

In fact, this symbol does appear on many food labels. It is called a pareve symbol. Sometimes it is represented by a K in a circle, a P in a circle, or just the word *pareve.* Producers use the pareve symbol to alert people who eat a kosher diet that the food has been prepared in accordance with Orthodox Jewish dietary restrictions. It is totally benign, but it is one powerful way to convince young naive recruits that unseen Jewish conspirators have a direct impact on their daily lives. Every good lie needs a grain of truth to make it believable.

These white supremacist groups also believe far more deadly conspiracies are under way. For them the war is already on, and white people are the victims. David Lane reduced the white supremacist movement's goals to fourteen words: "We must secure the existence of our people and a future for white children."[7] While it does not sound particularly threatening, it is actually a call to arms. His implication is that "they" are challenging "our" existence and "our" children's future and that we must act to stop them.

Ben Klassen called the aggression against white people "Jewish Tyranny." His description of the threat revealed the intensity of his concern:

1. The Jewish race by choice has waged deadly, unrelenting warfare against us, the White Race, in order to destroy us.
2. The Jewish people are banded together in a vicious racial, religious and political conspiracy to gain control of all the money, all the economic and financial resources, all the land and territory and real estate of the world, in short, its total wealth.
3. The Jews have made it their primary goal to mongrelize, kill, decimate and otherwise destroy the White Race.
4. The Jews are determined to enslave all the races of the world, including the final mongrelized product of the White Race that they intend bringing about.
5. The Jews have in the past successfully and successively destroyed our White Racial ancestors, to name a few: the White Egyptians; the highly creative and gifted Greeks of Classical History; the great and noble Romans of ancient times.
6. The Jewish conspiracy now owns, and/or monopolizes the majority of the White Man's industry, finances, educational facilities, news media, television networks, government, religion, and monopolizes all or nearly all instruments of thought control.
7. The White Race is now an occupied and enslaved people under the cruel heel of the Jewish tyranny.[8]

But convincing white people that a threat exists is not enough to compel them to break all societal bonds and begin an armed resistance. In this huge country, white separatists, as they are fond of calling themselves when they want to soften their image, could surely find a place to set up a community where they could just be left alone; a retreat where they could govern themselves, free from the interference of the Zionist Occupied Government. They would argue that they have tried to do so, but ZOG is threatened by such displays of independence from the system and always responds with force.

Robert Jay Mathews, the founder of the Order, the most storied phantom cell the white supremacist movement ever produced (otherwise known as the "Bruders Schweigen," or Silent Brotherhood), wrote a letter that provided his perspective on the war of resistance he waged against the ZOG in the early 1980s. Mathews claimed to have moved to Montana with only "a desire to work hard and be left alone," but FBI agents tried to get him fired from his job. In response he and his Silent Brotherhood started a "secret war" against the government, robbing banks and armored cars and assassinating enemies of the race. Mathews's war finally led to a showdown with the FBI on Whidbey Island, Washington. After a two-day gun battle the house he barricaded himself in caught fire. Mathews chose to burn to death inside rather than surrender to the FBI.

Mathews knew where the path he chose was headed, and he talked about his death in his final letter.

> I am not going into hiding, rather I will press the FBI and let them know what it is like to become the hunted. Doing so it is only logical to assume that my days on this planet are rapidly drawing to a close. Even so, I have no fear. For the reality of my life is death, and the worst the enemy can do to me is shorten my tour of duty in this world. I will leave knowing that I have made the ultimate sacrifice to ensure the future of my children. As always, for blood, soil, honor, for faith and for race.[9]

The white supremacist movement reveres Mathews as a martyr to the cause.

And this shooting wasn't an isolated incident, they would argue. A former soldier named Randy Weaver also sought a place where he could live free of government interference. He bought a remote mountaintop property in northwest Idaho, about as far from civilization as he could get, and built a cabin in which his family planned to live a life of isolation. Shortly after my undercover case began, federal agents attempted to arrest Weaver for failing to appear in court in answer to a charge of selling a sawed-off shotgun to a U.S. Bureau of Alcohol, Tobacco, and Firearms informant. The shoot-out that followed left a U.S. marshal, Weaver's wife, and his twelve-year old son dead and Weaver and a family friend seriously wounded.

They would also talk about David Koresh, who in 1993 tried to set up a community of faith in Waco, Texas, outside the parameters of what ZOG found acceptable, and once again ZOG responded with military force. To people in the movement, these incidents prove that violent resistance is not only justified, it's necessary. Separation is not a solution.

Unfortunately, the supremacists know not everyone sees, or wants to see, how dire the situation has become. They believe the courageous few have to take it upon themselves to stand up for the race and fight until the Sheeple wake up. The leaders make clear that the race needs heroes to follow the example of martyrs like Bob Mathews. The race's survival is at stake. Those that recognize the conspiracy have a responsibility to act and to resist by any means necessary. That might involve manufacturing, collecting, and stockpiling weapons to be used by others. It might mean committing crimes to raise money for the cause. While they would never consider stealing from each other, they believe it's morally justifiable to rob an armored truck or bank as long as it is done on the movement's behalf. Stealing from the enemy during wartime is not immoral. Anyone participating in the system is supporting ZOG, so if people, even civilians, have to be killed, that's just one of the necessary, unavoidable consequences of war. Bombing a synagogue, a black church, or a government office once in a while is a legitimate act of resistance that shows the Sheeple that the resistance movement is alive and keeps ZOG on its heels. All this activity is considered illegal only because ZOG writes the laws. To them, it is not illegitimate. The crisis they see compels their action.

This prophesy is self-fulfilling: their fear of government repression compels them to take action, and their actions involve violations of the law that, in turn, drive the government to react and enforce the law. Thus the supremacists's preparations for a confrontation leads to the confrontation, because ultimately, the confrontation is what they seek.

As a law enforcement officer my interest in these groups was never to learn about their ideology's finer details. I had to learn about these beliefs to fit in, but my only purpose in infiltrating these groups was to identify the individuals who were already engaged in criminal behavior and to gather the evidence necessary to prosecute them. I wasn't interested in talking to people who were just expressing their beliefs, and I intentionally limited my time with them. I was there to find the criminals who act on their beliefs and carry out the violent acts their leaders so encourage.

Getting into the phantom cells was the challenge. In preparing for the assignment I tried to dirty myself up by growing my hair a little shaggy so I could resemble the criminal I was pretending to be, but this effort turned out to be less effective than I had imagined. These phantom cells' members do not consider themselves criminals—quite the opposite. None of the Order's members had histories of violence before they activated their cell. In their minds they are the good guys, striving to represent the white race in a positive manner, and they want to be recognized as defenders of community rights and community values. They are often prudish moralizers who pride themselves on their politeness even as they plan and carry out horrendous violent acts. Apart from frequently using racial epithets they almost never curse. They observe strict standards of conduct and appearance. They told me to cut my hair more often than my FBI supervisors did. They tolerate no misconduct or criminality within the group. The criminals, they say, are all outside the group, mostly in the government.

They consider themselves soldiers. When they form their operational cells they look for recruits with the qualities of a soldier: someone who would put himself in harm's way for others, who would risk his life to defend the principle of justice, who has a clean record, and who is reliable, competent, and mission oriented. It turned out the qualities that appealed to the FBI when they hired me four years before were the same qualities the white supremacist underground was looking for. I had the raw material they could mold into an Aryan soldier.

This revelation was important for me. I discovered I wasn't dealing with crazed fanatics whose next moves I couldn't predict. Instead I was meeting people like me, except they had very different ideas of how to improve this world. Their behavior was purposeful and predictable. If I wanted to guess their next move, all I had to do was think of what I would do in their position. This realization enabled me to mold my behavior to meet their needs. They didn't have to like me if they knew they needed me, and this was the weakness I exploited.

It wasn't that the members weren't careful; the vetting process took time. They were obsessively security conscious, and they made deliberate efforts to conceal their activities and obscure their associations. I was never sure if I was on firm ground with any of them. They never seemed to trust me completely, but then again, I never trusted them, either. Distrust is the natural product of a clandestine existence.

I made mistakes, plenty of them. Letting a skinhead borrow a small knife I was carrying led to a big row when he called everyone over to see the "Jew knife" I'd given him. I had never noticed the manufacturer's name, Levine & Company, engraved on the handle, but he did, and he didn't take kindly to it. This mistake was the type a true believer wouldn't make. And that one wasn't nearly as embarrassing as when I took a Christian Identity member out to breakfast and ordered bacon and eggs. As I said, Identity followers believe they are the Israelites of the Bible, and as such they follow scriptural prohibitions against eating pork. Bacon was a no-no.

Fortunately I could explain away these mistakes by my late introduction into the movement, and willing mentors schooled me on the errors of my ways. But many did not regard these mistakes as innocent social faux pas; instead, they were serious transgressions that might have had serious consequences. These people believe the world is literally divided into two camps—us and them. "Them" is made up of people intent on killing "us." Each mistake I made indicated that I wasn't really part of "us," which left only one troubling possibility. Some people would no longer have anything to do with me after these mistakes, and others kept a much closer eye. Their problem was everyone makes mistakes from time to time, and they can't afford to throw everyone out. In the end they needed me more than they feared me.

On an operational level the movement is much more practical. Members of the phantom cells cooperate more effectively across the different white supremacist ideologies. They often have disdain for the aboveground leaders, especially if the leaders are perceived to be living well off the movement, and they view the internal ideological turf wars as counterproductive. At times they will even cooperate with groups outside the movement, whether it's buying guns from Mexican street gangs or supporting the anti-government violence of other non-white terrorist groups. The operational-level cells have more of a mission orientation. Anyone willing to fight the big enemy is their friend for the day.

They exercise operational discipline just like the military (often relying on military instructional manuals). They do not share information with each other or between cells except on a need-to-know basis. Within a three-person cell there could be several different active conspiracies that not each of them would know about. In other words, there can be cells within cells. One person could also be a member of many different cells, operating independently of one another. He would not share what he was doing with one cell with the others, nor would he be expected to.

They follow Beam's operational plan exactly as written. They communicate through automated phone messaging systems, short-wave radio, and e-mail. (They had to explain e-mail to me, because the FBI didn't have it then and in some cases still doesn't.[10]) They usually have little or no direct contact with movement leaders, but they subscribe to their newspapers, listen to their radio broadcasts, or view their websites to get regularly updated information, advice, and support for their activities. Bomb-making instructions are widely available at any radical bookstore, swap meet, or gun show. Their trade in illegal weapons is only limited by their resources. When they can't afford to buy them they make their own. One skinhead took me on a thirty-minute drive around his suburban Southern California neighborhood, where we were able to pick up all the components to make a pipe bomb for less than twenty dollars.

Their operations are simple but efficient. If something happens with a group in the Midwest, they know about it in California the next day.

When meeting new people it was customary to provide references or to drop names indicating who you knew and where you'd been. Nothing substantive would be discussed until everything checked out. Sometimes the second meeting never came, with no explanation, no calls, no further contact. I would never know if something spooked them or whether they just got tied up with other things. They always had an overriding fear of infiltration and surveillance. They all assumed they were being followed and their phone calls were monitored. The first time I was accused of being a "Fed" I was worried, but I soon realized they challenged everyone else the same way and it became routine.

They also constantly updated their tactics. When Harold von Braunhut, one of the elder statesmen of the white supremacist movement, spoke to Aryan youth in 1993 he advised them to abandon their skinhead uniforms, to grow their hair, to cover their tattoos, and to hide their racial beliefs. He told them that the Jews have so demonized Nazis that these symbols turn off too many people before they've even had a chance to hear the Aryans' message. Aryan youth should instead become "trench coat warriors," he said, and join what von Braunhut considered "mainstream" protest movements: the antiabortion movement, the anti-immigration movement, the anti–gun control movement, and the anti-tax movement. He said these trench coat warriors could identify the radicals within these organizations and bring them all together under one umbrella to form a huge antigovernment army. Once they were radicalized and mobilized to fight, they could start the war. There would be time to indoctrinate them into the racial beliefs later.

It sounded like an interesting plan, after looking out into a crowd of yawning skinhead youth, I thought it a bit too ambitious.

Some three months later my case ended with a series of arrests that broke up several different phantom cells, including one responsible for a string of racially motivated bombings. The FBI recovered dozens of illegal weapons and averted terrorist plots. Most pled guilty as a result of the overwhelming evidence the JTTF had gathered during the investigation. Some went to trial and were convicted in public by juries chosen from the community at large. The government presented its evidence, my conduct in the investigation was open to public scrutiny, and the jury spoke. The system worked as it was designed, and the subjects were afforded the protection of all the rights guaranteed under the U.S. Constitution. One subject availed herself of the appeals process and had her conviction overturned by the Ninth Circuit Court of Appeals and the prosecutors chose not to seek a retrial. I disagreed with the opinion, but I was satisfied that the legal process took its course. In the end it was a case the FBI could be proud of, a proactive criminal investigation that solved bombings, prevented planned acts of terrorism, and protected the civil rights in the minority community. I joined the FBI to do work like this.

I learned a great deal through this investigation. I learned how terrorist groups organize and operate. I learned about organized racism and fascism. I learned that the government could prevent terrorism using constitutionally sound criminal procedures and that the government could win against terrorism by protecting the civil rights of the community at large without violating the civil rights of those who would do them harm.

The FBI reassigned me to white-collar crime investigations. I called the Domestic Terrorism Unit at FBI Headquarters to schedule a debriefing so I could pass on the lessons I learned. They told me a debriefing would not be necessary; they had everything under control.

In 1995 a former U.S. Army soldier named Timothy McVeigh imitated a story in a racist novel called *The Turner Diaries* and detonated an ammonium nitrate–fuel oil truck bomb in front of the Alfred P. Murrah Federal Building in Oklahoma City, Oklahoma. The protagonist of the novel (written by William Pierce, a physics Ph.D. and founder of the neo-Nazi organization the National Alliance) sparked a race war by blowing up the J. Edgar Hoover FBI Building in Washington, D.C., with a truck bomb. McVeigh, a devotee of the novel, probably hoped for the same result. While he didn't succeed in starting a race war, he did introduce Americans to the antigovernment militia movement.

In 1996, based on my earlier success with white supremacists, the FBI asked me to go undercover again to infiltrate a militia group in Washington State that was experimenting with explosives. The FBI had laid siege to a "Freeman" compound in eastern Montana, and expectations of other similar confrontations were high.

To be sure, the militia movement had been around long before McVeigh put a face on it. Many white supremacist groups did paramilitary training, dressed up in camouflage uniforms, and gave themselves military designations. They all considered themselves soldiers. But when I went undercover again in 1996 I noticed something different. The militia movement didn't openly express racist beliefs like the white supremacists; in fact it went to great lengths to hide them (although a quick look around the room at one of the meetings revealed little diversity). Its anti-Semitism was masked. They didn't complain about "Jews," but rather "internationalists," "bankers," or "financiers." The United Nations and the New World Order replaced ZOG as the all-powerful enemy.

The members referred to themselves as Patriots, and they had adopted symbols of the American Revolution rather than those of Nazi Germany. They used the Constitution of the United States as their holy book, albeit with a focus on the Founding Fathers' intention that the rights they guaranteed only applied to white males. They immersed themselves in arcane U.S. legal histories and obscure reference books to "prove" the illegality of the parts of the Constitution they didn't like—particularly the Fourteenth and Fifteenth Amendments—and to establish their status as "sovereign citizens," who were required to obey only the laws they liked and endowed with the right to enforce the ones they chose. They sometimes espoused religious theories akin to that of the Christian Identity movement, but they were careful about how and where they expressed them. They were open to antigovernment sentiments of any type, but they were particularly incensed by gun control, abortion, taxes, and immigration. They didn't refer to race but rather to "heritage," and they defined their war as a culture war as opposed to a race war. I presented myself as a former neo-Nazi and was welcomed with open arms.

I quickly recognized the militia movement was the realization of von Braunhut's vision for the future of the white supremacist movement. The militia's rhetoric had a different focus designed to appeal to a broader audience, but everything else was just the same. Its identity group was Christian Patriots, whose members found themselves under siege by a satanic one-world government led by the Bilderbergers, the Illuminati, and the Trilateral Commission cabals of international financiers who controlled the U.S. government through corruption and vice. Their organizational and operational strategies were identical to those of the white supremacists. They even used the same strategic manuals and reference books. They had much greater and less marginalized aboveground support because of the better public relations that came with calling themselves "Patriots" rather than "Nazis," just as von Braunhut suggested they would. They had fewer leaders of national prominence, and because their ideologies were more inclusive, moving among the different groups was easier. This openness proved both a strength and a weakness, because while they could recruit more members, they were also more open to infiltration.

The criminal conduct they were involved in was the same as well: the manufacture and transfer of illegal weapons and explosives in preparation for a cleansing war and the conspiracy to commit acts of violence designed to ignite their war. This time I knew exactly what the extremists were looking for, and the investigation moved very quickly. Within six months I had recovered live explosives from two different phantom cells that had joined forces for operational purposes. Once again the FBI prevented terrorist acts with proactive criminal law enforcement techniques. Public trials then laid bare the "big lies" behind the militia movement: the Constitution of the United States was null and void and the Christian Patriots' rights were being abused. When the tapes I had made were played in court, even militia sympathizers attending the trial admitted the defendants had done wrong and deserved punishment.

When the prosecutions ended I began studying other domestic terrorist groups in preparation for future assignments. Left-wing antiglobalization groups were growing and becoming more violent, as demonstrated in the Seattle World Trade Organization riots of 1999. So, too, were the Animal Liberation Front (ALF) and its cousin the Earth Liberation Front (ELF). I went back and studied the revolutionary movements of the 1960s and 1970s. Once again the rhetoric was different, but the methodology was the same: separate a victimized "us" from an oppressive "them," and hype a crisis that necessitates using violence to redress a grave injustice. I'd heard it all before. Just exchange "Jewish tyrant" for "industrialist pig" or "vivisector," and you have the same arguments to justify the use of violence.

After 9/11 I focused on Islamic fundamentalist groups and found the same to be true with the jihadists. Osama bin Laden even railed against the New World Order, just as my former colleagues in the militia movement had.[11] The anti-Semitism was familiar, as was the anticapitalism and the anti-Americanism. I recognized this jihadist movement for what it was—fascism.

As I heard American politicians, media commentators, and counterterrorism officials discuss this new threat of terrorism, I began to realize how little they understood about who these terrorists are, how they think, what they want to accomplish, and how they can be most effectively countered. I took a teaching position at the FBI Academy, where I began to catch up on the academic literature regarding terrorism, which I had neglected while I was operational in favor of reading what the terrorists themselves were writing. Then I knew why the politicians so misunderstood this enemy. The behavioral and psychological studies weren't really "studies" at all, because these academics did not have access to terrorists. They were mostly a mishmash of improvable theories, assumptions, and biased opinions aimed at trying to explain how someone could do something so evil as commit an act of terrorism.

What was missing from the studies was the human element, or an acknowledgment that terrorists are human beings just like the rest of us. They are motivated to act by the same human emotions that drive us and are plagued by the same human weaknesses—fear, anger, prejudice—that drive our response to them.

In *Art of War* Sun Tzu said, "If you know the enemy and know yourself, you need not fear the result of a hundred battles."[12] If we want to defeat this enemy we need to put our fear, anger, and prejudice aside and learn to understand our enemy. We need to learn how to think like a terrorist.

Part I:
The Trouble With Terrorism

2
The Difficult Definition

The difference between a terrorist and a patriot is control of the press.

—David Lane, "88 Precepts of Natural Law," former member of the
Order, convicted of racketeering and civil rights violations
in the 1984 murder of Jewish radio host Alan Berg

Terrorism is like obscenity—we know it when we see it, but it's difficult to define. If you pick up any book about terrorism you'll almost always find a whole chapter, like this one, devoted entirely to trying to define the word *terrorism.* The lawyer in me likes the idea of defining all the terms up front, but with terrorism it's an exercise in futility.

Usually the chapter starts with a definition of terrorism taken from a dictionary, followed by a short history of the term's use in literature, then a comparison of different official government definitions, and finally an attempt to craft a new definition by culling all of this combined wisdom into one definitive meaning. Despite these efforts, whenever the experts who write these books come together, they still can't agree, and their debates inevitably spiral into endless arguments.

An old adage states that religion and politics are two subjects that should never be discussed in polite company. The saying comes from an acknowledgment that discussing religion and politics usually involves more faith and passion than fact and reason, and there's just no point in arguing with a true believer. The trouble with terrorism is that it is all about religion and politics. And yet we argue.

Part of the problem in defining terrorism is semantic. We use one word to describe too many different things, which, as German philosopher Ludwig Wittgenstein warned in his *Tractatus Logico Philosophicus,* inevitably leads to unnecessary confusion.[1] We use the word *terrorism* to describe the extremist violence of neo-Nazi groups, the vandalism and economic sabotage of environmental rights groups, and the hoax anthrax letters sent by antiabortion extremists. Terrorism is also used to describe the murders serial killers such as Unabomber Ted Kaczynski and D.C.– area snipers John Muhammad and Lee Boyd Malvo have committed, the armed resistance of such groups as the Irish Republican Army and the Palestinian Liberation Organization, and the guerrilla warfare conducted by indigenous insurgents in Vietnam and Iraq.

To add to the confusion, some nations set up and support terrorist organizations to act as their proxies, so these countries can attack their enemies but avoid responsibility. Certainly these state sponsors of terrorism must themselves be considered terrorists. Some argue that the definition of terrorism should also include the oppressive acts of tyrannical governments that maintain power by terrorizing their own citizens. The previous century saw attempted genocides of European Jews, Bosnian Muslims, and Rwandan Tutsis. Many people would consider these atrocities terrorism as well.

That's a great deal of territory to cover with just one word.

Clearly a Ku Klux Klan lynching, an Irish Republican Army (IRA) bombing, and an Earth Liberation Front arson can all be correctly described as acts of terrorism. But what if the Klan kills one of its own members as a suspected informant, or if the IRA bombing is directed at British military forces, or if the ELF member wields nothing more than a can of spray paint? Are these acts of terrorism? Is there any meaningful similarity between the terrorists Osama bin Laden and Ted Kaczynski? What is the difference between a Jewish member of the Zydowska Organizacja Bojowa (ZOB) throwing Molotov cocktails at Nazi staff cars in the Warsaw ghetto[2] versus an animal rights activist firebombing a university laboratory or a serial arsonist burning churches? All of these violent acts terrorize their victims, to be sure, but are they all terrorism? Are any of them? These questions lead to a thousand philosophical arguments but rarely result in any definitive answers.

Wittgenstein posits that it is often a failure of language rather than of logic that causes philosophical arguments:

> In the language of everyday life it very often happens that the same word signifies in two different ways—and therefore belongs to two different symbols—or that two words, which signify in different ways, are apparently applied in the same way in the proposition. . . . Thus there easily arise the most fundamental confusions (of which the whole of philosophy is full).

If we could craft one word, and only one word, to symbolize each of the separate acts described above, the confusion would disappear. Under

Wittgenstein's theories, to argue about the meaning of the word *terrorism* is nonsense, because the argument is really more about the word we have chosen to describe these things than about the nature of the things themselves.

Wittgenstein wasn't talking about terrorism, of course, but his theories are useful in separating what is essentially a semantic argument from a more substantive discussion of the issues. Wittgenstein believed having a logical language was important because "the limits of my language mean the limits of my world." A logical language can describe the world and everything in the world, but that is all. What Wittgenstein refers to as "the metaphysical," or what I would call "religion and politics," falls outside the bounds of what can be accurately described with a logical language. Therefore, according to Wittgenstein, it cannot be discussed: "Whereof one cannot speak, thereof one must be silent." In other words, there's no use arguing over religion and politics!

Another problem is most terrorism experts distinguish terrorism from regular crimes by focusing on the political or religious motives that inspire the violence. The most obvious definition for terrorism would be simply "an act intended to terrify." But serial killers and serial rapists terrify the neighborhoods they prey on, as do mafias and street gangs, yet we don't consider them terrorists. Only if the violence is ideologically driven to achieve some political or religious end do we consider it terrorism. We intuitively recognize the inherent difference between a mafia don planting a bomb to blow away his crosstown rival and Timothy McVeigh blowing up a federal building. We know what terrorism is when we see it, even if we have difficulty explaining it. To explain it we must talk about the political and religious justifications driving the violence, and once politics and religion enter the discussion, the arguments begin.

Clearly we view some violence as entirely justifiable. Thomas Jefferson wrote:

> We hold these truths to be self-evident, that all men are created equal, that they are endowed by their Creator with certain unalienable Rights, that among these are Life, Liberty and the pursuit of Happiness. — That to secure these rights, Governments are instituted among Men, deriving their just powers from the consent of the governed, — That whenever any Form of Government becomes destructive of these ends, it is the Right of the People to alter or to abolish it, and to institute new Government, laying its foundation on such principles and organizing its powers in such form, as to them shall seem most likely to effect their Safety and Happiness.[3]

We know this document as the Declaration of Independence, but it was really a declaration of war. When Jefferson argued it was not just a person's right but his duty to "throw off" a government that did not serve his interests, he was not talking to the king, but to his fellow colonists. This document was a call to arms. If we accept that people have the right to overthrow a government they disagree with, how can we argue that terrorists are somehow acting improperly?

Certainly King George III would have regarded the upstart colonists as terrorists, although that term was not yet in vogue. The Boston Tea Party staged by the Sons of Liberty in 1773 was economic sabotage, a criminal act no different from the Earth Liberation Front's vandalism that today destroys property in the name of saving the environment. So what makes the ELF members sinners and the Sons of Liberty saints?

The question seems to turn on our perception of whether the political or religious ends are justified. Who is a terrorist and who is a freedom fighter? Who gets to decide? Unfortunately this debate is exactly how the terrorist wants to frame the discussion, because as we've learned, religious and political questions have no definitive answers. Questions like this just result in arguments and passionate ones at that. As long as the terrorists have an argument to make, they will keep the debate going. Consider David Lane's lament about poor press coverage at start this chapter. Is it because of a poor public relations campaign that Lane is considered a murderer rather than a hero? Certainly not. He's in prison for gunning down a radio talk show host in his own driveway, hardly an act of self-defense.

But to a certain extent Lane makes a point. He recognizes his ideology is currently unpopular. But we can't fairly judge the legitimacy of a political position by its level of popular support. The Ku Klux Klan had plenty of popular support in the South for most of the twentieth century. Hitler's brand of anti-Semitic racism found support in the United States from groups like the German-American Bund. If Lane had committed his crimes in the 1920s instead of the 1980s, he might never have been charged, much less convicted. But the KKK's popular support didn't legitimize their cause any more than the lack of support for black suffrage and later for the civil rights movement made these causes illegitimate. According to Jefferson's theory, though, Lane is within his rights to resist a government he feels does not serve his ends.

While I understand the logic of Lane's argument, I have trouble sympathizing with him. It's not that I think he's disingenuous. I have spent enough time with people Lane inspired to know they truly believe their cause is just and they will be regarded one day as patriots. And right-wing terrorists aren't the only ones who think this way. Brazilian

Communist revolutionary Carlos Marighella described terrorists, which he called "urban guerrillas," in glowing terms: "The urban guerrilla is a person who fights the military dictatorship with weapons, using unconventional methods. A revolutionary and an ardent patriot, he is a fighter for his country's liberation, a friend of the people and of freedom." The methods Marighella advocates, however, include such nefarious activities as, "sabotage, terrorism, expropriations, assaults, kidnappings, executions."[4] I don't sympathize with Lane because I simply don't care why he did what he did.

As a criminal investigator, I know accurately discerning the true motives underlying any human behavior, let alone judging the veracity of a perpetrator's self-justification for his or her conduct, is difficult. I don't doubt the sincerity of either of these terrorists' beliefs that their crimes were necessary acts of resistance against an unjust oppressor. I just believe, like Wittgenstein said of the metaphysical, that we shouldn't be talking about it. Religion and politics are the source of the conflict, not its solution. Their ideology is irrelevant.

The United Nations has struggled for decades to develop a universally acceptable definition for terrorism, with little success. The idea is that if the nations of the world can come to an agreement on what terrorism is, they can then more easily pass international conventions that outlaw it. All governments naturally want to prohibit any political violence directed against them or their allies, and they want the international community to cooperate in their pursuit of those who would do them harm. The problem is these governments also want to reserve the right to use violence themselves when they deem it necessary and perhaps even to support a revolutionary movement against nations they oppose. Once again the argument focuses on political questions—who's right, who's wrong, and who gets to decide—which benefits no one as much as the terrorists.

The international community is not alone in finding difficulty defining terrorism. The U.S. government has codified at least three different official definitions of terrorism. The Department of Defense has one definition, the Department of State another, and the FBI a third, each varying slightly from the others depending on each agency's role in responding to terrorism. Thus the "official" definition of terrorism changes depending on which government agency responds to it. This lack of objectivity again plays into the terrorists' hands. If terrorism is considered a subjective notion that can change depending on the perspective of the actors involved, then the terrorist's point of view is as relevant as anyone else's. And if one government can't develop a single definition of terrorism, what hope is there for the international community to come to agreement?

Yet the desire to establish a universally acceptable definition of terrorism is so strong the international community expends an overwhelmingly disproportionate amount of intellectual energy, despite the little clarity it produces. While no final definition has yet to materialize, scholar A. P. Schmid of the United Nations Office on Drugs and Crime did craft the "academic consensus" definition of terrorism:

> Terrorism is an anxiety-inspiring method of repeated violent action, employed by (semi-) clandestine individual, group or state actors, for idiosyncratic, criminal or political reasons, whereby—in contrast to assassination—the direct targets of violence are not the main targets. The immediate human victims of violence are generally chosen randomly (targets of opportunity) or selectively (representative or symbolic targets) from a target population, and serve as message generators. Threat- and violence-based communication processes between terrorist (organization), (imperiled) victims, and main targets are used to manipulate the main target (audience(s)), turning it into a target of terror, a target of demands, or a target of attention, depending on whether intimidation, coercion, or propaganda is primarily sought.[5]

When you need an entire paragraph to define one word, you know have problems. Luckily, Schmid also came up with a "short" definition: "[an] act of terrorism = the peacetime equivalent of a war crime."[6] To break it down even further, we know peacetime is a state or condition without war. A war crime without a war, of course, is simply a crime. So, following Schmid's logic, terrorism = a crime.

I like this definition, because this approach is how I viewed terrorism as an FBI agent. The FBI's definition of terrorism is codified in Title 28 Code of Federal Regulations Section 0.85: "the unlawful use of force and violence against persons or property to intimidate or coerce a government, the civilian population, or any segment thereof, in furtherance of political or social objectives."[7] This definition goes too far into that forbidden area of discussing politics, but the first part of the definition is what drives the counterterrorism efforts for FBI agents on the street. "The unlawful use of force and violence against persons or property" would have been enough for me. The second half, which discusses the intent driving the terrorist's use of unlawful force, unnecessarily complicates the issue.

As a practical matter the second part of the FBI's definition would never come into play in actual counterterrorism investigations anyway. Title 28 Code of Federal Regulations is not a criminal statute; it is an administrative statute establishing the Department of Justice as the judicial administrative agency of the U.S. government. The practical purpose of defining terrorism in this statute is simply to give the FBI jurisdiction over investigations involving acts of terrorism. As an FBI agent my counterterrorism investigations never resulted in anyone being charged with terrorism. The terrorists I arrested were charged with specific criminal offenses; possessing and transferring illegal firearms and explosive devices, illegally using firearms and destructive devices, conspiring to use illegal firearms and destructive devices, and conspiring to violate civil rights. Terrorists use these crimes to accomplish their political goals. Once I had evidence of their illegal activities, I could bring charges against them. Certainly the motive behind their conduct came into play to prove they had the requisite criminal intent, but the laws I enforced had absolutely nothing to do with the terrorists' ideology.

By focusing the prosecution of terrorists on the underlying criminal activities we deny them a platform for their political or religious arguments. Their ideology, which is protected under the First Amendment to the Constitution in the first place and impossible to criminalize in the second place, is irrelevant to prosecuting their underlying crimes. Perhaps the defendants in my cases did commit their crimes for noble purposes, at least in their own minds, but that motive does not matter to a law enforcement officer. Do the crime and do the time. The terrorists can argue their just cause to the judge and to the jury, and even to the public if they want to, but the law enforcement officer's only concern is to prove they committed the crime. Cops just present the facts. If the judge wants to throw the case out of court or the jury wants to acquit or the people want to petition their government to change the law based on the terrorist's ideological arguments, that's their prerogative.

The United Nations has actually come a long way toward adopting this sort approach. Several international conventions prohibit the underlying criminal conduct terrorist groups typically engage in—hijacking airplanes, taking hostages, assaulting diplomats, bombings, and terrorist financing, among others—all ratified without much controversy. By concentrating on criminalizing the specific conduct terrorist groups engage in rather than trying to define terrorism, the international community can avoid unproductive arguments that divide it. The focus of the discussion should always be on addressing the violent means terrorists use, rather than on the ends they hope to achieve. With such an approach the United Nations can perhaps begin to build consensus on which means are never justified by any ends and to put terrorist organizations out of business.

But the reason I like treating terrorism as a crime is that I know the one thing terrorists hate more than anything else: they hate being called criminals.

3

Getting Beyond Good and Evil

That which is done out of love always takes place beyond good and evil.

—Friedrich Nietzsche, *Beyond Good and Evil*

*We're not fighting a nation; we're not fighting a religion;
we're fighting evil.*

—U.S. president George W. Bush

The difficulty with treating terrorism as a crime is that it is just too unsatisfying. Terrorist attacks are outrageously heinous. They are acts of war against an unprotected citizenry. To call terrorism a "crime" simply doesn't do justice to the act's despicable nature. Terrorism victimizes an entire nation, an entire population, an entire culture. It is a crime against humanity. As a result most people want to treat terrorism as more than just a crime and to punish terrorists more severely than we treat common criminals. Terrorism is evil, and terrorists are evil personified.

The evil nature of a terrorist attack might even justify a departure from normal legal and moral restraints in our response. The U.S. government can work on "the dark side," as Vice President Dick Cheney once said after 9/11, without ceding the moral high ground:

> That's the world these folks operate in and so it's going to be vital for us to use any means at our disposal, basically, to achieve our objective. . . . It is a mean, nasty, dangerous dirty business out there, and we have to operate in that arena.[1]

Yet even as we Americans willfully go beyond traditional bounds of acceptable conduct, we are unable to see our own actions as terroristic. We

37

don't have a Terrorist Unit in the Department of Defense, the Central Intelligence Agency (CIA), or the FBI. The enemy engages in terrorism; we only engage in counterterrorism.

But the groups we consider terrorists don't regard themselves as terrorists either. They call their organizations "armies," "brigades," "militias," and their members "soldiers," "mujahideen," or "holy warriors." They defend their actions as morally justifiable, necessary responses to oppression. They call us the terrorists. In 1998 an interviewer asked Osama bin Laden what he thought about being called a terrorist, and he said,

> They rip us of our wealth and of our resources and of our oil. Our religion is under attack. They kill and murder our brothers. They compromise our honor and our dignity and dare we utter a single word of protest against the injustice, we are called terrorists. This is compounded injustice.[2]

Terrorists firmly believe they are the persecuted victims of an evil injustice, and they have the right to resist their oppression by any means necessary.

This confidence in the righteousness of their cause is what drives terrorist groups to write their manifestos and publish their declarations of war. For a clandestine group to announce itself to a government before it attacks is counterproductive at best. These declarations clearly compromise the terrorist group's ability to operate without detection, and they establish a prima facie case of treason against any members caught and arrested. As a military strategy, producing such a document is pure folly. Why provide a warning to your enemy? But almost all terrorist groups, regardless of their ideology, sit down and write out a declaration of war that announces their presence, identifies their targets, and warns of the violence to come.

The Weather Underground's "Declaration of a State of War" called for a Communist revolutionary struggle against "Amerikan imperialism,"[3] the Creativity Movement's *White Man's Bible* included a "Declaration of Independence against Jewish Tyranny,"[4] and al Qaeda issued a fatwa against the "crusader-Zionist alliance."[5] These documents all read like criminal indictments. The terrorists list the charges against their oppressor, just as the U.S. Declaration of Independence laid out the American colonists' grievances against King George III.

The Weather Underground's declaration vowed to attack "a symbol or institution of Amerikan injustice" in response to the war in Vietnam and "the attempted genocide against black people."[6] The Creativity Movement complained that "Jews have made it their primary goal to mongrelize, kill, decimate and otherwise destroy the White Race" and threatened a racial holy war (RAHOWA), which it described as "total war against the jews and the rest of the goddamned mud races of the world—politically, militantly, financially, morally and religiously."[7] Osama bin Laden originally declared war against "Americans Occupying the Land of the Two Holy Places" in 1996 and specifically only justified attacks against American military forces: "Terrorising you, while you are carrying arms on our land, is a legitimate and morally demanded duty. It is a legitimate right well known to all humans and other creatures."[8] In 1998 he expanded this fatwa:

> [T]o kill the Americans and their allies—civilians and military— is an individual duty for every Muslim who can do it in any country in which it is possible to do it, in order to liberate the al-Aqsa Mosque and the holy mosque from their grip, and in order for their armies to move out of all the lands of Islam, defeated and unable to threaten any Muslim.[9]

No matter what the ideology or the era, these manifestos are strikingly similar in form. They identify the aggrieved class, recite crimes committed against them, review their futile attempts to resolve the conflict without violence, and finally offer an argument supporting the legitimacy of using force as a necessary last resort to end the oppression. The different groups often rely on historical texts, philosophical works, historical charters, or Holy Scriptures to justify using violence to accomplish their goals.

The manifesto is a critical document for the terrorist group, because it establishes the necessary elements for waging a "just war": just cause, proper authority, and proper intentions. Without this document the terrorists would appear to be just a gang of violent criminals. To reach their ultimate goals, terrorists need to prove to their wider audience that they are more than that. They need to show they are the victims of an awful injustice or at least that they represent these victims. The terrorist's violence is designed to serve a strategic purpose—to elicit a repressive reaction from the government they attack. The manifesto lets the government know who is responsible, so they will know who to repress. Once the cycle of violence starts, each side can argue over who is the true victim as they label their own increasingly violent reactions as necessary and legitimate defenses against injustices committed against them. Like kids in a sandbox, the other kid always started the fight.

As a simple matter of fact, most governments come to power through violence and, as White Aryan Resistance leader Tom Metzger once said,

"All governments rule by force or by implied force."[10] So what makes one entity's use of force legitimate and the other's evil arguably becomes a matter of perspective.

America's Founding Fathers declared all men were "endowed by their Creator" with the "unalienable" right to violently oppose any government that failed to serve their interests. The brave men who affixed their signatures on this Declaration of Independence realized it was essentially a suicide pact, and without victory their signatures would evidence their treason and seal their fate. Or as Benjamin Franklin put it at the time, if they did not "hang together" they would assuredly "hang separately." Indeed, we consider their act heroic because of what they risked to build their "more perfect" society. Patrick Henry's famous line, "Give me liberty, or give me death," exemplifies the nobility of self-sacrifice in furthering a worthy cause. We revere our martyrs. We erect statues, plaques, and memorials to honor their efforts to ensure our freedom, as we should.

But many of the brave men who spoke and wrote so eloquently about liberty and who took such enormous personal risks to establish a nation based on the "self-evident" principle that "all men are created equal" owned other people as property. Jefferson himself, the author of those immortal phrases, owned almost 200 slaves. This hypocrisy is deeply disturbing.

The Constitution of the United States, which was designed to protect the essential civil liberties of the American people, codified slavery as a legitimate institution in this new nation, and relegated the status of a black man to that of "three-fifths" of a person. Certainly the Founding Fathers had to recognize that their slaves' right to violently resist their bondage far exceeded their own comparatively insignificant grievances against King George. What is "taxation without representation" compared to captivity and forced labor? Yet slave revolts were routinely put down with force, at times exercised by the very men who fought so bravely for their own freedom during the revolution.

Slaves weren't the only ones who violently resisted slavery. The abolitionist John Brown wasn't a slave, he wasn't black, and he wasn't even from the South. Brown wasn't personally affected by slavery, but he found the institution an affront to his intense Christian faith and felt a religious calling to destroy it by any means necessary. Brown's militia was responsible for some gruesome violence in Kansas, including the butchering of unarmed pro-slavery settlers at Pottawatomie Creek, before the ill-fated 1859 raid on the Harper's Ferry armory in West Virginia that made him famous. He may have been on a mission from God, but he did devil's work to get there.

Many modern terrorists, particularly terrorist leaders such as Osama Bin Laden, do not come from the oppressed classes they claim to represent.

Commentators often regard such an anomaly as evidence of hypocrisy; as proof that there is no validity to the terrorists' cause and that the leaders are merely opportunists clutching at someone else's misery to justify their own lust for violence. But while many historians question John Brown's methods (and even his sanity), no one doubts John Brown's sincerity. He came to believe that the evil institution of slavery could not be abolished except through force, and he gave his life to bring an end to others' suffering. He was a visionary willing to fight for a just cause, a hero. That he didn't suffer in bondage didn't make his cause or his commitment to it less legitimate, quite the opposite.

Before he went to the gallows he wrote,

> I John Brown am now quite certain that the crimes of this guilty, land: will never be purged away; but with Blood. I had as I now think: vainly flattered myself that withought very much bloodshed; it might be done.[11]

Brown was hanged as a traitor, but just two years later his nation became engulfed in a bloody civil war over the abolitionist cause for which he forfeited his life. Today the many slaves who fought and died for their own freedom are all but forgotten, while John Brown is still revered for sacrificing himself for the freedom of others.

But Brown's heroism at Harper's Ferry does not erase the stain of his behavior at the Pottawatomie Creek massacre. A woman whose husband Brown shot that night wrote about this horrific event in a letter:

> Altho' vengeance is not mine, I confess that I do feel gratified to hear that you were stopped in your fiendish career at Harper's Ferry, with the loss of your two sons, you can now appreciate my distress in Kansas, when you then and there entered my house at midnight and arrested my husband and two boys, and took them out of the yard and in cold blood shot them dead in my hearing. You can't say you done it to free slaves. We had none and never expected to own one. . . . My son John Doyle whose life I beged of you is now grown up and is very desirous to be at Charlestown on the day of your execution.[12]

The Civil War that followed Brown's adventure saw more than its share of irregular warfare, or what could be considered terrorism. Whether they were called Partisan Rangers, guerrillas, or simply bushwackers, the unconventional methods irregular rebel forces used caused even the Confederate leaders who unleashed them to debate the legality of such tactics.

The vicious Missouri-Kansas border war that produced John Brown primed that region for some of the most savage atrocities committed during the Civil War. Organized Confederate forces were driven out of Missouri early in the war, but small bands of pro-slavery border ruffians formed an insurgency. These independent raiding parties harassed the federal troops occupying or traveling through Missouri and sacked pro-Union communities in both Kansas and Missouri, as often for their own enrichment as for any strategic military purpose. When the local population in Missouri appeared to support these insurgents, federal authorities ordered civilians imprisoned, sometimes tortured, and finally banished from the territory. Winning hearts and minds wasn't on the agenda.

One of the most notorious insurgents was a former horse thief named "Bloody Bill" Anderson, who rode under the black flag of Capt. William Quantrill, no stranger to a life of crime himself. Anderson was infamous for scalping, eviscerating, mutilating, and even beheading his victims.[13] By any definition most would consider Anderson a war criminal. But his defenders would argue that he and other Missouri partisans simply responded in kind to the horrific war crimes committed by pro-Union Kansas Jayhawkers and Red Legs, who had their own grim record of abusing civilians and plundering property.[14] In fact, one of Anderson's sisters had been killed and another seriously wounded when a building housing imprisoned civilians suspected of supporting the partisans collapsed. Some argue this event led to Anderson's excesses. Indeed, in this conflict each side gave as good as it got, with only one mutual guarantee: "no quarter." Anderson eventually met his own bloody end at the hand of Union soldiers, who then staged his mutilated corpse for publicity photos. No quarter.

After the Confederate surrender at Appomattox, many of these irregular forces continued their bushwacking ways. Infamous bank robbers Jesse James and Cole Younger got their start riding with Quantrill and Anderson. James later defended his criminal behavior, according to at least one sympathetic source, as a continuation of his legitimate resistance to the Union's occupation of his state.[15] Certainly the James-Younger gang's behavior didn't change after the Confederate surrender, so why should the perception of their behavior change? Does James's self-justification for his conduct matter, or did he rightly go down in history as just an outlaw? If he had died with Anderson before the Confederate surrender, would it have changed the way history remembers him?

Elsewhere in the south, other veterans of the defeated Confederate Army came home to form their own resistance organizations. Secret societies, such as the Knights of the White Camelia, the White Brotherhood, and most famously, the Ku Klux Klan, formed to resist the social and political changes forced upon the South after the war. This "Invisible Empire" employed masked night riders to terrorize blacks, northern carpetbaggers, and white Republicans in a campaign to restrict black suffrage, defeat Reconstruction, and reestablish white supremacy throughout the South. It worked. Their campaign was highly successful, but the tactics they used caused even the battle-hardened Gen. Nathan Bedford Forrest, the Klan's first Grand Wizard, to resign his position and order the Klan disbanded.

The Klan didn't disband, of course. It saw a resurgence in the early twentieth century, and at the height of its power the KKK served as a shadow government in many parts of the country, regulating virtually all aspects of social and political life through violence and intimidation. People running for public office once sought the Klan's endorsement, and Klansmen made it to the halls of Congress and even to the Supreme Court bench. *Birth of a Nation,* D. W. Griffith's landmark 1915 film homage to the Klan, was screened in the White House to outstanding reviews.

All this evidence demonstrates that guerrilla warfare, insurgency, and terrorist violence have been part of our national experience since the country's inception. The impulse to violently resist a perceived oppressor seems to be ingrained in human nature, as is the impulse toward extremism in crushing such resistance. Why then do we have so much trouble understanding it? And why do we now pretend the current war on terror is all brand new?

Thomas Jefferson wrote, "The tree of liberty needs to be refreshed from time to time with the blood of patriots and tyrants."[16] As the author of the Declaration of Independence and president of the United States Jefferson is justifiably regarded as a patriot, but as a slave owner he can only be considered a tyrant of the worse sort. Reportedly the only slaves he ever freed were his own illegitimate children and then only on his deathbed.

Timothy McVeigh wore a T-shirt bearing Jefferson's "tree of liberty" quotation on the day he blew up the Murrah Federal Building in Oklahoma City, obviously in a conscious effort to add an air of legitimacy to the destruction he was about to unleash. The other side of the T-shirt bore another quote, "Sic semper tyrannis," which is the motto of the Commonwealth of Virginia and is loosely translated as "Death to tyrants." John Wilkes Booth shouted this slogan from the stage of Ford's Theater after assassinating President Abraham Lincoln. The same theme justifying violence as resistance to tyranny plays out repeatedly, regardless of the era and regardless of the ideology.

Ben Klassen studied historical political conflicts and came to the "obvious conclusion" that "terrorism and violence works." He went on:

Yes, terrorism is bloody, cruel and victimizes innocent people, but it is a traditional power device and has been used consistently "from above" by politicians in power, and "from below" by those who would like to be in power. The latter have succeeded surprisingly often, and even the American Revolution itself was a power play of violence "from below" against the British who used terror "from above."[17]

Osama bin Laden likewise sees political violence as a two-way street:

[T]errorism can be commendable and it can be reprehensible. Terrifying an innocent person and terrorizing him is objectionable and unjust, also unjustly terrorizing people is not right. Whereas, terrorizing oppressors and criminals and thieves and robbers is necessary for the safety of people and for the protection of their property. There is no doubt in this. Every state and every civilization and culture has to resort to terrorism under certain circumstances for the purpose of abolishing tyranny and corruption. Every country in the world has its own security system and its own security forces, its own police and its own army. They are all designed to terrorize whoever even contemplates to attack that country or its citizens. The terrorism we practice is of the commendable kind for it is directed at the tyrants and the aggressors and the enemies of Allah, the tyrants, the traitors who commit acts of treason against their own countries and their own faith and their own prophet and their own nation. Terrorizing those and punishing them are necessary measures to straighten things and to make them right. Tyrants and oppressors who subject the Arab nation to aggression ought to be punished.[18]

These positions should not be mistaken for moral relativism. Neither of these men is a nihilist. Klassen might seem so when he argues that in nature there is no "righteousness, or morality or fair play."[19] But where the law of nature rules, the struggle for survival creates a moral imperative to do whatever is necessary to live and procreate. To Klassen, "what is good for the White Race is the highest virtue; what is the bad for the White Race is the ultimate sin."[20] Klassen created a movement with the most comprehensive set of rules to live by, regulating everything from diet to dating.

Likewise, bin Laden is no moral relativist. He's a moral absolutist and like all absolutists he relies on what has been written down—the Koran in his case—as inviolable law. In his writings and speeches bin

Laden uses liberal references to passages from the Koran to justify every action. Christian Identity white supremacists also use scriptural passages to justify their conduct, while the Weather Underground referenced the revolutionary writings of Karl Marx, Ernesto Che Guevara, and Chairman Mao to the same effect. To members of the Weather Underground revolution was their religion.

Most commentators distinguish immoral terrorist violence from moral counterterrorist violence by the terrorist's deliberate targeting of innocent civilians, but making such a distinction is being argumentative. Determining who is innocent, who is guilty, and who is a civilian, brings us back to the same dispute over who started it. Bin Laden makes his case:

> The Americans started it and retaliation and punishment should be carried out following the principle of reciprocity, especially when women and children are involved. Through history, America has not been known to differentiate between the military and the civilians or between men and women or adults and children. Those who threw atomic bombs and used the weapons of mass destruction against Nagasaki and Hiroshima were the Americans. Can the bombs differentiate between military and women and infants and children? America has no religion that can deter her from exterminating whole peoples. Your position against Muslims in Palestine is despicable and disgraceful. America has no shame. . . . We believe that the worst thieves in the world today and the worst terrorists are the Americans. Nothing could stop you except perhaps retaliation in kind. We do not have to differentiate between military or civilian. As far as we are concerned, they are all targets, and this is what the fatwah says. . . . The fatwah is general (comprehensive) and it includes all those who participate in, or help the Jewish occupiers in killing Muslims.[21]

An American veteran of the first Gulf War, McVeigh made the same argument in an essay explaining his rationale for bombing the Murrah Federal Building:

> Remember Dresden? How about Hanoi? Tripoli? Baghdad? What about the big ones—Hiroshima and Nagasaki? (At these two locations, the U.S. killed at least 150,000 non-combatants—mostly women and children—in the blink of an eye. Thousands more took hours, days, weeks, or months to die.) . . . Hypocrisy when it comes to death of children? In Oklahoma City, it was family convenience that explained the presence of a day-care center placed

between street level and the law enforcement agencies which occupied the upper floors of the building. Yet when discussion shifts to Iraq, any day-care center in a government building instantly becomes "a shield." Think about that. . . . When considering morality and mens rea [criminal intent] in light of these facts, I ask: Who are the true barbarians?[22]

I do not present these arguments because I find them persuasive. I don't need to have sympathy for my adversaries' arguments to understand them. But I do need to understand them if I am going to develop effective strategies to defeat them.

I personally believe neo-Nazism is an inherently evil ideology, rivaled only by Satanism for its intentional embrace of evil. I would argue that neo-Nazism is even more evil than the original National Socialism under Adolf Hitler. The original Nazis could at least argue they thought the atrocities they were committing were necessary to achieve some higher end, even though history ultimately proved them horribly wrong. Neo-Nazis know the horrendous scale of the atrocities Hitler's Third Reich perpetrated.[23] They know Nazi crimes against humanity produced no glory for the Aryan "supermen" and only misery for the entire world, yet they embrace this ideology anyway.

But the neo-Nazis I knew weren't evil personified. They were human beings—fathers, sons, mothers, and daughters—not caricatures. They clearly had plenty of flaws and they harbored beliefs I found abhorrent, but as an American, as a lawyer, and as an FBI agent sworn to uphold the Constitution, I respected their right to hold beliefs I disagreed with. They did not have the right to commit crimes to further their beliefs, however, and my job was to prevent that. But their criminal activities were purposeful, not pathological, and they sincerely believed they were acting for the greater good.

As a criminal investigator I spent time with various criminals: sociopaths, murderers, degenerate drug fiends, gang members, and white-collar criminals. I actually found the white-collar criminals I investigated more evil than the terrorists were. I investigated multimillionaires who could have comfortably retired in luxury but instead chose to defraud poor people out of the little money they had and for no other reason than to prove they could get away with it. I will never understand how they could destroy someone's life just for the hell of it. Not that the terrorists I met weren't intent on destroying lives—they were—but they at least believed, however erroneously, they were serving noble ends. As misguided as I know they were, they were at least sincere in their beliefs and they acted honorably within the context of their ideology. They believed their cause was just and required them to take action, often at great personal risk. They were not fanatic or insane. Theirs was a mentality I could understand.

Certainly they treated me more kindly than I treated them. They welcomed me into their community, tried to educate me to the dangers around me, and armed me so I could protect myself. They invited me into their homes, fed me, and vouched for me so I could make connections within the movement. They shared their confidences and trusted me with their most closely held secrets, secrets that could cost them their liberty and potentially even their lives. In return I lied to them every day and every time I opened my mouth. I tricked them into thinking I shared their cause. I recorded what they thought were our private conversations. I cajoled them into telling me more than they normally would have. I abused their trust and betrayed them to their greatest enemy in a premeditated plan carried out with the full force and authority of the federal government. I wasn't nice to them.

No, I am not a victim of Stockholm syndrome, the psychological condition in which hostages begin to sympathize with their captors. I didn't sympathize with any of the terrorists then, and I don't now. I have no qualms about what I did, and I would do it all again. In fact I did do it again, and I repeatedly volunteered for more undercover cases. I was willing to take the risk, because I knew these people were preparing to do evil things and someone had to stop them. The government is obligated to protect its citizens, and as a government agent I accepted that responsibility. I also know that if these people had discovered who I really was they would have treated me far worse than the justice system I represented ultimately treated them.

From an objective viewpoint, I understand how the terrorists would view my actions differently and feel that I victimized them. I can even accept that they would think what I did was evil. Perhaps the lying and betrayal was part of the "mean, nasty, dangerous dirty business" Vice President Cheney was talking about. Cheney justifies the government's jaunt into "the dark side" as a necessary means to a just end, but I reject this argument. Necessity is the justification terrorists use to defend their actions.

I'm not saying the argument doesn't have merit, but it's an argument I don't want to make. In the first place it's fruitless. I'm not going to convince the terrorists that they're the evildoers, and they aren't going to convince me that I am. Second, the question of who is right and who is wrong is the source of the conflict, not its solution.

Terrorism, simply put, is a pejorative term, a label we use to describe actions our enemies take against us. Terrorism is always discussed in a context where the moral wrongness of the act is a given. We never talk about "good" or "justifiable" terrorism. Using the term *terrorist* is little more than name-calling between adversaries.

This name-calling creates serious impediments to conflict resolution, however. It polarizes the parties, making objective analysis of the conflict difficult and negotiation impossible. If our side is "good" and the other side is "evil," there is little room for understanding and no room for compromise. We need to take the moral question out of the analysis precisely because it impedes clearly understanding our enemy.

Any victims of violence will naturally view their attacker as unjustified. This is only more true with terrorism, where, simply by definition, we are declaring the victims to be innocent. We only call violence "terrorism" if we are looking at it from the victim's perspective. This victim bias pollutes the study of terrorism. Behavioral and psychological studies of terrorism mostly focus on trying to figure out how someone could do something so evil and self-destructive. Behavioral scientists see terrorist violence as fanatical, deviant, and immoral behavior that can only be explained as some sort of psychological abnormality. They wonder whether terrorists are mentally ill or even brainwashed by their terrorist leaders. Yet our police and our military are authorized to use violence. We expect them to put themselves in harm's way when necessary, but we don't consider them brainwashed by their leaders.

Most psychological or behavioral studies of terrorism start with a disclaimer that acknowledges the lack of empirical evidence from which one could derive a scientifically valid conclusion about the psychology of terrorists. Rex Hudson explained the reasons for this lack of data in an analysis of the literature on terrorism written for the Federal Research Division of the Library of Congress:

> A principal reason for the lack of psychometric studies of terrorism is that researchers have little, if any, direct access to terrorists, even imprisoned ones. Occasionally, a researcher has gained special access to a terrorist group, but usually at the cost of compromising the credibility of his/her research. Even if a researcher obtains permission to interview an incarcerated terrorist, such an interview would be of limited value and reliability for the purpose of making generalizations. Most terrorists, including imprisoned ones, would be loath to reveal their group's operational secrets to their interrogators, let alone to journalists or academic researchers, whom the terrorists are likely to view as representatives of the "system" or perhaps even as intelligence agents in disguise. Even if terrorists agree to be interviewed in such circumstances, they may be less than candid in answering questions.[24]

Despite not having data to support scientifically valid psychological studies of terrorism, many terrorism researchers offer their opinions anyway. Although they are based on nothing more than conjecture, they're still accepted as legitimate. And then we wonder why we have trouble understanding terrorists.

Hudson goes on to explain that what little evidence does exist seems to indicate terrorists are not psychologically abnormal:

> Some specialists point out, in fact, that there is little reliable evidence to support the notion that terrorists in general are psychologically disturbed individuals. The careful, detailed planning and well-timed execution that have characterized many terrorist operations are hardly typical of mentally disturbed individuals. There is considerable evidence, on the contrary, that international terrorists are generally quite sane. . . . It seems clear that terrorists are extremely alienated from society, but alienation does not necessarily mean being mentally ill.[25]

Yet despite this evidence behavioral scientists still want to try and figure out what's psychologically wrong with these people.

Dr. Jerrold Post is one of the foremost proponents of the theory that terrorists are primarily driven by psychological factors. He argues that terrorists have a peculiar psychological mind-set he calls "terrorist psycho-logic" that compels them to engage in terrorism.[26] "The cause is not the cause," he argues, "[t]he cause, as codified by the group's ideology . . . becomes the rationale for the acts the terrorists are driven to commit." In defending his thesis that terrorists are driven by psychological factors, Post says that "individuals become terrorists in order to join terrorist groups and commit acts of terrorism," turning his argument into a semantic word game Wittgenstein would have hated. That individuals become football players in order to join football teams and play football is also true but only because if football players joined a quilting bee they wouldn't be called football players anymore, they'd be called quilters. I wonder if there's a "football player psycho-logic."

Although Post recognizes the lack of any studies identifying a particular "terrorist mind" and even cites his own comparative research, which found no major psychopathology among terrorists, he still believes "a great deal has gone wrong in the lives of people who are drawn to terrorism."[27] Citing no empirical data as evidence Post describes terrorists as "outcasts . . . from the margins of society," with "personal feelings of inadequacy," who join terrorist groups simply "to belong," to feel "that what they did mattered," and to "heal their inner wounds by attacking the outside enemy." Post focuses on the terrorists' absolutist mentality, or "their core belief that 'it's us against them and they are out to destroy us,'" as proof of their damaged psychology.[28] Compare that mentality to the rhetoric the Bush administration used in justifying the Global War on Terrorism: "either you are with us or you are with the terrorists."[29] Is there a "counterterrorist psycho-logic" as well?

Post also contemplates whether terrorists love or hate their parents, which he believes would alternatively predispose them to either right-wing "national-separatist" terrorism or left-wing "anarchic-ideologue" terrorism. Based on my experience inside terrorist organizations I find this concept absolute nonsense. Some of the neo-Nazi skinheads I knew had the complete support of like-minded parents while others broke their parents' hearts. I knew some terrorists' children who supported their parents' extremism while others would have nothing to do with the movement. Some people cannot accept that terrorists are psychologically normal even when the evidence clearly supports this conclusion. But more to the point, this type of analysis is irrelevant to counterterrorism efforts. Even if we could evaluate all right-wing national-separatist terrorists and find out how many of them did love their parents, they would still make up such a tiny percentage of the total number of people who love their parents as to be statistically meaningless. Imagine the new set of questions agents at the airport ticket counter might ask if profilers adopted such theories: Did you pack your own bags? Have they been out of your possession since you packed them? Do you love your parents?

But Post makes valid points when he focuses on terrorist behavior rather than on terrorist psychology. In explaining his analysis of the nature of "terrorist psycho-logic," Post describes many of the individual and group behaviors I saw while working undercover. He describes the absolutist "us versus them" mentality, the "action-oriented" and "stimulus-hungry" nature of the terrorist operators, and the terrorist leaders' authoritarianism. He describes the pressure to conform to group mores, the intolerance for dissent, and the quasi-religious devotion terrorists have to their ideology. Finally he describes the pressure to commit acts of violence. As you will recall, in chapter 1 I described each of these behaviors in specific detail as I recounted my experiences living with terrorists.

But Post's concept of a "terrorist psycho-logic" mind-set resonated with me, if only because it described me. I have always been action oriented and stimulus hungry. I joined the FBI to a certain extent for a sense of belonging, and I liked feeling that what I did mattered. I felt pressure to conform; I wore a white shirt, tie, and dark suit with wing-tip shoes whenever I was working in the office, in keeping with the Bureau's traditions. I also felt compelled to act, to make cases, and to volunteer for dangerous assignments. And finally when I questioned some FBI managers' improper conduct in one of the counterterrorism investigations I was involved in, I was shunned. It turns out the FBI has a low tolerance for dissent within the ranks as well. Post's description of a terrorist group could easily fit the FBI.

In fact Post could use the same terms to describe any mission-oriented organization, whether a law enforcement agency, the military, a football team, or a quilting bee. When quilters meet at a quilting bee I'm sure they feel compelled to make quilts. And if they've always quilted in a certain way they wouldn't like a new quilter to come in and tell them that they should do things differently. The behavior Post describes is simply human nature, and any study of small groups, even those that have absolutely nothing to do with terrorism, will reveal the same behaviors.

Other behavioral scientists make similar mistakes. Dr. Thomas Strentz, an FBI supervisory special agent with the Behavioral Science Unit, wrote a paper describing the characteristics of right-wing terrorist groups:

> [They] continue to attract the people who are easily manipulated to their rank and file . . . we see evidence of the insecure male who . . . does not consider a female equal. These groups generally surface in times of economic and social change. They provide quick-fix solutions to complex problems for the easily manipulated. Their self-proclaimed messiah, who is usually very intelligent and well spoken has the answer to their problems.[30]

This profile is a generally correct, though stereotypical, description of a white supremacist recruit (again, of the soup variety), but it could just as easily describe a U.S. Marine recruit. Military recruiters would certainly attest that a slow economy helps recruiting, and if the "self-proclaimed messiah" label doesn't fit a Marine drill sergeant, I don't know what does.

Strentz is actually better than most in that he at least recognizes different roles within terrorist groups exist and that the leaders should not be expected to have the same psychosocial characteristics as their recruits. Here are some of the general characteristics Strentz suggests would be found in a right-wing terrorist leader:

> college educated
> thirty-five to fifty years old
> urban and sophisticated
> literate

highly verbal
well-trained and perfectionist
politically active

Below are some of the followers' characteristics:

a limited formal education
twenty to fifty-plus years old
unsophisticated
not verbal
untrained with poor work skills
politically naive[31]

But once again, the leadership characteristics Strentz identifies generally describe the qualities that would be found in a good leader in any environment. A politically naive, poorly educated, and unsophisticated person with poor verbal skills and poor work skills would rarely be asked to lead anything.

These studies are all skewed, because we just don't want to admit terrorists are human beings. But they are people just as we are. They may not be like all of us, but they're certainly like me.

Actually they're not exactly like me. As a law enforcement officer, I was in the business of saving lives, not taking lives. I was trained to use lethal force if I had to, but I made every effort to ensure I'd never have to. Terrorists are really more akin to soldiers, whose mission in a war is to take life, to actually kill the enemy. In his article "Are Terrorists Mentally Deranged?" Dr. Charles L. Ruby, a retired Air Force lieutenant colonel, describes how many of the psychological characteristics behavioral scientists often use to describe terrorists—"obsessive, compulsive, suspicious, grandiose, self-centered, and remorseless"—may be a product of their clandestine lifestyle rather than psychopathy. And, as Ruby points out, it is a lifestyle soldiers share:

> Military officials who are responsible for highly classified information and who perform sensitive missions may display obsessive, compulsive, and suspicious behaviors as a result of rigid adherence to security policies. In fact, these "pathological" characteristics enhance one's suitability for highly sensitive positions (personal experience of author). Also, high-ranking officials, individuals involved in special operations, and others who have a considerable amount of independence and power may develop a sense of grandiosity and egotism. These psychological consequences of military

experience may also apply to the competitive corporate world as well. Finally, military members who are personally responsible for killing people (including the "collateral damage" of noncombatants) in wartime probably feel remorse yet may not show it. Rather they may cope by orally justifying their violent behavior and may even resort to demonizing the enemy to ease the horror of their actions. Their verbalized justification for killing and apparent lack of remorse can be interpreted as psychopathy or sociopathy.[32]

Again, neither I nor Ruby make any moral comparison between terrorists and soldiers. I have the highest regard for the military, and I'm sure as a former Air Force officer Ruby does as well. The point is that the question of morality clouds our perceptions, making it impossible for us to see the terrorists as they are, which we must if we want to create sound policies to stop them. In fact, the terrorists are not evil monsters. They are rational, thoughtful people making conscious, predictable strategic decisions, albeit in a completely abnormal environment. Their environment is their weakness.

Terrorists resemble soldiers in their mentality, but the clandestine lifestyle required by their chosen occupation severely restricts their capabilities. They usually cannot afford to be particularly discriminating in their recruiting; they are further limited in their ability to organize, in their ability to train, and in their access to military hardware. A true picture of terrorists would show poorly selected, poorly trained, and poorly equipped soldiers in a poorly organized army. That describes our enemy, but because we don't know our enemy or understand their strategy, our policies hand them victories they never could have won on their own.

4

Compounding Confusion

Even the best states are a protection racket.

—Tom Metzger, founder, White Aryan Resistance

For a victim government, terrorism presents a political problem as well as a security problem. Terrorist acts represent a direct challenge to the governing authority's legitimacy, and as a result, political considerations rather than valid security concerns sometimes drive the government's response to terrorism. Governments can overstate the threat from a terrorist group to justify strengthening their grip on power and cracking down on dissent, or conversely, understate the problem to avoid acknowledging a legitimate political opposition's existence. All too often government reactions driven by political considerations inflame the conflict rather than resolve it.

The prime example of overstating a threat to seize illegitimate power was Adolf Hitler's reaction to the Reichstag fire. Germany's Weimar Republic was a constitutional democracy when Hitler came to power in January 1933. The Nazi Party had won the largest number of seats in the Reichstag, or the German House of Parliament, but did not hold a full majority, so President Paul von Hiddenburg struck an agreement to form a coalition government with Hitler as the chancellor. Almost immediately Hitler dissolved the government and scheduled new elections for early March 1933. On the evening of February 27, 1933, the Reichstag Building went up in flames in an obvious case of arson. The police arrested a Dutch Communist named Marinus van der Lubbe, who confessed to setting the fire. Van der Lubbe claimed to have acted alone, but Hitler used the fire to foment fear of an impending Communist revolt.

The day after the fire Hitler requested an emergency measure, the "Order of the Reich President for the Protection of People and State," temporarily suspending constitutionally protected civil rights until the impending terrorist uprising could be averted. Thousands of Communist leaders, including many of Hitler's political opponents, were immediately arrested. Not surprisingly the Nazis fared better in the new elections, and when the new government was installed, Hitler consolidated his power by pushing through another emergency measure, the "Law to Remedy the Distress of the People and the Reich," also known as the "Enabling Act," which gave Hitler the dictatorial powers he claimed were necessary to stabilize the nation's security situation.

Controversy lingers over whether the Nazis set the fire as part of a conspiracy to seize power, but Hermann Goering strenuously denied it after the war.[1] Whether the fire was staged or just fortuitous in its timing, the Nazis clearly took full advantage of the opportunity to establish a police state under the guise of protecting the Fatherland.

But under the threat of terrorism, even a government with the best intentions might react in a manner that abrogates the civil rights of the citizens it is trying to protect without necessarily adding to the nation's security. In 1919 a series of anarchist bombings, strikes, and labor riots in the United States caused a general panic, which later became known as the "Red Scare." To combat this threat U.S. attorney general Mitchell Palmer authorized a young J. Edgar Hoover, director of the Bureau of Investigation's General Intelligence Division, to conduct a series of warrantless raids targeting anarchists, Communists, Socialists, and even labor unions. These "Palmer raids," as they became known, rounded up the "alien agitators" thought to be instigating the violence—mostly eastern European and Russian immigrants, such as self-avowed anarchists Emma Goldman and Alexander Berkman—for deportation.

Palmer described his perspective on the "red" threat in an over-the-top rhetorical style:

Like a prairie-fire, the blaze of revolution was sweeping over every American institution of law and order a year ago. It was eating its way into the homes of the American workmen, its sharp tongues of revolutionary heat were licking the altars of the churches, leaping into the belfry of the school bell, crawling into the sacred corners of American homes, seeking to replace marriage vows with libertine laws, burning up the foundations of society.

Robbery, not war, is the ideal of communism. This has been demonstrated in Russia, Germany, and in America. As a foe, the anarchist is fearless of his own life, for his creed is a fanaticism that admits no respect of any other creed. Obviously it is the creed of any criminal mind, which reasons always from motives impossible to clean thought. Crime is the degenerate factor in society.[2]

The bureau arrested thousands of people and ordered them deported, but few ever faced criminal charges. Louis Post, the assistant secretary of the Department of Labor who was responsible for processing the Justice Department's deportation requests, began denying them when he discovered the bureau had no evidence that many of these immigrants had done anything wrong. As a reward for his strict adherence to the constitutional principal of due process during this time of crisis, Attorney General Palmer insisted Post be impeached. But Palmer's plans backfired when Post's vigorous defense of the rule of law during his impeachment trial exposed the widespread abuses of civil liberties that resulted from Palmer's crackdown.

Scholars regard the Palmer raids as a classic example of excessive government overreach during a crisis, but imagine what would happen today under similar circumstances. At the turn of the twentieth century, radical anarchists had already committed several acts of terrorism. A bombing and shootout during a Chicago labor protest at Haymarket Square in 1886 had left more than six police officers dead. In 1901 a young Communist assassinated U.S. president William McKinley after attending a speech in which Emma Goldman justified the use of political violence. Goldman's boyfriend, Alexander Berkman, was released from prison in 1906 after serving a lengthy sentence for his own assassination attempt against industrialist Henry Clay Fricke during the Homestead Mill strike in 1892. Berkman immediately returned to writing and speaking out in support of anarchism. Bolshevik radicals seized power in Russia with a bloody revolt in 1917, and the idea that this event might be the start of a worldwide Communist revolution was not unimaginable. When mail bombs arrived at the homes of prominent U.S. government officials living on opposite sides of the country in April 1919, a search of the postal system revealed sixteen additional bombs addressed to prominent business and political figures around the nation, including Attorney General Palmer himself. Two months later more bombs were detonated in eight different cities, and one bomber blew himself up on Palmer's front lawn, perhaps unintentionally. Palmer had good reason to start taking this unrest personally. Meanwhile, nationwide strikes involving hundreds of thousands of workers took place all across the nation. Martial law was declared in Omaha, Nebraska, and Gary, Indiana, after widespread rioting. The threat to national security appeared genuine.

Certainly the fear was real. Cartoons drawn during this period depicted bomb-wielding anarchists as swarthy, bearded enemies in foreign garb lurking dangerously in the shadows, waiting to attack symbols of American freedom. Xenophobia was on the rise. The Ku Klux Klan reformed as a political force throughout the country by presenting itself as a protector of the white Christian values increasingly under threat from a wave of new immigrants. The Klan expanded its enemies list during this period to include Jews and those they called "papists." That these new targets included the eastern European and Italian immigrants who made up much of the leftist movement in the United States at the time was no coincidence.

Ultimately the Palmer raids were little more than the Justice Department's attempt to assuage the public's fears and give the appearance that the government was doing something about the anarchist threat. By overtly targeting immigrants the department reduced the chances of any serious public resistance to its heavy-handed tactics. It's impossible to know whether the Palmer raids were successful in preventing other, perhaps even more serious terrorist acts. For his part, even after his methods were denounced, Palmer was unrepentant:

> I apologize for nothing that the Department of Justice has done.
> . . . I glory in it . . . and if agents of the Department of Labor were
> a little rough and unkind . . . with these alien agitators . . . I think
> it might well be overlooked in the general good to the country.[3]

Judging from the evidence recovered during the thousands of arrests and searches, however, there is room for doubt about Palmer's threat assessment. The only weapons reportedly seized during the raids were three pistols.[4] Some revolution.

Anarchists continued to pose a threat, however. In September 1920, shortly after the Red Scare subsided and Palmer's aggressive tactics were abandoned, a horse cart loaded with scrap metal and 100 pounds of dynamite blew up on Wall Street, in the heart of New York's financial district, and killed thirty-three people. Law enforcement suspected anarchists but never solved the crime. More anarchist-related bombings were reported over the next decade. Clearly Palmer's raids had not swept up all the agitators, despite the free hand law enforcement was given to trample civil liberties in the name of increased security. The dragnet didn't work, and the terrorists remained free to strike.

But a Bolshevik revolution in the United States never materialized, either. The government's abusive counterterrorism tactics appear to have been ineffective and unnecessary. The controversy ended Palmer's political career and brought public disrepute to the Justice Department and the fledgling Bureau of Investigation. But the question was always more one of competence rather than an intentional abuse of power. Palmer and Hoover had nothing to gain by rounding up innocent aliens and everything to lose by failing to solve the bombings. They believed the threat was real and did what they thought necessary to protect the nation. They just happened to be wrong. Although Hoover promised to reform the FBI and do away with the "radical activities" department when he became director,[5] he remained genuinely concerned—obsessively so—about the threat communism posed to American values during his reign.

Questions about the U.S. government's competence to properly evaluate and effectively manage a terrorist threat are not new. Our history shows that officials responsible for countering asymmetrical threats to national security often misjudge the risk posed by different types of social movements, primarily when biased perceptions drive the policies rather than an objective analysis of the threat's nature or scope. The anti-immigrant government policies in the early twentieth century were borne out of fear of the "alien agitator" and the threat from abroad. But these policies gave tacit encouragement to the rebirth and growth of the largest, deadliest, and longest-lasting terrorist organization ever to exist in America, the Ku Klux Klan.

Alas, this trend was repeated. Another example the government's overreaction to a perceived national security threat, which also saw few arrests and prosecutions of terrorists, was the outrageous and sometimes bizarre FBI response to the radicalization of the New Left student protest groups in the 1970s. As student-activist organizations advocating for civil rights and for an end to the Vietnam War became more disruptive, the FBI began using techniques originally designed to counter the activities of hostile foreign intelligence agents. The FBI made this decision in part out of "frustration with the apparent inability of traditional law enforcement methods to solve the problems presented."[6]

The FBI's Counterintelligence Program (COINTELPRO) included many different aggressive and even illegal techniques—the Senate Committee investigating these abuses would later call them "tactics of wartime"—to "expose, disrupt, and otherwise neutralize" the activities of U.S. dissident groups. FBI assistant director William Sullivan described the program as

> a rough, tough, dirty business, and dangerous. It was dangerous at times. No holds were barred. . . . We have used [these techniques] against Soviet agents. They have used [them] against us. . . . [The same methods were] brought home against any organization against which we were targeted. We did not differentiate. This is a rough, tough business.[7]

COINTELPRO is most infamous for the dirty tricks campaign waged against Dr. Martin Luther King (which were designed to prevent him from becoming a "black messiah," according to official records) and other nonviolent civil rights groups. It consisted of five separate programs: the Communist Party USA (CPUSA) program, initiated in 1956; the Socialist Worker's Party program, 1961; the White Hate program, 1964; the Black Nationalist program, 1967; and the New Left program, 1968.

That COINTELPRO started with the Communist Party USA makes sense. The program's original purpose was to counter the intelligence-gathering activities of hostile foreign nations, and the CPUSA had been "blatantly" involved in past Soviet espionage, according to the FBI.[8] The FBI had become responsible for foreign counterintelligence investigations during World War II, and the FBI developed a National Security Division to deal in these highly classified investigations, which rarely, if ever, resulted in public charges. Using foreign counterintelligence techniques in domestic security investigations would have dire consequences, however, when these covert techniques were exposed to public scrutiny. Some COINTELPRO files were stolen during the burglary of an FBI office in Media, Pennsylvania, and released to the public, resulting in a scandal that saw several FBI agents themselves charged with criminal offenses. Meanwhile many terrorists escaped prosecution because COINTELPRO techniques couldn't stand up in federal court. Most evidence gathered during COINTELPRO was ultimately worthless to a criminal prosecution.

Some COINTELPRO techniques were mundane: "anonymously mailing reprints of newspaper and magazine articles . . . to group members or supporters to convince them of the error of their ways" and "attempting to arrange for reporters to interview targets with planted questions." Other methods were simply inappropriate: "mailing anonymous letters to a member's spouse accusing the target of infidelity" and "using informants to raise controversial issues at meetings in order to cause dissent." Finally there were some practices that were absolutely illegal, such as "encouraging street warfare between violent groups."[9]

But the problem wasn't just that these techniques were illegal and inappropriate for investigating domestic terrorist groups; they were ineffective as well.

The FBI started the COINTELPRO program with three stated purposes in mind: to protect national security, to prevent violence, and to maintain the existing social and political order. While protecting national security and preventing violence were viewed as entirely appropriate goals, the Church Committee expressed concern about the FBI seeing itself as a protector of "social and political order."

The five separate COINTELPRO programs did not all operate in the same manner. The Senate Select Committee that investigated COINTELPRO, better known as the Church Committee, found:

> The White Hate program, for example, was very precisely targeted; each of the other programs spread to a number of groups which do not appear to fall within any clear parameters. In fact, with each subsequent COINTELPRO, the targeting became more diffuse. The White Hate COINTELPRO also used comparatively few techniques which carried a risk of serious physical, emotional, or economic damage to the targets, while the Black Nationalist COINTELPRO used such techniques extensively.[10]

The nastiest of those techniques carrying a risk of physical damage was "the snitch jacket," in which agents leaked false information suggesting one of the targeted group's members was a police informant. The leak's purpose seems obvious, but the FBI claimed no deaths ultimately resulted from this practice. Another risky COINTELPRO technique was to try and instigate violence between radical groups. FBI offices actually claimed "credit" for at least four assaults as proof of this method's effectiveness in the Black Nationalist program.[11]

The Church Committee found the New Left program "had the highest proportion of proposals aimed at preventing the exercise of free speech. Like the progression in targeting, the use of dangerous, degrading, or blatantly unconstitutional techniques also appears to have become less restrained with each subsequent program."[12]

The specifically stated purpose of the FBI's New Left program was to "expose, disrupt, and otherwise neutralize" the activities of an ill-defined group of student-activists in response to the growing unrest on college campuses around the country. But FBI officials the Church Committee interviewed couldn't even articulate what they meant by "the New Left." One FBI supervisor quoted in the Senate report talked about the political pressure exerted on the FBI:

> During that particular time, there was considerable public, Administration—I mean governmental Administration [and] news media interest in the protest movement to the extent that some groups, I don't recall any specifics, but some groups were calling for something to be done to blunt or reduce the protest movements that were disrupting campuses. I can't classify it as exactly an hysteria, but there was considerable interest [and concern]. That was the framework that we were working with. . . . It would be my

impression that as a result of this hysteria, some governmental leaders were looking to the Bureau.[13]

Once again, the government expected that the FBI "do something," and from its inception, the New Left program appeared to focus more on protecting "the social order" than on national security. The Church Committee cited an example of the FBI using COINTELPRO techniques against two students who demonstrated for their right to use a four-letter word in a free-speech rally because the FBI felt their demonstration showed an "obvious disregard for decency and established morality."

The New Left program started on October 28, 1968, which in hindsight was incredibly fortuitous timing. It preceded the first bombing attributed to the Weather Underground Organization (WUO), the militant offshoot of Students for a Democratic Society (SDS), by almost a full year. The "Days of Rage" rampage through the streets of Chicago, which WUO leaders had billed as the beginning of the armed revolution inside the United States, was kicked off with the bombing of the Haymarket Square Police Statue on October 7, 1969. One would think that a year-long, aggressive counterintelligence program would have developed significant inroads with this group by that time, but the bombing remains unsolved, as do most of the other forty or so bombings or attempted bombings attributed to the WUO over the next six years.[14]

A July 1968 strategy memo from FBI headquarters outlined the counterintelligence techniques agents could use to neutralize the New Left:

(1) preparing leaflets designed to discredit student demonstrators, using photographs of New Left leadership at the respective universities. "Naturally, the most obnoxious pictures should be used";
(2) instigating "personal conflicts or animosities" between New Left leaders;
(3) creating the impression that leaders are "informants for the Bureau or other law enforcement agencies";
(4) sending articles from student newspapers or the "underground press" which show the depravity of the New Left to university officials, donors, legislators, and parents. "Articles showing advocation of the use of narcotics and free sex are ideal";
(5) having members arrested on marijuana charges;
(6) sending anonymous letters about a student's activities to parents, neighbors, and the parents' employers. "This could have the effect of forcing the parents to take action";
(7) sending anonymous letters or leaflets describing the "activities and

associations" of New Left faculty members and graduate assistants
to university officials, legislators, Boards of Regents, and the press.
"These letters should be signed 'A Concerned Alumni,' or 'A Concerned Taxpayer'";

(8) using "cooperative press contacts" to emphasize that the "disruptive
elements" constitute a "minority" of the students. "The press should
demand an immediate referendum on the issue in question";

(9) exploiting the "hostility" among the SDS and other New Left groups
toward the SWP (Socialist Workers' Party), YSA (Youth for Socialist Action), and Progressive Labor Party;

(10) using "friendly news media" and law enforcement officials to disrupt New Left coffeehouses near military bases which are attempting to "influence members of the Armed Forces";

(11) using cartoons, photographs, and anonymous letters to "ridicule"
the New Left, and

(12) using "misinformation" to "confuse and disrupt" New Left activities, such as by notifying members that events have been cancelled.[15]

As might be expected, these measures proved useful neither in actually preventing the WUO or other New Left groups from committing
violent crimes, which was the stated goal of the COINTELPRO program, nor in successfully investigating and prosecuting their criminal
activities (other than for marijuana possession). Overall the FBI agents
interviewed during the Senate investigation described the New Left program as ineffective and misdirected. The Church Committee concluded:
"Upholding decency and established morality, defending the correctness
of U.S. foreign policy, and attacking those who thought the Chicago
police used undue force have no apparent connection with the expressed
goals of protecting national security and preventing violence."[16]

Making the situation worse, when the COINTELPRO investigations' unlawful nature became public, several criminal cases that could
have been made against WUO terrorists had to be dismissed.

Was the WUO a threat to national security? Its often-stated goal
was to overthrow the "imperialist" U.S. government, but the organization never had more than thirty or forty members (although they claimed
several hundred).[17] It was a small army if it was an army at all. After a
WUO bomb factory in New York City blew up, killing three WUO
members, the group took efforts to ensure that no one was actually killed
in its bombings, timing them when no one was likely to be around and
calling in bomb warnings to the authorities. In fact only one death possibly attributable to the WUO occurred, when a police station in San Francisco was bombed and a police officer was killed. The WUO did not

claim credit for this bombing, and the area was home to other left-wing radical organizations that were less squeamish about murder than the WUO was, so we may never know. The WUO, however, did successfully bomb the U.S. Capitol, the U.S. State Department, the Pentagon, local police stations throughout the country, National Guard facilities, and the offices of multinational corporations. These attacks certainly demonstrated technical proficiency, uncommon bravado, and a reckless disregard for human life (in spite of phoned-in bomb warnings). With the 1973 U.S. withdrawal from Vietnam, the WUO's primary justification for using violence was gone, and by the late 1970s the WUO disbanded. Fugitive members began turning themselves in by the early 1980s. Some who remained underground joined with other radical groups or formed their own and continued their armed resistance. Most of those who came out of hiding received little jail time and successfully reintegrated into society. A few even serve as faculty at U.S. universities, including former WUO leader Bernardine Dohrn, who works at my own alma mater, Northwestern University Law School.

Now the public generally regards the WUO not as a terrorist group but as a group of misguided kids who got carried away in expressing their idealism during an intense period of civil conflict over the Vietnam War. A review of FBI records released under the Freedom of Information Act paints a much different picture, however. In fact, WUO members made numerous trips to Vietnam, Cambodia, Eastern Europe, and Cuba to receive training in revolutionary techniques and to meet with Communist leaders, including officials from the National Liberation Front in Vietnam and the Cuban government. According to the 1976 FBI summary, WUO members maintained contact with Vietnamese and Cuban intelligence officials after returning to the United States.[18]

The WUO engaged in these activities during a period of hostility with Cuba and an active war with Vietnam. To put its activities in today's context, imagine American student-activists traveling to Iraq or Afghanistan, training with al Qaeda, and then returning to the United States with the stated purpose of "bringing the war home." Would we be concerned with their civil liberties and their free speech rights?

The FBI meticulously documented the WUO's contacts with these hostile foreign nations. The 1976 FBI report summarizing the WUO's foreign influences is more than 400 pages long. This evidence would have been inadmissible in a criminal court though, and because it was classified it remained hidden from the American public for decades. Thus, it would have been impossible for the average policeman, much less the average citizen, to have drawn accurate conclusions about the threat posed by the Weather Underground.

The Church Committee report also described the FBI's perception of their success against the Klan, which provides an interesting comparison. The FBI officials interviewed during the Church Committee investigation generally regarded the White Hate program as extremely effective. One FBI official said:

> I think the Bureau got the job done. . . . I think that one reason we were able to get the job done was that we were able to use counterintelligence techniques. It is possible that we eventually could have done the job without counterintelligence techniques. I am not sure we could have done it as well or as quickly.

His boss seconded this view:

> I think from what I have seen and what I have read, as far as the counterintelligence program on the Klan is concerned, that it was effective. I think it was one of the most effective programs I have ever seen the Bureau handle as far as any group is concerned.[19]

On the one hand, the FBI perceived its New Left program as ineffective, although only one death was possibly attributable to the WUO and the New Left movement disintegrated by the late 1970s. On the other hand, the FBI viewed its White Hate program as very effective, despite the steady numbers of hate crimes, bombings, and murders attributable to white supremacist groups continuing right up to the present day.

Underestimating the threat from white hate groups might have been understandable for the FBI in the 1970s. After all, the FBI resisted hiring blacks as special agents until after J. Edgar Hoover died in 1972. Not many supervisors at FBI Headquarters during that period were likely to feel personally threatened by white supremacist groups. Conversely, the much smaller Black Nationalist groups, such as the Black Panther Party and the Black Liberation Army, directly targeted law enforcement officers. That agents found themselves in the crosshairs may explain why the FBI used more aggressive techniques against the Black Nationalist groups. Unfortunately, the FBI's skewed perception of the relative seriousness of the different groups' threats still exists.

Today the FBI ranks eco-terror groups as the number one domestic terrorist threat in the United States, despite the fact that not one death has been reported as a result of eco-terrorism. Meanwhile the Southern Poverty Law Center documented almost sixty right-wing terrorist plots in the ten-year period following the 1995 Oklahoma City bombing.[20] A Department of Justice Bureau of Justice Statistics study published in

November 2005 revealed that an average of 191,000 hate crimes occur every year, 85 percent of which involve violent crimes. While not all these crimes can be attributed to white hate groups, it is revealing that the Bureau of Justice Statistics' averages are more than fifteen times higher than the number of hate crimes reported annually by the FBI.[21] The FBI still doesn't have an accurate grasp of the scope of racial violence in this country.

Part of the reason the FBI considered its White Hate COINTELPRO successful is that instead of focusing on the Klan's political ideology, which Director Hoover and many of his white agents apparently had some sympathy for, it targeted those Klan extremists who actually committed acts of violence.[22] The FBI's New Left program, by comparison, focused almost exclusively on countering the subversive ideology of the student groups, almost to the exclusion of addressing their criminal activities. Why waste investigative resources on a program to send newspaper articles to college professors and to harass students who want to use four-letter words when Communist-trained radicals are bombing the Capitol? An approach directly focused on the New Left's violent criminal element would have been a far more effective, efficient use of bureau resources and ultimately would have resulted in far less consternation for the nation as a whole. Exposing an aggressive law enforcement program directed against Vietnamese- and Cuban-trained American bombers who attacked symbols of democracy here in the United States would likely have generated little public concern.

Combined with the Bureau's misperception of the nature of the threat different terrorist groups pose is its lack of understanding of how terrorist groups actually organize and operate. This ignorance debilitates countererrorism operations.

For example, the FBI uses the term *domestic terrorism* to define terrorism committed by groups indigenous to the United States and the term *international terrorism* to define terrorism committed by groups based abroad. But terrorist groups don't behave differently just because they live in different parts of the world. As a matter of fact, most extremist movements that the FBI categorizes as domestic terrorists, such as neo-Nazis and the Animal Liberation Front, originated overseas and still maintain an international dimension to their activities. Nazism began in Europe, not the United States. In 2005 prominent white supremacist and former Klan leader David Duke traveled to Syria and the Ukraine to speak to audiences eager to hear his anti-Semitic message. Likewise, as we saw too vividly on September 11, 2001, and more recently in the train bombings in Madrid (2004) and London (2005), international terrorist groups are able to recruit terror cells who can plan and execute operations domestically.

The FBI's distinction between international and domestic terrorism has more to do with allocating administrative resources than with assessing the different groups' threats. Such bureaucratic organizations as the FBI often need to create arbitrary categories to distribute and track resources for internal administrative purposes, and that's perfectly understandable. The problem arises when the FBI allows its arbitrary administrative distinction between domestic and international terrorists to actually affect the way it conducts investigations of the different groups. Today in FBI, domestic terrorists are treated as a local crime problem while international terrorists are treated as national security threats. Just as during the Red Scare, external threats are seen as more dangerous than local threats, even though Americans are far more likely to be killed by domestic terrorists than by international terrorists.

The U.S. intelligence failures that preceded the al Qaeda terrorist attacks of 9/11 are well documented. The 9/11 Commission blamed the FBI's failures in part on the proposition that the FBI "has long favored its criminal justice mission over its national security mission."[23] But this conclusion conflicts with the facts. After the COINTELPRO disaster in the 1970s, the Department of Justice issued guidelines mandating that domestic terrorism investigations would be exclusively treated as criminal matters. The FBI has always treated international terrorism as a national security matter, however, and it still does.

The FBI primarily investigates international terrorism using the counterintelligence techniques it designed for use against Soviet agents, not criminal investigations. Just as in the pre-COINTELPRO days, the bureau's counterintelligence methods are highly classified; therefore, the intelligence collected in these investigations was segregated from the FBI's criminal investigators by an "intelligence wall." This "wall" (really a set of bureaucratic rules) was built to protect criminal investigations from being tainted with evidence collected through inadmissible means, and to prevent the exposure of classified information, sources, and methods in public trials. In fact, the three FBI investigations that the 9/11 Commission identified as missed operational opportunities to have interdicted the attack—the Phoenix Memo requesting an investigation into the large number of terrorism suspects taking flight lessons, the failure to locate hijackers Khalid al Mihdhar and Nawaf al Hamzi when they traveled to the United States, and the failure to properly investigate the activities of Zacarias Moussaoui—were all being investigated by the FBI as counterintelligence matters and not as criminal matters. These failures occurred because the intelligence collectors didn't pass their intelligence to the FBI's criminal investigators. Our intelligence agencies were so concerned about protecting their sources and methods that they forgot that their mission was to protect the nation's security.

One special agent assigned to criminal investigations even complained to FBI headquarters about its failure to share information regarding Mihdhar and al Hamzi in an e-mail: "Someday someone will die—and . . . the public will not understand why we were not more effective and throwing every resource we had at certain 'problems.'"[24] Contrary to the 9/11 Commission's assertions, the FBI didn't rely too heavily on its criminal investigators—it didn't rely on them at all. And it turns out counterintelligence techniques are no better suited to international terrorism investigations in the twenty-first century than they were to domestic terrorism investigations in the 1960s and 1970s.

All this confusion has an unnecessarily debilitative effect on counterterrorism operations, because these misperceptions are allowed to drive our policy. Instead of learning the lessons of COINTELPRO and of 9/11, we now use almost exclusively counterintelligence methods in our counterterrorism efforts. The intelligence wall has supposedly been torn down by the Patriot Act, which contained provisions authorizing the sharing of intelligence with criminal investigators, but the information collected using counterintelligence techniques is all still highly classified, which limits its dissemination and compromises its use as evidence. State and local law enforcement officials, the front line of defense within the United States, often are not cleared to see critical intelligence affecting their communities. Even where select local officers are allowed to participate in FBI Joint Terrorism Task Forces they are forbidden from sharing the classified intelligence they learn with their own agencies. Many post–9/11 terrorism prosecutions have experienced difficulties because of the increased use of classified methods in criminal terrorism investigations. The government still protects its sources and methods to the detriment of our national security. As we saw during COINTELPRO, terrorists benefit from government secrecy.

This problem is not just with the FBI. The FBI, the CIA, and the Department of Defense are all Industrial Age, bureaucratic, hierarchal organizations with formal chains of command and procedural rules. When these organizations analyze terrorist groups, the investigators look for and expect to find the same type of structure. They want to know the name of the organization, who is in charge, who the lieutenants are, and the role each member plays. In a statement released as part of Zacarias Moussaoui's criminal trial and then quoted in the *New York Times,* Khalid Sheikh Mohammed, mastermind of the 9/11 attack, seemed to ridicule the U.S. investigators interrogating him after his 2003 arrest in Pakistan:

> I know that the materialistic Western mind cannot grasp the idea,
> and it is difficult for them to believe that the high officials in Al
> Qaeda do not know about operations carried out by its opera-
> tives, but this is how it works. . . . We do not submit written
> reports to our higher ups. I conducted the September 11 opera-
> tion by submitting only oral reports.[25]

Clandestine groups simply don't have the luxury of formal organization. To avoid detection they must spread authority, especially operational authority, and disguise associations. This paradigm is not new.
Long before al Qaeda, Louis Beam urged his followers to use leaderless
resistance and phantom cells to limit detection and criminal liability, and
Tom Metzger went one better by recommending "lone wolf" tactics—
the creation of one-person terror cells—that would appear to eliminate
organizational structure altogether and even further limit operational
exposure. But these practices are actually much older. David Cunningham,
author of *There's Something Happening Here: The New Left, the Klan, and
FBI Counterintelligence,* outlined the challenge the FBI faced when investigating the Weather Underground. He described it as "an underground
organization that had eschewed centralization for small isolated cells
often operating autonomously. Since Weatherman in its underground
incarnation involved an extreme lifestyle and total commitment, a vast
informant network proved impossible to develop for this target."[26]

Al Qaeda is executing a time-tested strategy, and its members are
doing it by the book. Plus it is much easier now, as the Internet has made
communication simple and instantaneous and formal organization all
but unnecessary. Terrorists groups of all kinds now use this technology to
its fullest capability. Today's terrorists can recruit, indoctrinate, and communicate without even meeting each other. Terrorism has become an
Information Age threat, but our intelligence agencies still examine it
through an Industrial Age lens.

In all my time working inside terrorist groups, I never went through
any formal induction ceremony or officially signed on as a member of
any organization. Some of the terrorists I worked with didn't even know
my name. Yet they sold me illegal arms and explosives, and I was present
during the planning of terrorist attacks. So was I a member of a terrorist
organization? I certainly acted like one but proving it would have been
difficult had I not been taping all of my conversations.

The problem counterterrorism agencies face is terrorist groups do
not act like corporations. There are no rules for obtaining membership,
no employment contracts, no membership cards. Cellular structures, leaderless resistance, lone wolf strategies, and Internet communications make

it very difficult for intelligence or law enforcement officials to understand or to even see the group's organization. But just because these techniques mask the organization doesn't mean there isn't an organization.
The FBI made this mistake with the Ku Klux Klan during the
COINTELPRO era, when it focused too narrowly on the group's vio-
lence-prone members to the exclusion of the group's leaders. Once again,
David Cunningham explains:

> In many communities the local Klan chapter served mainly as a
> fraternal civic organization . . . , and only a small percentage of
> members were prone to violence. In 1964 when the FBI began
> active attempts to repress the Klan, agents recognized these facts,
> devoting special attention to what they termed "action groups,"
> or "the relatively few individuals in each [Klan] organization who
> use strong-arm tactics and violent actions to achieve their ends
> . . . without the approval of the organization or membership."
> The dangerous individuals were indeed "relatively few," though
> the Bureau's characterization managed to seriously underestimate
> the complicity of Klan leaders in the action groups' misdeeds. Far
> from being renegades operating without the formal organization's
> consent, members of action groups (referred to in some Klaverns
> as "wrecking crews") tended to be the Klan's elite members, those
> who had proven their loyalty and toughness. In many cases the
> Klan leadership recruited and cultivated these crews, and it was
> considered an honor to be selected to participate in their violent
> missions.[27]

In the 1960s the Klan presented itself as a benign social club with
just a few bad apples who acted out once in a while to mask its organized
criminal activities. Today's white supremacist organizations use lone wolf
techniques and Internet websites to the same effect. But just as the FBI
fell for the Klan's "civic organization" ruse in the 1960s, it has fallen for
the myth of the lone extremist. Then–FBI director Robert Mueller testi-
fied before Congress in 2003 about threats posed by domestic terrorists:

> I am particularly concerned about loosely affiliated terrorists and
> lone offenders, which are inherently difficult to interdict given
> the anonymity of individuals that maintain limited or no links to
> established terrorist groups but act out of sympathy with a larger
> cause. We should not forget the Oklahoma City bombing in 1995,
> for example, which was carried out by individuals unaffiliated with
> a larger group.[28]

The problem with this statement, of course, is that Timothy McVeigh and his accomplices were not unaffiliated with a larger group. They were just not affiliated in a way that Director Mueller recognized or understood. In fact McVeigh associated with a number of extremist groups, much the way I did when I was undercover. McVeigh sold *The Turner Diaries* at gun shows, and he reportedly associated with different right-wing extremist groups in at least three states. Of course, today you can buy *The Turner Diaries* at big chain book stores or over the Internet, largely because McVeigh made it so famous, but in 1995 you had to go to its source—William Pierce, the founder of the white supremacist organization the National Alliance—who sold it in bulk to vendors such as McVeigh. The book is not good literature, but it is an informative manual for carrying out a terrorist truck bombing. That McVeigh had photocopied pages from the book with him in his car on the day of the bombing should have been a clue about his affiliations with extremist groups. That one of McVeigh's accomplices, Terry Nichols, had a copy of *Hunter*—Pierce's sequel to *The Turner Diaries*—should have been an even bigger clue that their plot involved more than the whims of a couple of "lone extremists."[29] In *Hunter* a lone extremist acts on behalf of the white supremacist cause.

McVeigh was not a lone extremist; instead, he was trained to make himself look like a lone extremist, just as I was. Lone extremism is not a phenomenon; it's a right-wing terrorism technique that comes complete with written instruction manuals. It's a ruse the FBI bought, hook, line, and sinker. In his 1999 analysis of the academic research on terrorism, Rex Hudson found a gem of a quote on the subject of lone terrorism from criminologist Franco Ferracuti, who postulated there was "no such thing as an isolated terrorist—that's a mental case."[30]

Now I am not suggesting that any other person was culpable for the Oklahoma City bombing itself. To involve more than two or three people in an operation's details would violate lone wolf tactics. What I am suggesting is that the bombers were affiliated with a larger group or groups. These groups trained, supported, and encouraged McVeigh to his commit criminal acts, the same way they did with me, and just as in the 1960s, the FBI should not make the mistake of ignoring the movement leaders' role in the criminal activity.

Labeling terrorists *lone extremists* serves two important functions for the government: first, the FBI could be forgiven for not having foreseen and prevented a bombing by a lone actor, and second, the FBI could reassure the public that with the bomber in custody there was not a continuing threat. Just a little over a year later, however, the FBI labeled another bomber from the right-wing antigovernment movement, Eric Rudolph, as a lone extremist. I guess the next one will be, too.

To be sure, terrorism presents the FBI, or any law enforcement agency, with a difficult challenge. They have to limit their counterterrorism efforts to focus exclusively on the violent criminals within the organization, rather than on the ideology or on the organization as a whole, and still gather enough intelligence about the organization to recognize how it supports and encourages the violence. It's a difficult task, but it can be done effectively using constitutionally sound law enforcement procedures. I know, because I've done it—twice.

Unfortunately, the FBI doesn't know what I learned about how to infiltrate terrorist groups and successfully prosecute terrorists. Despite my repeated requests, the Domestic Terrorism Unit at FBI headquarters never debriefed me.

But perhaps I flatter myself. Perhaps my insights and analyses of the terrorist groups I infiltrated aren't valuable and wouldn't be useful to an organization whose number-one priority is preventing terrorism. Fortunately all of my meetings with terrorists were recorded, so people much smarter than I could analyze the evidence for its intelligence value. The tapes aren't secret; they were introduced as evidence in public trials. Surely FBI counterterrorism experts and behavioral scientists, who recognize how their work suffers from the lack of reliable data about terrorist group behavior, would find a wealth of information in these recordings—namely, how extremist groups recruit, how operational cells are organized and directed, and how targets are selected. But the tapes have never been analyzed either. This neglect is the true intelligence failure, the failure to recognize the value of the intelligence we already have.

Part II:
Mind-set and Methods

5
Understanding Political Violence

I only regret that I have but one life to lose for my country.

—NATHAN HALE

In the campy 1984 John Milius film, *Red Dawn,* Cuban and Russian military forces invade the United States in a brazen Cold War sneak attack and occupy America's heartland.[1] A few plucky high school students with skills developed from exercising their Second Amendment rights decide to take to the mountains and form a ragtag insurgency rather than submit to Communist enslavement as the rest of their community does. Under the war cry "Wolverines!" (their high school mascot), they attack the unsuspecting oppressors, using guerrilla tactics that bog down the invaders and ultimately force their retreat.

Red Dawn is the militia movement's favorite film.

The militias see twenty-first-century America under the influence of a much more sinister foreign occupation, one led by a cabal of satanic internationalist bankers who've succeeded in corrupting and weakening America with a godless multicultural value system. These internationalist forces are even more sinister than invading armies because they don't show themselves. They invade with stealth, pulling the strings behind the action, like puppet masters. To prove their assertions, the militias use the old propaganda trick of peppering their fables with well-established facts. One of their conspiracy theories suggests fluoridated water is a plot to dull American minds by poisoning the water supply. Everyone knows the government puts fluoride in the water and that fluoride is a poison, so drawing the conclusion that the government is poisoning us seems reasonable. The militias' proof of the existence of a satanic cult controlling the government involves an examination of the Great Seal on the back of a U.S. dollar bill. They say *Annuit Coeptis Novus Ordo Seclorum* means "announcing the conception of a secular [i.e., without God] New World Order" and point out the picture of Satan's "evil eye" overseeing the thirteen levels of hell. In fact these are two separate phrases. *Annuit Coeptis* means "He (God) has favored our undertakings," and *Novus Ordo Seclorum* means "a new order for the ages."[2] The eye represents the eye of providence and the thirteen levels of the pyramid the thirteen original colonies. But why would you believe me and not them?

The militias see themselves as true patriots who take to the mountains (figuratively) to resist these evil forces when no one else dares, just like those plucky high school kids in the movie. This fantasy would be just a silly diversion from otherwise ordinary lives were it not for their penchant for acting on these odd beliefs with real guns and explosives.

I mention *Red Dawn* whenever I lecture to police or military audiences about the terrorists' mind-set because the movie is instructive to understanding how they justify and legitimize the use of violence, even terrorist violence. Most Americans, particularly police officers, initially can't picture any circumstances in which they would resort to terrorism. The film presents a circumstance in which they would. It starts with images of the quintessential, American small town: red-cheeked, happy, athletic children; big blue skies; majestic purple mountains; and amber waves of grain. Seeing this idealized vision of America under foreign military occupation—a Communist occupation no less—would be enough to drive any red-blooded American, even police officers, to engage in violent resistance. Immediately someone in my audience will object and argue that the violent resistance depicted in the film is not terrorism because the Communists invaded the United States first. Terrorists make this exact argument: our violence is legitimate because it is a justifiable response to an injustice committed against our people.

The point is some imaginable circumstances would allow for and in fact would even compel us to engage in violent resistance. Why is it, then, that we have such a hard time understanding the mind-set of the politically motivated terrorist?

In *The Leviathan* political philosopher Thomas Hobbes imagined what a world without law, an uncivilized "natural state," would look like.[3] He pictured people driven by unrestrained self-interest living in a perpetual state of war over the finite resources required for survival. Neither great physical strength nor superior intellect allows one person to rule over another, because these advantages are easily overcome by the secret machinations of others or by a confederacy of enemies. Hobbes argued that without law there was no justice or injustice, only the struggle for survival. He described the quality of a person's life in this world as "solitary, poor, nasty, brutish and short."[4]

To escape this fate people enter into an agreement, each of us sacrificing our own right to do as we please in exchange for the peace and security that comes with others promising to restrict their own behavior and "be contented with so much liberty against other men as he would allow other men against himself."[5] This agreement, codified through the law, serves as the basic foundation for social order. As a lawyer I have great faith in the law, but clearly the law as established through Hobbes's social contract is not enough to eliminate violence altogether. Hence he presents two fundamental laws of nature: "the first . . . which is: to seek peace and follow it. The second, the sum of the right of nature, which is: by all means we can to defend ourselves."[6]

Not everyone lives up to their obligations under our social contract; some cheat, break the law, and victimize their neighbors. We have a name for those who refuse to obey the law—"criminals." Criminals are a danger to society not just because they threaten and attack individuals, but because they threaten the social contract and risk unraveling the very fabric of society.

> But if other men will not lay down their right, as well as he, then
> there is no reason for anyone to divest himself of his: for that were
> to expose himself to prey, which no man is bound to, rather than
> to dispose himself to peace.[7]

If the government does not deal with criminals properly, the social contract itself is at risk. Thus the law allows for and actually legalizes certain kinds of violence.

The most fundamental human right, or "law of nature" as Hobbes would say, is the right of self-defense—namely, the right to use force, even deadly force, as necessary to resist and repel an attacker. That self-defense is a right only makes sense, of course, because without the right to protect your own life, no other rights would have meaning. Terrorists fill their manifestos with self-defense arguments.

But the right to use violence in self-defense is strictly limited. Under common law a person under attack can use force only as a last resort, the amount of force used in self-defense must be proportionate to the attacker's force, and the violence must end as soon as the threat is mitigated. The doctrine of self-defense prohibits using force either to avenge a previous attack or to punish an attacker.

But even with these strict limitations, legalizing the right to use force in self-defense raises some difficult questions. When can force be used? Do we have to wait for assailants to actually strike us before we can fight back? Can we resist when they raise their clubs? How about when they just threaten violence? And who gets to say what force is reasonable under the circumstances? If these questions aren't fairly resolved we might find ourselves slipping into the perpetual warfare state that Hobbes envisioned, where it's every man for himself.

So we create a proper authority, a government, to establish a rule of law and resolve these lingering questions. Government, at least according to the Constitution of the United States, is created to "establish justice, ensure domestic tranquility, [and] provide for the common defense."[8] To establish justice, governments write laws and set up courts of law to resolve disputes. They create police forces to ensure domestic tranquility and raise armies to provide for the common defense.

To fulfill these duties governments have the authority to use force in ways individuals cannot. They authorize the police to use a reasonable amount of force necessary to capture and arrest criminals. Police can even apply lethal force not only in self-defense but also to protect the lives of others. Police don't have a duty to retreat and they can intervene in the disputes of private parties to prevent harm from being done to innocent people.

Through the courts governments can use force punitively—that is, to punish people who break the law. Even Hobbes noted, after all, that the social contract's bonds "have their strength, not from their own nature (for nothing is more easily broken than a man's word), but from fear of some evil consequence upon the rupture."[9] Punishment is meant to serve as both a deterrent and a form of retribution or revenge. The courts also use force as prophylaxis. They protect society from criminals by physically restraining them and locking them in prison to prevent them from committing other crimes. California has a "Three Strikes and You're Out" law: once a criminal is convicted of three violent offenses, that person automatically receives a life sentence to protect society. Under current U.S. law, the government can even use lethal force—the death penalty—as a form of punishment.

But is a government's use of force necessarily legitimate? The word *legitimate* has two meanings. The first meaning is "legal," or "accordant with the law."[10] A government can always claim its actions are legal; after all, it writes the laws. If the government wants to do something that's illegal, it just writes a law that says it's legal. When Hitler wanted to usurp dictatorial powers, for instance, he just had the Reichstag draw up the Enabling Act. When the Confederate Army needed the tactical flexibility of units like Quantrill's raiders, the Confederate Congress passed the Partisan Ranger Act to legalize their dubious conduct. Having the power to write the law can often be convenient, but situations like these render the rule of law all but meaningless.

Another meaning of the word *legitimate* is "proper," or "conforming to recognized principles or accepted rules and standards."[11] That meaning guides this discussion. How does a government establish its "proper" authority? With a manifesto, of course. In the Declaration of Independence, Jefferson wrote that governments derive "just powers" from "the consent of the governed." A legitimate government's proper authority, according to Jefferson, is established through the common agreement of the people. The only problem is Jefferson goes on to say the people have the right to overthrow their government when they decide it no longer serves their interests and is, therefore, no longer legitimate. And this right is where all the trouble lies.

If "the people" decide a government's exercise of force is improper, or illegitimate, then "the people" against whom that force is used have the right to defend themselves, violently if necessary. Terrorists always claim to represent "the people." In their *Green Book,* the Provisional Irish Republican Army declared themselves "the legal representatives of the Irish people . . . morally justified in carrying out a campaign of resistance against foreign occupation forces and domestic collaborators."[12] Likewise, the Black Panther Party's Ten Point Platform and Program asserted "the power to determine the destiny of our Black Community."[13] White supremacist groups claim to represent the entire white race; Osama bin Laden, the entire Muslim world. But do they really?

The question becomes, who legitimately represents the will of the people? If anyone can legitimize an attack against the government simply by claiming to represent the will of the people, how could a government ever establish domestic tranquility and provide for the common defense? Who gets to speak for the people?

This dilemma appears not just in U.S. law but in international law as well. After Nazi Germany's military aggression cast the entire world into a catastrophic war, the international community came together to form the United Nations in an attempt to create an international institution that would regulate the use of force among nations and guarantee the human rights of all people. The founding purpose of the United Nations was to "maintain international peace and security, and to that end: to take effective collective measures for the prevention and removal of threats to the peace, and for the suppression of acts of aggression" by promoting "the principal of equal rights and self-determination of peoples."[14] The problem came when the United Nations defined the "acts of aggression" it would act to suppress by excluding any action that would "prejudice the right to self-determination, freedom and independence . . . of peoples forcibly deprived of that right . . . particularly peoples under colonial and racist regimes or other forms of alien domination: nor the right of these peoples to struggle to that end."[15]

Just as with the U.S. Declaration of Independence, the United Nations Charter specifically guarantees the people's right to resist oppression. In case a question remained as to what form a struggle for freedom could legally take, the Organization of African Unity and the Organization of the Islamic Conference ratified regional terrorism conventions that repudiated terrorism but affirmatively distinguished "armed struggle against colonialism, occupation, aggression and domination by foreign forces" and "armed struggle to liberate their territories and attain their rights to self-determination and independence," respectively, from acts of terrorism.[16] It is perhaps not surprising that organizations representing regions where equal rights and self-determination are not yet guaranteed for all people would want to retain the right to support an armed struggle to achieve those goals. Armed struggle, then, remains a legitimate means for the people to attain self-determination under international law, which is exactly what the terrorists claim to be doing.

In essence, a war on terrorism is not a war in the conventional sense as much as it is a contest over who can legitimately claim to represent the will of the people. This battle makes establishing a rule of law all the more important.

The U.S. government was founded on the proposition that all people have inalienable rights, which are enumerated in the Bill of Rights, or the first ten amendments to the Constitution. It is important to remember that the Constitution did not create these rights. The Founding Fathers maintained that all people are born with them, for they are "endowed by our Creator." The Constitution establishes the government, gives it powers, and outlines the process by which it exercises those powers. The three branches of government work independently to check the power of the others. This process ensures the government remains a servant of the people, because it compels accountability and transparency. This process is the rule of law.

When I was an FBI agent I had the authority to enforce the law, but the government constantly scrutinized my exercise of that authority. If I wanted to search someone's house I had to get a warrant from a judge; if I wanted to arrest someone I had to get an indictment from a grand jury; and if I wanted to incarcerate someone I had to convince a jury of his or her peers that the defendant was guilty of a crime in a public trial. The Constitution guarantees the defendant the right to an attorney, and the adversarial process permits the defendant to challenge every piece of evidence and to cross-examine every witness. A jury of average citizens gets to weigh the evidence, judge the defendant's conduct, and more important, judge the government's conduct before determining its verdict. The transparency of the legal process protects the defendant's rights and allows the people to accurately judge the legitimacy of the government's methods. The people, through the jury, have the right to repudiate those methods if necessary.

This transparency and accountability are more important in terrorism cases, where terrorists defend their conduct by challenging the governing authority's legitimacy. How better to determine which side truly represents the people's will and which is truly just and legitimate than to allow both sides to present their evidence and their arguments in a public forum? And in what better forum could the government expose the terrorists' true criminal nature than in a courthouse?

The truth is terrorists commit all sorts of crime. Terrorist acts—murders, kidnappings, bombings, arsons—are all crimes, of course, but terrorists commit other crimes before they engage in terrorism. They traffic in or manufacture illegal weapons and explosives, and they conspire with others to commit acts of violence. Because they have to live a clandestine existence, they are often involved in identity theft and document fraud, and they often use illicit methods to raise money, such as selling drugs or other contraband, extorting legitimate businesses, or pulling off armed robberies. Simply belonging to a terrorist group is not illegal in the United States yet, but it is in such other countries as the United Kingdom. After 9/11, however, the U.S. government made providing any material support, such as training or financial aid, to a terrorist group a criminal offense.

As I said in chapter 4, the U.S. government treats domestic terrorism, or terrorism committed by U.S.–based groups, purely as a law enforcement matter. The war on domestic terrorism is fought by the police and prosecutors.

International terrorism—or terrorism committed by groups based outside the United States—also involves criminal acts that, along with domestic terrorism, violate domestic U.S. law. But because it originates beyond the nation's borders, an act of international terrorism can rightfully be considered an act of war, which might justify a military response. But is war a legitimate response to an act of terrorism?

Philosophers and theologians have long debated the morality of war. According to the "just war" principles arising from this debate, a war is only "just" if there is both a "just cause" and the war is carried out in a "just" manner. Wars of aggression or conquest are always unjust. Under international law, a nation has the right to use armed force to defend itself and its allies from foreign aggression but only as a last resort, much as an individual has the right to use force in self-defense. And just as in self-defense law, a nation can use armed force only with the "right intention"—that is, to defend itself and recover what was lost by the trespass against it but not to punish or seek revenge. The force used to repel the attack must also be proportionate to the injury suffered, and the violence must end as soon as the threat is mitigated.

Perhaps the most critical principle of the Just War tradition when discussing terrorism is that armed force can only be directed at combatants, not civilians.

I have spent a great deal of time with terrorists. I can tell you they sincerely believe they have a just cause and that their actions are a necessary response to an injustice committed against them. Because of these beliefs, they go to the trouble of writing their declarations of war, listing their grievances, and documenting their "right intentions." Even the neo-Nazis I worked against, who have arguably one of the most despicable, discredited ideologies in the world, still think they're the good guys.

But even if the terrorists could argue they have a just cause, that's only half the equation. Terrorists deliberately attack civilians, which Just War principles strictly prohibit. The terrorists would argue, however, that they are not civilians but taxpayers who financially support an illegitimate government and benefit from its illegitimate policies. The terrorist would argue these supporters of injustice are not innocent, and we would have to admit their logic is sound because the U.S. government uses the same argument to criminalize those who materially support terrorist groups.

Certainly we believe terrorists are war criminals. In fact some U.S. government officials have argued the terrorists' refusal to abide by traditional rules of armed conflict gives the United States the right to ignore those rules in its response.

So who gets to decide who's right? Is there an ultimate judge, or as an international community are we still in Hobbes's natural state of perpetual war, where even a strong nation can be overcome by secret machinations or a confederacy of enemies? Does a universal rule of law exist? The U.N. Declaration of Human Rights guarantees "every person has the right to recognition everywhere as a person before the law."[17] But does the rule of law have a place in the Global War on Terrorism, or is this war simply a nasty, brutish fight for survival?

How can societies protect themselves if terrorists have an internationally recognized right to engage in an armed struggle for equal rights and self-determination?

6
Grading the Government

If you know neither the enemy nor yourself,
you will succumb in every battle.

—Sun Tzu, *Art of War*

The United Nations has been notoriously ineffective in addressing international terrorism. As we have seen, the United Nations has not even succeeded in agreeing on a definition of terrorism, a problem driven at least in part by the ongoing conflict between Israel and the Palestinians. According to Anne Beyefsky of the Hudson Institute:

> [United Nations] Member states are essentially divided into two camps. In one corner is the Organization of Islamic Conference (OIC) composed of 56 states insisting that terrorism excludes the "armed struggle for liberation and self-determination." More precisely, blowing up Israelis of all ages in cafes, synagogues, buses, and discotheques is considered legitimate. In the other corner is the rest of the world.[1]

Ironically the United Nations and the State of Israel, which seem diametrically opposed on the issue of terrorism versus armed struggle, were both created by the international community out of the same desire: to redress the grievous crimes Nazi Germany committed against humanity in general and the Jews in particular and to ensure they would never happen again. I think it is important to remember this commonality and to recognize, as dire as the international situation may seem today in terms of the Global War on Terrorism, the present turmoil pales in comparison to the misery Adolf Hitler's fascist aggression in World War II and his attempted genocide of European Jewry foisted on the world.

Hitler's crimes were of such an extraordinary scale that to even discuss Nazi fascism in the context of a contemporary political debate brings howls of protest from people who believe such correlations do disservice to the Holocaust's victims. This reaction is entirely understandable where such references are gratuitous, such as when a politician recently likened stem cell research to human medical experiments performed in Nazi death camps, a statement for which he later apologized.[2] But as someone who was trained in fascism by self-avowed Nazis I have a unique perspective on the phenomenon and I feel it's important to explore the topic to gain a better understanding of how terrorism works.

First let me say a word about the terms I use. I have used the term *Nazi fascism,* which may appear redundant in that all Nazis are indeed fascists, but Nazism and fascism are two different things. Nazism, or more formally National Socialism, is a militant, racist, anti-Semitic political philosophy first articulated by Adolf Hitler in *Mein Kampf.*[3] From the start it sounds like something that would be hard for anyone to like, but one must remember National Socialism was a populist movement. In fact, it promoted numerous civic values that could be considered appealing, even compelling: a patriotic love of country; respect for the working man's role in driving a vibrant national economy; admiration for national service, particularly military service; reverence for traditional values and the promotion of excellence; the voluntary subordination of one's individual interests to the greater interests of the nation as a whole; and dynamic leadership with the will to aggressively confront any threats to the nation's security. I'd wager that a candidate running on this platform could draw a crowd of supporters anywhere in the world.

But for all its otherwise compelling aspects Hitler's National Socialism could never be separated from its militant racism and virulent anti-Semitism. His vision of a triumphant Germany centered on cultivating and bringing to dominance an Aryan master race. His plan to perfect the Aryan race naturally required subjugating "inferior" peoples, Jews in particular. This was not an unpopular concept. Hitler published *Mein Kampf* years before he came to power, so his philosophy's more troubling aspects were never secret. Yet he and his Nazi Party came to power in a democracy. Could the German people have been so drawn in by National Socialism's promise of a glorious future that they simply ignored the uglier aspects of Hitler's ideology? Perhaps no one read his book.

One might try to imagine a different National Socialism, one that would take advantage of the populist elements but eliminate the racism. But even a softer National Socialism would eventually have to find a societal schism to exploit: sectarianism, nativism, nationalism, classism. Respecting "traditional values" in a diverse environment raises the question, whose values are being respected? In America would "traditional values" include the attempted genocide of Native Americans and slavery? Would the pursuit of excellence mean casting aside the disabled and the deviant? National Socialism requires the identification of a superior "us," which naturally implies an inferior "them." "Our" advancement would logically demand usurping resources and power (rights) from "them." Division is inherently discriminatory. Separate is unequal.[4] But National Socialism, abhorrent as it is, is still just an ideology, and ideas alone can't hurt anyone.

Fascism, by contrast, is not an ideology but rather a behavior—a method of securing and exercising political power. The writer and philosopher Umberto Eco learned about fascism firsthand, as I did, trained by fascists growing up as a boy in Mussolini's Italy. He describes fascism in ephemeral terms, as something "behind a regime and its ideology . . . a way of thinking and feeling, a group of cultural habits, of obscure instincts and unfathomable drives."[5] In his 1995 essay, "Ur-Fascism," Eco postulates that *Ur-Fascism* (eternal fascism) can't be defined, rather only described by the features that are commonly found in regimes called "fascist."[6] These features include the following fourteen elements:.

1. A cult of tradition
2. The rejection of modernism
3. A compulsion to action for action's sake
4. The inability to withstand analytical criticism
5. An exploitation of the fear of difference
6. An appeal to a frustrated middle class
7. The obsession with a plot
8. Humiliation at the wealth and force of the enemy, yet conviction the enemy can be defeated
9. An acceptance of life as permanent warfare, for pacifism is considered trafficking with the enemy
10. Popular elitism exhibiting contempt for the weak
11. The possibility that everybody can become a hero
12. A machismo ethic implying both disdain for women and intolerance and condemnation of nonstandard sexual habits, from chastity to homosexuality
13. A selective populism that disdains parliamentary government
14. Ur-Fascism speaks Newspeak (a reference to George Orwell's *1984*)[7]

According to Eco, the existence of just one of these elements is enough to form the nucleus of an emerging fascist regime.

In *The Anatomy of Fascism,* Robert O. Paxton takes a similar approach and distills the essence of fascism from a meticulous study of fascist governments. Paxton takes a stab at a short definition:

> Fascism may be defined as a form of political behavior marked by obsessive preoccupation with community decline, humiliation, or victim-hood and by compensatory cults of unity, energy, and purity, in which a mass-based party of committed nationalist militants, working in uneasy but effective collaboration with traditional elites, abandons democratic liberties and pursues with redemptive violence and without ethical or legal restraints goals of internal cleansing and external expansion.[8]

Paxton then lists the "mobilizing passions" that drive the political behavior that marks fascist regimes:

- a sense of overwhelming crisis beyond the reach of any traditional solutions;
- the primacy of the group, toward which one has duties superior to every right, whether individual or universal, and the subordination of the individual to it;
- the belief that one's group is a victim, a sentiment that justifies any action, without legal or moral limits, against its enemies, both internal and external;
- dread of the group's decline under the corrosive effects of individualistic liberalism, class conflict, and alien influences;
- the need for closer integration of a purer community, by consent if possible, or by exclusionary violence if necessary;
- the need for authority by natural chiefs (always male), culminating in a national chieftain who alone is capable of incarnating the group's historical destiny;
- the superiority of the leader's instincts over abstract and universal reason;
- the beauty of violence and efficacy of will, when they are devoted to the group's success;
- the right of the chosen people to dominate others without restraint from any kind of human or divine law, right being decided by the sole criterion of the group's prowess within a Darwinian struggle.[9]

It turns out that fascism is even harder to define than terrorism. But understanding the features and the passions that lead to fascism is important because although fascism in its mature form was the antithesis of

democracy, fascism was conceived, born, and nurtured within democratic governments, often with the support of politically and economi-
cally powerful segments of society. Although George W. Bush's administration often states that democratic nations are inherently peaceful, the
most aggressively militant nation that ever appeared on earth grew out of
a democracy. Hitler took fascism to such extreme depths of inhumanity
that he forever distorted our perception of what fascism looks like in its
infancy. But our inability to recognize fascism when it is forming is critical to stopping it before it becomes too strong. Indeed Paxton warns
"Stage One" fascism is present in all democracies.National Socialist ideology provided fertile ground in which fascism could take root because it
already divided a good us from a bad them.

People's desire to define themselves as part of a distinct community
or tribe is ingrained in human nature. We identify ourselves by many
different attributes: race, religion, citizenship, national origin, political
affiliation, profession, sexual preference, and a thousand other traits. But
do the attributes we use to define ourselves have any meaning? I am an
American. If an American is attacked anywhere in the world, I regard it as
an assault against me personally. I am willing to fight to defend my country, and I certainly put myself in harm's way to protect it from an internal
threat. But why? Nationality is just one aspect of my identity; there are
many others. If a white person is attacked in South Africa, or a Roman
Catholic in Northern Ireland I don't take it personally, even though I'm
white and Catholic.

I choose to identify most strongly with my nationality, while Osama
bin Laden obviously identifies most closely with his religion and David
Lane with his race. Is there anything that makes my identification with
nationality more valid than their identification with religion or race? White
supremacists would argue they focus on the more meaningful aspect of
identity because race is an attribute we cannot change. This argument
can be persuasive because in a struggle for survival the ability to quickly
determine who is on your side is critical. Someone looking at me wouldn't
know my nationality or my religion, but they would know my race. But
the opposite argument is also compelling. Perhaps because we can make
a conscious choice about our citizenship and our religion our identification with those attributes is more meaningful.

There's no one answer to the identity question, of course, and terrorists enjoy these types of arguments. We do need to understand how
identity works, however, because identity is what the terrorists exploit.
They use our natural affinity for identifying ourselves into distinct communities as a wedge to divide the world along fault lines they choose.
When a nation comes under threat from someone claiming to represent

a particular community, naturally the government would want to protect us by taking action against that community.

The seeds of fascism that Paxton says exist in all democracies germinate slowly, but once they start growing they are difficult to control, as the Germans discovered. Eco ends his "Ur-Fascism" article with words of warning:

> Ur-Fascism is still around us, sometimes in plainclothes. It would be so much easier, for us, if there appeared on the world scene somebody saying, "I want to reopen Auschwitz, I want the Black Shirts to parade again in the Italian squares." Life is not that simple. Ur-Fascism can come back under the most innocent of disguises.[10]

It is particularly important to clearly understand fascism and how it works when discussing terrorism because terrorists justify their violence as a legitimate armed struggle against an unjust oppressor. No regime is more oppressive than a fascist regime. An oppressed person's politically motivated act of violence against a fascist regime, or any other totalitarian regime for that matter, could almost always be objectively regarded as a legitimate act of resistance.

Imagine Jewish members of the ZOB living in the Warsaw ghetto during the Nazi occupation. If they bombed a café where off-duty Nazi soldiers were having lunch, this terrorist act would be viewed as justifiable under the doctrine of self-defense, because the Nazis were engaged in an active genocide against the Jews. In this circumstance, the use of violence is most legitimate, for the right to self-defense is a fundamental human right.

Now imagine the same Jews joined the Zionist movement after the war and used the identical terrorist technique against British military forces occupying Palestine. Certainly the Jewish terrorists would have argued this action was justifiable in an "armed struggle against colonialism, occupation, aggression and domination by foreign forces,"[11] but this action's legitimacy is not quite as clear as the previous case. Certainly Thomas Jefferson, the OIC, and the Organization of African Unity would agree that the armed struggle for self-determination is a legitimate right, but others in the international community might not agree this action was necessary to secure those rights or that the victims, off-duty British soldiers in a nation not at war, were legitimate targets for an act of war.

Finally imagine the same Jews immigrated to the United States and became U.S. citizens. After a few years they joined the Jewish Defense League and detonated a bomb in a New York City café frequented by Soviet diplomats and military attachés. They might have argued that because Russian Jews were being persecuted in the Soviet Union they had a legitimate right to commit this act on their behalf. This argument would not have been nearly as persuasive as the previous two and would have clearly violated both U.S. and international law.

In all three incidents the Jewish bomber's actions, his intentions, and his results were the same, yet we would judge the relative legitimacy of each bombing differently. What this scenario tells us is that a terrorist attack's underlying legitimacy has less to do with the terrorists' actions or ideology and more to do with the nature of the governing authority they attack. This news is good because the nature of our government is something we can control. We cannot control what terrorists do or think, but we can make their actions more or less legitimate by controlling what we do and think.

First we need to find a way to evaluate the relative legitimacy of different governments using objective criteria. We know that a fascist government is the most repressive type of government, and thanks to Paxton and Eco we know the attributes of a fascist regime. Thus we can plot a fascist regime at the most extreme end of a line scale measuring the legitimacy of different governments, which we'll call the Government Accountability Scale. But what type of government exists at the scale's other end? What is the antithesis of fascism?

Per Jefferson, a government can only derive just powers from the will of the people, so a democratically elected government would be more legitimate than any other form of government. But Saddam Hussein held a referendum shortly before Operation Iraqi Freedom in which he supposedly received 100 percent of the Iraqi people's vote, yet his rule was one of the most brutal fascist regimes of modern times.[12] And even where the people are free to choose their candidate a majority faction could vote to suppress the rights of a minority group. American white supremacists ruled the South in the early part of the twentieth century by pushing through Jim Crow laws that guaranteed whites' control of local governments. Clearly popular elections alone are not sufficient to guarantee a government "of the people."

Perhaps as with Paxton and Eco, rather than trying to define a "just government," we should instead describe its features. Popular elections are certainly a necessary step in creating a government of the people, albeit not a sufficient one. Meaningful elections must also be open, free, and fair. A wide choice of candidates must be free to run for office, and all of the people must have the freedom to vote for those candidates they like, based on a clear understanding of each candidate's political positions. Many other rights must be guaranteed for this process to occur: the candidates must have the freedom to present their ideas in public forums and to challenge traditional belief systems; the people must have the right to assemble and to listen to the candidates, to organize into parties to support the candidates they choose, and to challenge the government policies they oppose; the press must be free to cover the issues and to report on the candidates' positions; and finally these freedoms must be guaranteed by law. Such a law might look like this one:

> Congress shall make no law respecting an establishment of religion, or prohibiting the free exercise thereof; or abridging the freedom of speech, or of the press; or the right of the people peaceably to assemble, and to petition the government for a redress of grievances.[13]

You may have recognized this proposal as the First Amendment to the Constitution of the United States. I do not present it with the ethnocentric attitude that the U.S. constitutional system of government is better than other systems, but in attempting to list a free society's necessary elements, the Bill of Rights is not a bad place to start. There is nothing wrong with any form of government as long as it truly represents the will of the people. Hobbes's *Leviathan*, after all, was an argument in support of a monarchical government. But the whole concept of a social contract, the knowing and voluntary exchange of personal liberty for a promise of greater security, is inherently democratic. The Constitution merely documents that social contract.

The right of free speech and a free press ensures an informed citizenry; the right to bear arms (Second Amendment) guarantees that the citizenry can defend itself from an oppressive government or a hostile threat; the legal protection of personal property from arbitrary seizures (Third and Fourth Amendments) prevents the military and police authorities from abusing their power; the right to avoid self-incrimination (Fifth Amendment) prevents the government from extracting false confessions through coercive interrogations; the right to due process of law (Fifth Amendment) and a speedy and public trial (Sixth Amendment) ensures a prisoner's access to the legal system; and the right to counsel (Sixth Amendment) guarantees the meaningful protection of those legal rights. Beyond the Bill of Rights, a free country must guarantee suffrage for all of its citizens (Fifteenth and Nineteenth Amendment) and ensure the rights and privileges protected by the law apply equally to all citizens (Fourteenth Amendment).

Of course these rights don't mean anything without a fair and open legal process overseen by an independent judiciary. If the legal system is corrupt or simply complies with the governing authority's will, all these rights are meaningless. If the legal process, or any other government process for that matter, is closed to the public, the people will have no way of knowing what the government is doing and therefore will be unable to give meaningful consent. Government secrecy jeopardizes the social contract and compromises the government's legitimacy. Transparency and accountability are the hallmarks of a free government.

Many other documents identify other features of a free government, particularly the United Nations Universal Declaration of Human Rights; the International Covenant on Economic, Social, and Cultural Rights; and the International Covenant on Civil and Political Rights.[14]

The following list distills the features of a free government:

- Respect for the supremacy of the law
- Free and fair elections
- Freedom of speech and assembly
- Freedom of the press
- Freedom of religion
- Due process of law and an independent judiciary
- Legal protections of minority rights
- The right to a publicly funded education
- The right to private property and free markets
- Civilian control of the military
- Open access to government records
- The freedom to emigrate

Just as with Paxton's and Eco's lists of a fascist government's attributes, a government does not need to incorporate all these features to be considered a free government. But the more features it adopts the more evident the government in question expresses the will of a free people and is, therefore, legitimate.

Now we have described both ends of the spectrum on the Government Accountability Scale. On the one side we have a fascist or totalitarian state, characterized by Paxton's and Eco's features, and on the other is a free government with the features I identified here. Most governments would not have all of the attributes of one or the other but would fall somewhere in between. The more fascist features the government has, the more closely it would fall toward the fascist end of the scale; and the more features of a free government, the closer it would place toward the free government end of the scale. When a terrorist attack against a government occurs, rather than trying to evaluate the terrorist's argument that his violence was justifiable, we could just look where the victim government fit on the Government Accountability Scale.

A terrorist attack against a government on the fascist end of the scale, where individual or group rights are suppressed, is more likely to be justifiable as a legitimate act of self-defense. A terrorist attack against a free nation, where the terrorist enjoys the right to speak his mind, petition the government, and vote and where the government protects minority rights and only exercises authority through the due process of the law, would be impossible to justify as a legitimate strike for self-determination. Thus the legitimacy of the terrorist's actions actually is more easily judged by the victim government's behavior than by the terrorist's.

The Government Accountability Scale serves several crucial purposes. First, it shifts the discussion from argument to analysis. As we have seen, arguing the merits of conflicting political and religious positions with a terrorist yields no objective solution. The Government Accountability Scale allows us to objectively analyze our own behavior and to make a more accurate assessment of who we are as a nation "of the people." The Government Accountability Scale also shifts the focus away from the terrorists, because it enables a government to objectively evaluate the legitimacy of its own policies without regard to the terrorists' actions or arguments. Therefore, it removes the concern over "negotiating" with the terrorists. Finally, the Government Accountability Scale gives all control over the situation to the government. If a government can objectively analyze its own behavior it can amend its policies to reduce the legitimate cause for dissent, or it can explain those policies and open a channel for the people to express their dissent through a peaceful political process, or it can keep its current policies and simply tolerate a certain level of dissent, even violent dissent. But the power rests entirely with the government. By putting in place policies and institutions that demonstrate transparency and accountability, a government can validate its own legitimacy and make it impossible for a terrorist group to emerge with a credible message. And with terrorism, it's all about the message.

Here's what the Government Accountability Scale does not do: it does not stop terrorism. Free countries are not exempt from terrorism. In fact, some have argued that democracies are even more susceptible to terrorism than dictatorships because terrorists take advantage of democracies' freedoms. President Bush has suggested that terrorists "hate our freedoms."[15] To support this way of thinking, I have heard people suggest that terrorism didn't exist under Hitler and Stalin, but this assertion simply isn't true.[16] Many people attempted to assassinate Hitler and other officials in his government, and numerous anti-Nazi resistance groups existed. These people were typically not considered terrorists because of the ongoing war, but that is just a matter of semantics. Stalin was a notorious paranoid, and for good reason. Dictators have a great ability to suppress dissent and aggressively exercise that power (which is why they're called dictators), but dissent doesn't go away. Police states such as Stalin's only provide the illusion of stability.

The United States is currently a nation at war, yet I and everyone around the world know where the president sleeps at night: 1600 Pennsylvania Avenue. I'm even allowed to print it in a book. Saddam Hussein, however—the once all-powerful dictator of Iraq with his notoriously brutal Intelligence Service and Republican Guard to protect him—had to sleep in a different place every night and employ body doubles to throw off potential assassins. If the dictators aren't safe, neither are dictatorships. I once asked a foreign military officer who had grown up under a dictatorship in Eastern Europe whether totalitarian regimes experienced problems with terrorism. He replied, "Yes, the terrorists were in the government."

Yes, citizens of free countries are victims of terrorism as well. But they are also victims of murder, robbery, rape, and other violent crimes and at a much higher statistical rate. The goal of a counterterrorist policy is not to stop every potential terrorist attack, as that would be impossible. The goal is to stop a terrorist group from turning into a terrorist movement.

The Government Accountability Scale will not stop terrorism, but it gives us objective information that will help us learn how to respond to terrorist attacks. Whether they know it or not, the Government Accountability Scale also plays an important role in the strategy terrorists use to build a movement.

But first we need to learn more about how the terrorists think.

7

Methods and Motives

*If you know yourself but not the enemy, for every victory
gained you will also suffer a defeat.*

—SUN TZU, *ART OF WAR*

For terrorists, terrorism is all about the message. The Weather Underground issued dozens of communiqués to explain the rationale behind their every violent act; contributed articles to underground newspapers; published a book, *Prairie Fire;* and even starred in a documentary film.[1] Likewise the *Al Qaeda Training Manual* emphasizes the parallel roles that communication and violence play in their struggle to establish an Islamic government:

> *by pen and gun*
> *by word and bullet*
> *by tongue and teeth.*[2]

And al Qaeda members write books, such as Ayman al-Zawahiri's *Knights Under the Banner of the Prophet*[3]; post messages on websites; issue strategy papers; make videotaped statements; give press interviews; and so on. As we have seen, almost all terrorist groups issue some kind of manifesto or declaration of war that explains the purpose of their actions.

As victims of terrorism we often mistakenly think the terrorists are trying to communicate with us, perhaps trying to force some kind of dialogue, but they are not. In justifying their resort to violence, the Weather Underground expressed its frustration after attempts to reform the system through dialogue with the government: "Tens of thousands have learned that protests and marches don't do it. Revolutionary violence is the only way."[4]

The *Al Qaeda Training Manual* also clearly states that words are wasted on the enemy:

> The confrontation that we are calling for with the apostate regimes does not know Socratic debates . . . , Platonic ideals . . . , nor Aristotelian diplomacy. But it knows the dialogue of bullets, the ideals of assassination, bombing, and destruction, and the diplomacy of the cannon and machine-gun.[5]

The whole point of committing a terrorist act is to demonstrate that the time for negotiating with the government is over. The first act of violence represents the group's final break from society.

But if the terrorists are not talking to us, to whom are they talking? In chapter 3, I introduced Dr. Jerrold Post's terrorist psycho-logic, which divides the world into us versus them.[6] I witnessed this phenomenon firsthand with right-wing extremist groups. The terrorists don't care about their opposition—them—their focus is on communicating with the us community, or what I call the terrorists' identity group. But why do terrorists have to work so hard to convince their own identity group of the righteousness of their cause? And why do they have to make their point in such a public fashion? The answer is because terrorists really don't have any political influence over their identity group. The identity group may not even know the terrorists, or their cause, exist.

The terrorists' first step is to identify their identity group in a manner that distinguishes it from mainstream society. Saadi Yacef, a leader of the Algerian terrorist group the National Liberation Front (NLF) during the Algerian War of Independence, explained, "Urban guerrilla warfare is generally divided into three phases. In the first, it is a matter of making oneself heard by stating one's identity."[7] It's as simple as that.

In separating and identifying an identity group, terrorists can exploit a division between ethnic or social groups, religious affiliations, economic classes, or any other characteristic, real or contrived, that distinguishes one person from another. Like the white supremacists I worked against, members of the Weather Underground went through a symbolic purification process to separate themselves from the corrupt mainstream society, albeit with altogether different rituals: by embracing the drug culture and by breaking sexual mores with "smash monogamy," or ritualistic group sex.[8] "Freaks are revolutionaries and revolutionaries are freaks" is the way Bernardine Dohrn explained it, which was not exactly a message mainstream society understood. But the freaks—her identity group—understood. She was trying to tell the dope smokers, the alienated students, and the young rebels of society who perhaps weren't politically active that they were part of her movement, the identity community of the Weather Underground, whether they knew it or not.

The Weatherman identity group of "revolutionaries" was just as expansive a category as race or religious affiliation. In the Underground's fourth communiqué, issued on September 15, 1970, shortly after breaking counterculture guru and LSD advocate Dr. Timothy Leary out of prison in California, Dohrn reiterated that the group considered itself in a state of war against the United States. She claimed to be working in tandem with

> the NLF [the South Vietnamese National Liberation Front, the political arm of the Viet Cong] and the North Vietnamese, with the Democratic Front for the Liberation of Palestine and Al Fatah, with Rap Brown and Angela Davis, with all the black and brown revolutionaries, the Soledad brothers and all the prisoners of war in Amerikan concentration camps.[9]

Such a geographically broad, ethnically, culturally, and ideologically diverse identity group would clearly be as difficult to manage and lead as the entire white race would be for the white supremacist groups or the entire Muslim world would be for the jihadists. These terrorist groups' leaders are all smart enough to know that they don't have the power to mobilize their identity communities with words alone.

We learned in chapter 4 that terrorists are like soldiers, just very poorly selected, poorly trained, and poorly equipped soldiers. By definition terrorists have neither military nor political strength. If a terrorist led an army we wouldn't call him a terrorist, we'd call him a "rebel general." Terrorist leaders do not have political control of a government, or else we would call them "president," "prime minister," "dictator," or maybe even "dear leader." Terrorists do not lead political parties of any significance; if they did we would call them "the opposition candidate" or, if the opposition was militant, "the rebel leader." So we know that if we're calling them terrorists they are poorly selected, poorly trained, and poorly equipped soldiers with little or no political power.

A terrorist resorts to terrorism only because he lacks the political power necessary to advance his cause through peaceful means and the military power to move it forward by force. The terrorist's life is the dangerous and difficult life of a fugitive, and no one would choose that path unless he or she felt the situation was so dire there was no alternative. Terrorism expert Martha Crenshaw has long argued that research shows that terrorism is the "product of strategic choice."[10] Terrorism is a tactic that rational but politically powerless people use to compel social change.

Three possible reasons explain why the potential terrorists lack political support: they lack political skills, or they have political skills but lack a popular cause, or they have political skills and a popular cause but are politically repressed by the government. Determining the terrorists' political case will be important in developing an appropriate government response to the terrorist action, but for the potential terrorists, all that matters is their realization that they are powerless to change their situation politically or militarily. Terrorism is a sign of weakness, not of strength.

But if terrorists are so weak, then why are they so dangerous? The answer is because they have a strategy, a very effective strategy.

In February 2006 the Combating Terrorism Center at West Point published Jarret M. Brachman and William F. McCants's report "Stealing Al-Qa'ida's Playbook," which analyzed various al Qaeda strategy documents and tried to develop an effective counterstrategy to defeat them.[11] The report summarizes an al Qaeda strategy to defeat the United States proposed by Abu Bakr Naji in *The Management of Barbarism* in 2004.[12] The CTC report states:

> The solution, Naji says, is to provoke a superpower into invading the Middle East directly. This will result in a great propaganda victory for the jihadis because the people will
>
> 1) be impressed that the jihadis are directly fighting a superpower,
> 2) be outraged over the invasion of a foreign power,
> 3) be disabused of the notion that the superpower is invincible the longer the war goes on, and,
> 4) be angry at the proxy governments allied with the invading superpower.
>
> Moreover, he [Naji] argues, it will bleed the superpower's economy and military. This will lead to social unrest at home and the ultimate defeat of the superpower [footnotes in original text omitted].[13]

If you're new to reading terrorist strategy, this obviously well-conceived, cogent plan seems, at least at the moment, to have been effectively executed to the jihadists' advantage. It could be considered a bit of Monday-morning quarterbacking in that the plan was published in 2004, after the U.S. invasion of Afghanistan and Iraq and just as the Iraqi insurgency started picking up steam. But Naji probably wrote this strategy much earlier, and as is the nature of clandestine group–produced documents, it only made its way into the public realm much later. As someone who has studied terrorist tactics, I recognize Naji's strategy as the classic mujahideen approach, well documented in earlier texts. As McCants and Brachman point out, Naji credits these same tactics for their success in resisting the Soviet occupation of Afghanistan.

The only problem with al Qaeda's strategy is that it's not original. They cribbed it. Here's part of a terrorist strategy document published in 1979:

> GUERRILLA STRATEGY:
> Many figures of speech have been used to describe Guerrilla Warfare, one of the most apt being "The War of the Flea" which conjured up the image of a flea harrying a creature of by comparison elephantine size into fleeing (forgive the pun). Thus it is with a Guerrilla Army . . . which employs hit and run tactics . . . while at the same time striking at the soft economic underbelly of the enemy, not with the hope of physically driving them into the sea but nevertheless expecting to effect their withdrawal by an effective campaign of continuing harassment contained in a fivefold guerrilla strategy.
> The strategy is: .
>
> 1. A War of attrition against enemy personnel which is aimed at causing as many casualties and deaths as possible so as to create a demand from their people at home for their withdrawal.
> 2. A bombing campaign aimed at making the enemy's financial interest in our country unprofitable while at the same time curbing long term financial investment in our country.
> 3. To make the [area of operations] . . . ungovernable except by colonial military rule.
> 4. To sustain the war and gain support for its end by National and International propaganda and publicity campaigns.
> 5. By defending the war of liberation by punishing criminals, collaborators and informers.[14]

Although Naji altered the strategy somewhat to fit the particulars of al Qaeda's current situation, the similarities in goals and methodology to this second document clearly demonstrate Naji's were not original ideas. The second piece is an excerpt from the Irish Republican Army's *Green Book,* which was written in the Maze prison H-blocks by interned Provisional IRA terrorists and published in 1979 (only the Irish would include a pun in their guerrilla strategy manual).[15] But before you feel sorry for those poor IRA lads who weren't given literary credits for their good ideas, review Carlos Marighella's *The Mini-manual of the Urban Guerrilla,* published ten years before the *Green Book:*

[T]he urban guerrilla bases himself on models of action leading to attack . . . with the following objectives:

a) to threaten the [area of operations] . . . where the giant indus-trial-financial-economic-political-cultural-military-police complex that holds the entire decisive power of the country is located;
b) to weaken the local guards or the security system of the dicta-torship . . . [by] catching the government in a defensive position with its troops immobilized in defense of the entire complex of national maintenance . . . ;
c) to attack on every side with many different armed groups, few in number, each self-contained and operating separately, to dis-perse the government forces . . . ;
d) to give proof of its combativeness, decision, firmness, determi-nation, and persistence in the attack on the military dictatorship in order to permit all malcontents to follow our example and fight with urban guerrilla tactics. Meanwhile, the government, with all its problems, incapable of halting guerrilla operations in the city, will lose time and suffer endless attrition and will finally be forced to pull back its repressive troops in order to mount guard over the banks, industries, armories, military barracks, prisons, public of-fices, radio and television stations, North American firms, gas stor-age tanks, oil refineries, ships, airplanes, ports, airports, hospitals, health centers, blood banks, stores, garages, embassies, residences of outstanding members of the regime, such as ministers and gen-erals, police stations, and official organizations, etc.[16]

The H-blocks must have had a pretty good library. And Marighella didn't invent these tactics either. The Partisan Rangers used them during the American Civil War, the Sons of Liberty before the Revolutionary War, and Zealots, Thugs, and Assassins throughout antiquity. This strat-egy is not new. Guerrillas, insurgents, and terrorists use it for one simple reason: it works!

Almost five years into the Global War on Terrorism the U.S. gov-ernment finally recognized the enemy does have a strategy. This acknowl-edgment is a positive development, and the counterstrategies suggested in the CTC report are steps in the right direction. But after realizing this strategy is not new—indeed, it has been used throughout history—tak-ing lessons from the historical record will be key to developing an effec-tive counterterrorism strategy.

First, before we can learn how the terrorist's strategy actually works, we must understand the dynamics of the terrorists' identity groups.

Terrorists make up a relatively tiny proportion of their identity group. In *Defeating the Jihadists: A Blueprint for Action,* former White House National Security Council counterterrorism adviser Richard Clarke described the jihad movement using a series of concentric circles. The smallest circle in the center represents hardcore al Qaeda members; and the outer circles, varying levels of support for the movement.[17] This schematic is helpful in describing the structure of a terrorist's identity group, but my version differs from Clarke's in that it is generic to any terrorist identity group rather than specific to one movement. I'll return to Clarke's circles in chapter 15.

Now imagine a series of concentric circles with the terrorist group located in the center. In the next circle appear the terrorist group's supporters, including those individuals indoctrinated into the group's ideology who assist the terrorists by providing training, material, and logistical support but who do not participate directly in terrorist attacks. The third circle contains sympathizers, or people who have sympathy for the terrorists' cause but who don't have any contact with the terrorist group, don't actively support them, and don't necessarily agree that an armed struggle is necessary or is even helpful to the cause.

In the fourth circle are people whom the terrorists consider part of their identity group but who do not support the terrorist cause or even identify themselves as part of the community represented by the terrorist group. For white supremacists, as an example, this group would make up all nonracist whites, namely, people who don't support white supremacy, aren't racist, and don't feel race is a significant aspect of their identity. As I mentioned in chapter 1, white supremacists call these whites "Sheeple," and I will adopt their terminology for this discussion. The Sheeple make up the largest portion of the terrorists' identity group.

Anyone outside the circles is considered them, or the nonidentity group. Them includes both the corrupt forces who oppress the terrorist's identity group and the general population of others who support the status quo, either directly or indirectly, and are seen as benefitting from it. This point is important, because so much of the discussion regarding terrorism focuses on innocent civilians, who, as we have seen, simply don't exist in the terrorists' mind-set. According to the terrorists if you're not supporting us, you are supporting them; therefore, you are not innocent. In an audiotape broadcast by Aljazeera in April 2006 Osama bin Laden reiterated this position:

> The war is a responsibility shared between the people and the governments. . . . The war goes on and the people are renewing their allegiance to its rulers and masters.

They send their sons to armies to fight us and they continue their financial and moral support while our countries are burned and our houses are bombed and our people are killed.[18]

Even when terrorists do appear to be speaking directly to the victims of their crimes, they are really not. Shortly before the 2004 presidential election, bin Laden appeared in a videotaped message. Rather than sitting in a cave with an AK-47 over his arm, as he had in previous videotapes, he dressed formally and stood behind a lectern as Americans would expect a world leader to do. After a short prayer, of course, bin Laden began, "People of America this talk of mine is for you and concerns the ideal way to prevent another Manhattan. . . ."[19] This introduction might have led some to believe he was actually talking to the American people, but an analysis of what he said makes clear he is not. Bin Laden rationalized the 9/11 attacks, touching on all of the usual themes common to terrorist manifestos—self-defense, just cause, proper authority, and so on—and seemingly reached out for some understanding and common ground from which both sides could move forward in a peaceful way, with each gaining security by not threatening the other. It seemed as if he was truly looking for compromise.

Except he exposed the charade when speaking about 9/11's aftermath: "As for its results, they have been, by the grace of Allah, positive and enormous, and have, by all standards, exceeded all expectations."[20] As I said, terrorists make poor politicians, but even the worst politician would not exult in his adversary's misery if his true purpose was to foster better relations. This message, like all of al Qaeda's messages, is for his supporters, his sympathizers, and the Sheeple who make up his identity group, not the American people. Bin Laden was trying to present himself to the Islamic world as the reasonable party in this conflict, the one seeking a peaceful solution while the West continues its belligerence against the Muslim world. Bin Laden was fulfilling the "duty to retreat" element of the self-defense argument. His purpose was not to convince his victims of anything; instead he was trying to build support within his identity group. Understanding the way terrorists interact with their identity groups is essential to interpreting the meaning of their public statements.

To establish a baseline of support within an identity group, the would-be terrorists must act on the community's behalf. Often the terrorists will provide some sort of protective security, perhaps ridding a neighborhood of a criminal nuisance, wherein the terrorist group starts to be seen as a legitimate authority within the community. This activity does not necessarily involve a use of force. It can be something entirely positive, like promoting the social welfare or providing social services that the governing authority does not address. In fact, the more involved the terrorist group is in non-security-related community services, the greater will be their level of support. Common sense dictates a group providing legitimate social services to a community has a much easier time establishing its proper authority within that community. If you have to call the terrorist group to get your garbage picked up, your electricity turned on, or your child enrolled in school then it is the government, whether it has been elected or not.

Once a baseline of support exists, the terrorist group looks to establish influence with sympathizers in the next circle. Getting the sympathizers' attention requires a more dramatic action, because sympathizers have no direct contact with the terrorist group and may not even know it exists. The terrorists must draw attention to themselves in a way that lets people sympathetic to the cause know there is someone ready to act on their behalf. Terrorists write their manifestos to reach out to this audience of sympathizers and try to convert them into supporters. The manifesto itself is not enough, however; the terrorists also need to express themselves through action; propaganda by the deed, as the old anarchists used to say. The Weather Underground's first act of violence was to bomb Chicago's Haymarket Square Police Statue, which was erected to memorialize the police victims of the anarchist riot there in 1886. This act sent as powerful a message to their sympathizer community as the Weatherman's "Declaration of a State of War" ever would. Despite what Dr. Post says, when the terrorists are talking to the terrorist sympathizers, they must recognize that "the cause is the cause," because that's all they share.

This stage is critical for the terrorists, because this action—as in the case of the Haymarket Square Police Statue bombing, which was purely symbolic and hurt no one—inevitably involves violating criminal laws. The criminal act represents a final break from societal values, demonstrating through deed that the cause is more legitimate than the law. In a sense it's a challenge to both the supporters and the sympathizers, as it forces them to choose a side—the law or the outlaw. But it's a risky play. If the supporters aren't ready for such a break from society, they may withdraw their support from the group, and if the sympathizers disapprove of the criminal action, they may reject not only the authority of the terrorist group, but the legitimacy of an armed struggle altogether. The terrorist's criminal conduct risks losing not only support but also the cause itself.

Distinguishing between a terrorist's crime and civil disobedience is important at this stage, because the terrorist deliberately attempts to confuse the two. Overtly violating or refusing to obey an unjust law to compel legal reform is a time-honored form of legitimate protest. To be clear, however, the operative word in the phrase *civil disobedience* is *disobedience*. It requires breaking the law, which has consequences. What makes an act of civil disobedience honorable is the activist's willingness to accept the legal consequences of that disobedience. Muhammad Ali's 1967 refusal to be inducted into the armed services, which led to his arrest, indictment, conviction, and the surrender of his boxing title, was an honorable act of civil disobedience. Running to Canada to avoid the draft in the 1960s and 1970s was not. Civil disobedience is only effective as a form of protest when it puts the government in the untenable position of having to enforce an unpopular law or to abandon it. Refusing to obey laws we don't like isn't civil disobedience, it's anarchy.

Terrorism is distinguishable from civil disobedience. Terrorists violate laws that are typically not in dispute. Sitting down at a "whites only" lunch counter when the law says you can't is civil disobedience. Bombing the luncheonette or murdering its owner is terrorism. Laws against bombing and murder are not unjust. Terrorists also don't willingly accept the legal consequences of their disobedience. All the complex operational methodology discussed so far is specifically designed so the terrorists can avoid responsibility for their criminal acts. Suicide terrorists certainly suffer the mortal consequences of their bombings, but the purpose of their suicide is to avoid the legal consequences.

At this point in a terrorist campaign, the terrorists appear to be little more than a gang of criminals, and if the government can successfully brand the terrorists as criminals, they will reduce the terrorists' ability to draw support from sympathizers in the third circle. So terrorists argue mightily that they are not criminals. Instead they call themselves "armies," "insurgents," or "militias." Imprisoned white supremacists call themselves "prisoners of war" (POWs) even after they've been convicted of criminal offenses having nothing to do with their armed resistance.

Marighella devoted the first two paragraphs of *The Mini-manual of the Urban Guerrilla* to an argument distinguishing the "ardent patriot" and "friend of the people"—that is, the urban guerrilla—from the criminals, outlaws, and counterrevolutionaries he so resembles.

Many times, actions by criminals are taken to be actions by urban guerrillas.

The urban guerrilla, however, differs radically from the criminal. The criminal benefits personally from his actions, and attacks indiscriminately without distinguishing between the exploiters and the exploited, which is why there are so many ordinary people among his victims. The urban guerrilla follows a political goal, and only attacks the government, the big businesses and the foreign imperialists.

Another element just as harmful to the guerrillas as the criminal, and also operating in the urban area, is the counterrevolutionary, who creates confusion, robs banks, throws bombs, kidnaps, assassinates, and commits the worst crimes imaginable against urban guerrillas, revolutionary priests, students, and citizens who oppose tyranny and seek liberty.[21]

This argument is interesting because Marighella later admits that "one of the fundamental characteristics of the Brazilian revolution is that, from the beginning, it developed around the expropriation of the wealth of the major business, imperialist and landowning interests . . . ," and he says that the "expropriated wealth" can be used for purchasing weapons and matériel to support the revolution and for "the daily maintenance of the fighters."[22] So maybe the urban guerrilla can benefit personally from the revolution after all (long live the revolution). To the casual observer, though, the urban guerrilla, the criminal, and the counterrevolutionary look alike, and this similarity is dangerous for the terrorist.

The Weather Underground was a notable exception to this rule. Bernardine Dohrn ignored Marighella's advice and openly embraced the "outlaw" moniker (although she still referred to imprisoned sympathizers as "prisoners of war").[23] She didn't use the name out of rhetorical excess but deliberately to extend the Weather Underground's identity group to include a decidedly criminal element. The FBI explained the genesis of this outreach in a 1976 summary of foreign influences on the Weather Underground Organization:

> So when Huynh Van Ba, representative of the Provisional Revolutionary Government of Vietnam (PRG), instructed the WUO to "look for the person who fights hardest against the cops. . . . Don't look for the one who says the best thing. Look for the one who fights," the campus base was forgotten and the WUO began to recruit greasers and assorted oddments who had displayed their hatred of authority in direct combat with police.[24]

This strategy may have well served the North Vietnamese in their efforts to create mayhem in the United States during the Vietnam War, but this advice proved disastrous for the Weather Underground. Although there was tremendous sympathy for the Weather Underground's stated causes—promoting civil rights, ending the war in Vietnam, and reforming U.S. foreign policy—that sympathy never translated into support for the revolution it tried to inspire. The WUO's extremism alienated the civil rights movement and the student protest groups, both of which included well-organized, articulate, and active people who could otherwise have provided a wellspring of support for the Weathermen. I believe the WUO's embrace of criminality drove that alienation. The Weather Underground once had a cause around which a movement could have been built, but its tactics failed to win over even their sympathizers. The WUO made a great impact, to be sure, but then it fizzled out to the point that the government could release the group's active terrorists, who had been jailed for a short period, back into society with little concern that they would renew the armed struggle.

Assata Shakur, formerly Joanne Chesimard, the "mother hen" of the Black Liberation Army,[25] was interviewed by Christian Parenti in Havana, Cuba, where Shakur is living in exile after escaping from a U.S. prison. Asked about the relationship between "gangsta rap" and the Black Nationalist movement, Shakur seemed to acknowledge the negative effect that embracing outlaw culture had on the Black Nationalist groups of her era:

> In the 1960s and the 1970s people like Huey Newton and Eldridge Cleaver, clearly exhibited aspects of that confusion, and mixed up revolutionary politics with gangsterism. The mind destroying machine works overtime, getting us to crave power and money instead of justice.[26]

Within a struggle for legitimacy, criminality is lethal. No group knew this better than the Provisional Irish Republican Army. In 1972 the British granted PIRA terrorists imprisoned in the H-blocks "special category status," which permitted them to wear their own clothing, to associate freely with each other, and to operate almost as if they were POWs, a status white supremacists like David Lane craved. In 1975 the British revoked these privileges under a get-tough policy known as "criminalization." After a series of escalating protests, the PIRA inmates started a hunger strike. The hunger strikers didn't demand an end to British rule in Northern Ireland or the release of PIRA prisoners; all they wanted was the restoration of their special category status privileges. Ten PIRA terrorists died in the hunger strike. They accepted being prisoners, but they starved themselves to death rather than be treated like common criminals. I will evaluate the PIRA's tactics in chapter 13, but from a longevity standpoint alone the PIRA members certainly appear to have better understood the nature of community support more than the Weather Underground did.

The next step for the terrorist group—gaining influence among the Sheeple—is the most difficult. To accomplish their goals the terrorists know they need the Sheeple because the Sheeple's numbers convert a movement into a revolution. But the Sheeple aren't interested in the terrorists' message, neither in the form of a manifesto nor in the form of a bombing. The terrorists need to somehow convince the Sheeple that they are part of the group's identity community, that there is a difference between us and them, and that the Sheeple are part of us and not part of them, no matter how integrated into the mainstream community they think they are. This lobbying is difficult, because the terrorists can say all they want but the Sheeple won't listen. The Sheeple are completely invested in the existing power structure.

The terrorist needs help to gain influence with the Sheeple, and that help can only come from one source—the enemy. The terrorist needs the government to do his work, and to expedite it the terrorist needs to commit an atrocity that will trigger a severe government reaction. Terrorists see the world at a tipping point, and they want to nudge it into chaos. The atrocity is designed to compel a reaction.

The terrorists hope the government will respond inefficiently, both in how it attacks and in who it attacks. Almost all terrorists talk about a terrorism as an economic strategy of attrition rather than a military strategy. They want the government to waste resources trying to protect every possible target. But more important to their success, they hope the government's inefficient reaction will impose hardships on the innocent as well as on the guilty. Such an injustice will stir resentment in the identity community and validate the terrorists' propaganda that "they" are persecuting "us."

The terrorists need the government to divide the world into "us" and "them" just as they do—to separate their identity community from the mainstream. The Sheeple would never choose to side with the terrorists, but if the government treats the entire identity community as its enemy, the Sheeple will have no choice. Only the government can compel the Sheeple to the terrorists' camp, and the terrorists are happy to let them do it.

Stephen Ulph, a researcher who tracks Internet traffic about the jihadist movement for the Jamestown Foundation, came across a colorful description of how this strategy works in analyst Sayf Allah's post on the Internet forum Risalat al-Umma. Ulph explains:

> He claims that al-Qaeda has, and has always had, a specific aim:
> to galvanize the sleeping corpse of the Islamic Nation and remove
> the corrosive body of Western influence. To that end, the 9/11
> attacks were designed "to force the Western snake to bite the sleeping body, and wake it up."[27]

The "sleeping corpse" is of course the Sheeple of the jihad movement, or the worldwide Islamic community called the umma. Al Qaeda could not wake the Sheeple on its own but had to rely on the "Western snake" to do its work.

But again, this strategy was not al Qaeda's invention. Marighella's *Mini-manual* laid it out decades ago:

> We repeat and insist on repeating—it is the way of insuring popular support. As soon as a reasonable portion of the population begins to take seriously the actions of the urban guerrilla, his success is guaranteed.
>
> The government has no alternative except to intensify its repression. The police networks, house searches, the arrest of suspects and innocent persons, and the closing off of streets make life in the city unbearable. The military dictatorship embarks on massive political persecution.[28]

The genius behind this strategy is the terrorist's recognition that the government has an identity group it must answer to as well. The government's primary obligation under the social contract is to provide security. When a terrorist threatens that security, the government's supporters, or its identity community, naturally demand action. If the government fails to respond, the people will look for a new leaders. The government's desire to retain power compels it to "do something."

Unfortunately that "something" is typically just what guerrillas and terrorists like Marighella want—for the government to "intensify its repression." The terrorist attack's purpose is to force the government to move closer to the fascist side of the Government Accountability Scale. The more the government moves down the scale the more legitimate the resistance movement becomes and the more support the terrorists will gain. Now the terrorists would argue that they are not really making the government move down the scale; rather that they are simply exposing the government's true fascist nature. Whether the government is actually becoming more repressive or is simply being recognized as more repressive is irrelevant. Once the general population perceives the government to be further toward the fascist end of the scale, the greater legitimacy the resistance will have. The Weather Underground highlighted this rebound effect in their "Declaration of a State of War:" "The insanity of Amerikan 'justice' has added to its list of atrocities six blacks killed in Augusta, two in Jackson and four white Kent State students making thousands more into revolutionaries."[29] A repressive government reaction only succeeds in driving more people into the revolution.

Unfortunately for the government, the terrorists realize this terrain is where they have a distinct advantage in the conflict. The terrorists have no territory to defend. Because terrorist groups are small and lack organization or equipment, they are difficult to detect. They can simply blend into their identity community, leaving no operational targets for the government to attack. Also, rather than being a disadvantage, the terrorists' lack of military hardware is actually an advantage. They have nothing so there is nothing for them to protect. For them, "Freedom's just another word for nothin' left to lose."[30]

The government interprets its inability to identify and locate the terrorists as evidence that the identity community is harboring and supporting them. This scenario may not be true, but the uncertainty causes the government to err on the side of caution and start treating all of "them" with suspicion, thereby lumping the Sheeple in with the terrorists.

Meanwhile the terrorists can strike wherever and whenever they want. According to Marighella, terrorism is only distinguishable from other guerrilla actions by "the apparent ease with which it can be carried out."[31] Marighella knows that terrorist attacks cost very little, can be carried out by very few or even a single operative, and can involve no more than one well-placed shot or a phoned-in bomb threat. A twenty-year-old skinhead I knew was able to obtain all the components we needed to make a bomb in a half-hour tour around his neighborhood, for less than twenty dollars. Terrorism is that easy.

The government, then, must protect every potential target. But any resources it spends hardening targets is ultimately wasted, because the terrorist can simply move to less protected targets. The government is in a no-win situation. Again Marighella explains:

> In spite of all this, the police systematically fail. The armed forces, the navy and the air force are mobilized to undertake routine police functions, but even so they can find no way to halt guerrilla operations or to wipe out the revolutionary organization, with its fragmented groups that move around and operate throughout the country.[32]

And this situation leads us to the final stage of the terrorists' strategy. When the government is unable to stop them, the terrorists begin to have influence over the government's identity group:

> The people refuse to collaborate with the government, and the general sentiment is that this government is unjust, incapable of solving problems, and that it resorts simply to the physical

liquidation of its opponents. The political situation in the country is transformed into a military situation in which the "gorillas" [government agents] appear more and more to be the ones responsible for violence, while the lives of the people grow worse.[33]

The government's primary purpose is to provide security, so the terrorists attack the government's legitimacy by proving it is incapable of protecting its citizens. This move, in turn, provokes a robust government response that validates the terrorists' claim that they are being persecuted.

I submit that this strategy is not the product of a damaged self. Terrorism is a cunning tactic that creates strengths out of weaknesses. The terrorists know they cannot win militarily, so terrorism is not a military strategy. The only way to describe terrorism in terms of a military strategy would be to say that the terrorists seek to provoke an overwhelmingly superior military force into attacking them with indiscriminate force sufficient to make them martyrs for their cause. Such a military strategy could never succeed. But terrorism works because it is not a military strategy. The military aspect of terrorism is a trick.

We must remember that the terrorists have neither the military nor the political power necessary to destroy a government on their own. The terrorists' strategy is to fool the government into destroying itself by becoming what the terrorists say it already is: illegitimate.

8
Case Study #1:
A Successful Terror Campaign

A lost battle is a battle one thinks one has lost.

—Ferdinand Foch

Perhaps an easier way of conveying the strategy behind the terrorist's activities is with examples rather than with theories. Gillo Pontecorvo's 1966 film, *The Battle of Algiers,*[1] is a useful model to explore the theories put forth in chapter 7, because it is a flawless account of how these strategies were used to wage a successful terrorist campaign from beginning to end. Film is an excellent medium for teaching about terrorism because it effectively conveys emotion, the driving force behind both terrorism and counterterrorism.

The Battle of Algiers so accurately depicts terrorist strategy because a former Algerian terrorist and freedom fighter, Saadi Yacef, produced it and wrote the book on which the story was based. Saadi also wrote an early version of the screenplay (which Pontecorvo reportedly called "awful")[2] and even played a fictionalized version of himself in the film. Yacef fought in the real Battle of Algiers (1954–57) as a colonel in the Algerian National Liberation Front, a terrorist organization known by its French acronym, FLN. The FLN fought an urban guerrilla–style terrorist campaign against French colonial forces that had ruled Algeria for over a hundred years.

The Battle of Algiers was just one conflict in a larger war of independence taking place throughout Algeria. The French military captured Yacef in 1957, and although he was promised prisoner of war status when he surrendered, he was tried and convicted of terrorist offenses and received a death sentence. His sentence was later commuted, and when

Algeria gained its independence in 1962, he was freed as part of a general amnesty. He returned to Algeria, where he went on to serve in the Algerian government. The film is historically accurate, with many scenes shot where the actual events took place. One building blown up during the war was even rebuilt for the movie.[3] Though the film is a dramatization it has an unquestioned authenticity, at least from the terrorists' perspective, that has made it a favorite among terrorist groups from the IRA and the Weather Underground to the Tamil Tigers in Sri Lanka.[4] The film was even introduced as evidence in a criminal trial against Black Panther Party members in New York in 1970.[5]

Perhaps because terrorist groups so enjoyed the film it developed a reputation as pro-terrorist propaganda, a reputation I believe is not deserved. The film does depict French paratroopers inflicting brutal torture on suspected FLN supporters, but it also shows cold-blooded FLN assassinations of unsuspecting police officers and the bloody aftermath of the FLN's terrorist bombings of French cafés and dance clubs. The fact of the matter is that the Algerians ultimately won their independence. That the film ends with scenes of Algerians celebrating victory is more a matter of historical record than a statement about the morality of the means they used to achieve it. I believe the French paratroopers are represented very well in the character of Col. Philippe Mathieu, who could not have framed the dilemma the French found themselves in more clearly (using screenwriter Franco Solinas's words, of course):

> We are soldiers and our only duty is to win. Therefore, to be precise, I would now like to ask you a question: Should France remain in Algeria? If you answer "yes," then you must accept all the necessary consequences.[6]

The film has not only been used as a training film for terrorists but for counterterrorists as well. It should be, in my opinion, required viewing for anyone working counterterrorism on any level, for any government facing a terrorist threat will find itself in this same dilemma. Once the policy driving the conflict is established, the government has the choice of altering the policy or accepting its consequences. The only other option is to do exactly what Colonel Mathieu does here—explain the policy and the consequences to the public, and let them decide. For the governing authorities, accepting the necessary consequences is the easy part. Determining which consequences are actually "necessary" is much harder. But I am getting ahead of myself.

The film accurately depicts three distinct parts of a terrorist campaign: terrorist group recruitment, terrorist group organization and operations, and the effects of the government's response.

The film begins with the arrest of a petty criminal, Ali la Pointe, after a French policeman spots la Pointe's game of three-card monte. La Pointe flees through the city streets of Algiers, quickly outpacing the police, but as he passes a group of young French pieds-noirs,[7] one of them trips him and la Pointe falls hard to the ground. La Pointe still has time to get up and outrun the police, but he instead stands and head butts the young Frenchman in the nose. He exacts his revenge but is beaten by the pieds-noirs and arrested in the process. La Pointe is the perfect terrorist recruit, someone willing to fight for a just cause, to fight dirty if he has to, and more than that, to throw that first punch knowing he is going to lose in the end.

La Pointe is radicalized in prison. Upon his release, he is no longer a petty criminal but an Algerian Islamic avenger. When we see him next he doesn't wear the Western clothes he wore as a street hustler but instead more traditional Arab robes, symbolizing his purification and separation from the corrupt colonial culture. Additional scenes of community purification play out with young Algerian children harassing a drunken Algerian, punishing vice, and demonstrating the development of a more morally pure generation under the FLN's tutelage. Then in a clandestine wedding ceremony an FLN representative performs what appears to be the bureaucratic functions of a county clerk, officially documenting the union as Islamic rites are read. This scene seems almost out of place in the film, and none of the major characters appear in it. It is important, however, because it demonstrates that the FLN is replacing the colonial government in providing legitimate social services to the community.

La Pointe meets his first comrade in arms, Petit Omar, a ten-year-old boy, who passes along instructions for la Pointe's first assignment: the assassination of a French police officer. His mission will be aided by a third member of his terror cell, a young woman named Djamila. This army—a street hood, a boy, and a young woman—is not what we picture when we think of a cabal of terrorists.

Women play a surprisingly prominent role in *The Battle of Algiers,* just as they did in the real battle. It may seem paradoxical for women to play a major role in an Islamic terrorist organization, but as Yacef explained in a 2004 interview:

> Normally women took the back seat. But when war broke out, we needed them. They fed us. They were lookouts on the terraces. . . . The women were totally implicated. . . . They wanted to participate directly in the struggle—plant bombs, hide weapons, do liaison work. They were exactly like the men. Sometimes better. A woman who plants a bomb is better than a man who does nothing or just hands out flyers.[8]

Misogyny and prejudice had to take a backseat to operational necessity. Just as with the white supremacists I worked against, circumstances prevented the FLN from being as selective as they might have wished regarding personnel. Terrorist groups have to take who they can get: women, children, and men who do nothing or just hand out flyers. A terrorist group always resembles a poorly selected army.

But this reality also demonstrates the futility of trying to develop a terrorist profile, a point made more dramatically later in the film. In response to increasing FLN terrorism the French authorities seal off the Arab quarter, known as the Casbah, with military checkpoints. Several scenes show long lines of Arab men, women, and children waiting to be searched by French troops, while young pied-noir couples pass through uninterrupted with just a wave and a smile. A few scenes later FLN bomb makers are seen placing bombs in women's handbaskets while three Algerian women dress and make themselves up to look European. A wave, a smile, and a little flirtation with the soldiers and they're through the checkpoints and on their way to the cafés and clubs with their deadly baskets.

Remember this film was made in 1966, long before international terrorism was even studied as a phenomenon separate from what was generally referred to as "insurgency," yet already the terrorists mocked the government's futile efforts at protective security. And this scene was not just for dramatic effect. They re-created events that occurred on September 30, 1956, when three female FLN operatives strode past checkpoints and planted their basket bombs in the city's European quarter. The French developed a profile they thought would prevent FLN terrorists from leaving the Casbah, so the FLN simply adjusted their operations. Like Marighella said, terrorism is similar to guerrilla warfare, only easier.

Efforts to wall off the enemy with cordons of protective security are not just ineffective; they are counterproductive because they impact the innocent among the terrorist's identity community and divide society as the terrorist wants it divided. Closing the Casbah showed the Algerian Arabs—the FLN's Sheeple—that the French considered them enemies rather than loyal French citizens. Yet decades later governments still fall into these same traps, putting up walls instead of building bridges.

It turns out la Pointe's first operation was just a ruse designed to test his mettle. His conversion into a full-fledged terrorist comes in another highly symbolic scene of ritualistic purification. La Pointe goes into a brothel, where he's clearly well known, and calls out the owner, a pimp named Hacene le Bonois. When they meet in the street Hacene calls la Pointe "my son," reinforcing their familiarity, but la Pointe has broken with that former life. He says the FLN, having twice warned Hacene to change occupations, has condemned him. Hacene practically raised La

Pointe, who gives Hacene one last chance to repent, demonstrating the FLN's reasonableness. Hacene resists and goes down in a hail of machine gun fire as la Pointe shouts a warning throughout the red-light district: "Look at him well! Now nobody can do whatever he wants in the Casbah. Not even Hacene."[9] In this one act la Pointe irrevocably breaks with his past life, cements his bond with the FLN in his new life, and begins the process of cleansing the community. La Pointe's recruitment and training are complete, and the terrorism starts in earnest.

Initially the FLN's targets are police officials. As the law enforcement officers of the colonial power, the police are the mechanism of government oppression, and therefore legitimate targets in an armed struggle for self-determination. They are not combatants exactly, but certainly not innocent. The police are technically civil authorities and not soldiers at war, so opinions would obviously differ. As we've seen, innocence is a tricky issue. In any event, the FLN's targeting of police draws an inefficient response. Frustrated by their inability to defend themselves, the police, led by the assistant police commissioner, plot and carry out a devastating terrorist bombing of their own at the Rue de Thebes home of an Algerian man implicated in a policeman's murder. The screenplay is vague as to the Algerian man's actual involvement—with the circumstances of his arrest seeming to suggest his innocence, but the police blotter indicating his guilt—perhaps subtly acknowledging the difficulty of assigning guilt or innocence in these situations.

The bombing at Rue de Thebes ends this subtlety, however. The bomb brings down several buildings and kills dozens of civilians, including women and children. This atrocity sparks a mass uprising, but the FLN quells it for the purpose of solidifying its role as the proper authority representing the Algerians of the Casbah. As he sends the crowd home, Yacef's character shouts, "The FLN will avenge you!" This scene, too, describes real events. In a 2004 interview with Gary Crowdus of *Cineaste* magazine, Saadi Yacef explained that this bombing was the catalyst for the FLN to start targeting civilians:

> At that point the Algerian population of the Casbah wanted to go into the European quarters to take revenge. We stopped them, just the way you see it in the film, by telling them that the FLN would avenge them. In order to keep our word, we had to arm ourselves in a way that was equal to that of our adversaries. That's why we brought in experts, chemists, who helped us devise bombs. Those were the three bombs that were carried and placed by the women, as you see them do in the film.
>
> In discussing the whole question of bombs and the placing of

bombs, you have to understand that at this time the ultracolonialists, the pieds-noirs, would often disguise themselves as paratroopers, and, because they were not interested in any mercy, they would place bombs indiscriminately, resulting in the death of civilians. So we too began to place our bombs indiscriminately, not really worrying about the consequences.[10]

One side's atrocities justify the other's. Each is the victim, each is the perpetrator.

The film doesn't flinch from the carnage caused by the FLN bombings, even depicting a child licking an ice cream cone in a café as the seconds tick away before an explosion. In a later scene the military captures FLN leader Ben M'Hidi and parades him before reporters. One asks him whether using ladies' baskets for bombs isn't a bit cowardly. Ben M'Hidi responds with words terrorists have used ever since to defend their conduct:

And doesn't it seem to you even more cowardly to drop napalm bombs on unarmed villages, so that there are a thousand times more innocent victims? Of course, if we had your airplanes it would be a lot easier for us. Give us your bombers, and you can have our baskets.[11]

With the increasing terrorism the authorities call in the French military. Colonel Mathieu, 3d Regiment, Colonial Paratroopers, makes his entrance by marching his men through the streets of Algiers.

Mathieu lays out the situation in a briefing for his newly arrived troops. First he describes the FLN's organizational structure as a classic pyramidal hierarchy broken into cells, an organizational structure common to clandestine terrorist groups of that era. Mathieu draws a triangle on the board with a number 1 at the top and a 2 at one corner and a 3 at the other corner. Each member is tasked with recruiting two new members below him, he says as he also draws a 3 and a 4 below corner 2 and a 5 and a 6 below corner 3. They then each recruit two more, and so on. Each member only knows the one who has recruited him and the two he has recruited in turn. This way if one person is captured he or she can only inform on three members, and the organization survives. Mathieu says, "That is why we do not know our adversaries: because, in practice, they do not even know each other."[12]

I actually received almost this exact briefing at a terrorism lecture twenty years later at new agents' training at the FBI Academy, but by then this organizational structure was no longer in use. Louis Beam's

"Leaderless Resistance" article had come out in 1983, demolishing the hierarchical pyramid in favor of phantom cells by the time I went through the academy.[13] In reality, the hierarchical cells never worked, not even in the movies. If the FLN had observed cellular discipline, each member would only know those two he recruited and the one who recruited him. Yet in the film la Pointe meets Petit Omar, Djamila, Jaffar (Yacef's character), Ben M'Hidi, and many others, including FLN supporters who run the various safe houses. Keeping cellular discipline is nearly impossible, even in a two-hour movie.

But just as the lone extremist myth, the idea of the magically talented enemy persists. Mathieu describes the FLN terrorist as if he is a spirit:

> He is an adversary who shifts his position above and below the surface with highly commendable revolutionary methods and original tactics. . . . He is an anonymous and unrecognizable enemy who mingles with thousands of others who resemble him.[14]

He recognizes, however, there are actually few terrorists among the Algiers population: "There are 80,000 Arabs in the Casbah. Are they all against us? We know they are not. In reality, it is only a small minority that dominates with terror and violence."[15]

For Mathieu, though, the FLN's organizational capabilities presents a challenge that cannot be handled with normal methods: "We find ourselves hindered by a conspiracy of laws and regulations that continue to be operative, as if Algiers were a holiday resort and not a battleground."[16] Forty years earlier U.S. attorney general Mitchell Palmer used this same reasoning to justify his Palmer raids, and in the 1970s FBI agents would echo Mathieu's words to describe why COINTELPRO was necessary. Mathieu explains to his troops that victory requires intelligence, and intelligence only comes through interrogation "conducted in a manner so as to always obtain a result, or rather, an answer."

The French military's use of torture against Algerians during the War of Independence is well documented. In the film the press put two and two together after the captured Ben M'Hidi is reported to have killed himself by tying his shirt into a rope and hanging himself in his cell, even though earlier press releases said he was kept bound hand and foot to prevent a possible escape.

In reality torture is exposed because its victims don't have any incentive to keep the government's secrets. French paratroopers arrested and tortured French journalist Henri Alleg, a supporter of Algerian independence. Aleg's written account of his experiences was smuggled out of prison and published under the title *The Question* in 1958.[17] The book described the French paratroopers' interrogation techniques in shocking detail, leading French authorities to ban it, but not before it forced the French public to acknowledge that crimes were being committed in its name. Some French officers involved in the torture have even penned memoirs of their own, defending their conduct. Their defense of these techniques is reflected in this exchange between a French reporter and Mathieu after the military's use of torture is leaked to the press:

> MATHIEU:
> What type of interrogation should we choose—
> the one the courts use for a crime of
> homicide which drags on for months?
>
> THIRD JOURNALIST:
> The law is often inconvenient, Colonel.
>
> MATHIEU:
> And those who explode bombs in public
> places, do they perhaps respect the law?[18]

French general Paul Aussaresses, who served as a high-ranking officer in Algiers, published *Special Services, Algeria: 1955–1957,* in 2001 in which he unabashedly and unapologetically admitted his role in torturing Algerian prisoners and strangling Ben M'Hidi during the Battle of Algiers..[19] He was charged in France with attempting to "justify war crimes," because the general amnesty declared after the Algerian War prevented his being charged with the actual war crimes themselves.[20] He was convicted in January 2004, almost fifty years after the war, proving that while justice is sometimes very slow, eventually there is a reckoning.

His conviction will do little to resolve the issue over what a government charged with protecting innocent lives must do when confronted by a deadly clandestine enemy. Indeed, counterterrorism expert Bruce Hoffman, writing in the *Atlantic* shortly after the 9/11 terrorist attacks on the United States, wrestled with these issues. He referenced the Battle of Algiers and the trade-off between the need for intelligence and democratic ideals. Hoffman said French general Jacqes Massu

> was forever unrepentant: he insisted that the ends justified the means used to destroy the FLN's urban insurrection. The battle was won, lives were saved, and the indiscriminate bombing campaign that had terrorized the city was ended. To Massu, that was

all that mattered. To his mind, respect for the law and the niceties of legal procedure were irrelevant given the crisis situation enveloping Algeria in 1957.[21]

And indeed torture did help France defeat the FLN, both in the film and in real life. In 1957, in the movie's climatic scene, intelligence gained through torture allows the French paratroopers to locate Ali la Pointe, and he is trapped with his ragged terror cell in a small hideout behind a false wall. Mathieu begs him to surrender, for the sake of the women and children, but they do not. Mathieu orders the building blown up, killing the last FLN leader still at large and ending the Battle of Algiers. It may seem surprising that terrorists enjoy this film so much when all the terrorists end up imprisoned, tortured, or killed.

The FLN's defeat is not the end of the film, though, nor the end of the story. Algeria won its independence five years later with mass uprisings. Yacef credits the abusive techniques the French used:

> Actually torture helped the FLN enormously because what it did was to expose the real face of the French military . . . you could say that Aussaresses was one of the FLN's most important assets because the more he tortured, the more militants we recruited.

Yacef believed the reports of torture not only united the Algerian people but undermined French support for the war, both among the French troops involved in the torture and at home. He said, "So torture is a problem that fell more on the shocked French conscience than on the conscience of the Algerians, who were its eternal victims."[22]

The French won the Battle of Algiers but lost Algeria. Academic experts such as Martha Crenshaw agree that the French military had as much to do with the Algerian victory as the FLN:

> There was no mass insurrection as a result of urban terrorism, but Pierre Montagnon concludes that nationalism took a decisive hold in the Algiers Muslim population as a result of French repression. Because the French authorities suspected all Muslims of being terrorists and persecuted them simply for their identity, the consciousness of separation grew.[23]

The film was released a few years before Marighella published *The Mini-manual of the Urban Guerrilla*. Even if he didn't see the film I'm certain Marighella studied the strategy that led the FLN to victory, because his writing conveys it exactly. The terrorists only win by forcing the government to oppress them; by adopting more and more repressive measures, the government loses its legitimacy with the people, and ultimately loses the war.

Unfortunately not everyone who sees the film gets this message. Hoffman writes in his *Atlantic* article about an acquaintance he calls "Thomas," who is a Sri Lankan army officer fighting one of the most formidable terrorist groups ever, the Liberation Tigers of Tamil Eelam, better known as the LTTE or the Tamil Tigers. After running off a litany of truly atrocious acts the LTTE carried out in recent years, Hoffman recounts a conversation with Thomas about the Sri Lankan counterterrorism interrogation techniques. Thomas recalled capturing three Tamil Tigers who had planted a bomb to target civilians somewhere in the Sri Lankan city of Colombo. After they refused to reveal the bomb's location and after he warned them about what he would do if they did not talk, Thomas shot one of the men in the forehead, killing him. Thomas said the others volunteered information quickly thereafter, and lives were saved.[24] On the one hand, Thomas saw a positive result. But, on the other, perhaps not surprisingly, the Tamil Tigers are still going strong.

Hoffman was clearly troubled by his conversation with Thomas, but he was not convinced such techniques are counterproductive:

> I am constantly reminded of Thomas—of the difficulties of fighting terrorism and of the challenges of protecting not only the innocent but an entire society and way of life. I am never bidden to condone, much less advocate, torture. But as I look at the snapshots and the lives of the victims recounted each day, and think how it will take almost a year to profile the approximately 5,000 people who perished on September 11, I recall the ruthless enemy that America faces, and I wonder about the lengths to which we may yet have to go to vanquish him.[25]

"A sense of overwhelming crisis beyond the reach of any traditional solutions" is how Paxton put it.[26] Unfortunately Hoffman is not alone in his ambivalence about torture. In 2005 the PBS *Frontline* series hosted a debate of preeminent legal scholars entitled "Is Torture Ever Justified?" This legal panel discussion should have been the shortest on record (even if they had replaced the word torture with the more popular newspeak euphemism "highly coercive interrogation"), with the question simply followed by a unanimous "no." And I won't even go into the issue of whether torture could ever be morally justified, because I promised to avoid moral arguments. My answer is based solely on whether the effectiveness of torture as a counterterrorism technique, as measured against the cost, is justifiable. All of the evidence demonstrates torture just doesn't work, especially in counterterrorism operations. Fortunately Tom Parker, a Brown University fellow and, more important, a former counterterrorism investigator in Great Britain, finally made the point that "those prepared to hold their noses and adopt such practices run the risk of purchasing (minimal) short-term tactical victories at the expense of long-term strategic success."[27] The reason torture doesn't stop terrorism is because terrorism isn't about a military victory. It's about legitimacy.

In a brilliant sequence in *The Battle of Algiers*, after all the brutal interrogations, torture, and abuse, Mathieu has finally extracted the information he was looking for: the FLN leaders' names. He calls his troops together to announce the victory. As he names the FLN leaders he displays their photographs and says, "I found these in the police archives."[28] The police had the terrorists' records the whole time, but the French were so focused on gathering new intelligence they didn't bother to evaluate the evidence they already had in their files. It was a mistake the United States would repeat, both before and after 9/11.

Perhaps the most ironic thing about *The Battle of Algiers,* which is almost never discussed, is that with all the death and destruction on both sides the central driver of the action is a peaceful protest, a general strike designed to convince the United Nations to take up the Algerian question. The French spend more effort trying to stop the general strike through most of the movie than they do trying to find the FLN, and the general strike has more of a visibly galvanizing effect on the Algerian people than do all of the FLN bombings. The United Nations does not take up the Algerian question in the end, at least not in time to help the Algerian people, and Franco Solinas later said he included these scenes to demonstrate that the Algerians could not have won their independence without the armed struggle.[29] I wonder if this scenario doesn't also represent an opportunity missed, though. The Algerian masses were not united behind the terrorists, but they were united in the strike, demonstrating their preference for a political solution over an armed struggle. The strike might have provided the French a more peaceful avenue to resolve their political issues in Algeria. If the French had encouraged the United Nations to take up the Algerian question, they may still have had to leave Algeria, but they could have left without sacrificing innocent lives on both sides, and without the loss of honor resulting from widespread violations of human rights, violations that are still being exposed in courts of law some fifty years later.

9

Ranking the Resistance

Insanity in individuals is something rare—but in groups, parties, nations and epochs, it is the rule.

—Friedrich Nietzsche, *Beyond Good and Evil*

Looking at terrorism as a tactic—or as the "product of a strategic choice," as Crenshaw would say—allows for a more objective analysis of terrorist behavior, because it most accurately reflects the terrorists' true nature as rational actors. I learned terrorists are rational actors from spending time inside terrorist organizations, discussing strategy, training, planning attacks, making bombs, and listening to them dream about the better future they felt they were fighting for. Most of the terrorist manifestos and strategy manuals I've read demonstrate a high degree of intellectual sophistication and logical reasoning, certainly much more than I would have given them credit for when someone first handed me *The White Man's Bible* so many years ago.

Many of the terrorist leaders I've heard speak are articulate and effective public speakers, keeping in mind that they were not trying to persuade us but instead a particular like-minded audience. Terrorists who skillfully execute their strategy often succeed in overthrowing the governments they oppose and become the leaders of the new governments they establish. They aren't stupid or mentally unstable people. We should regard terrorists first and foremost as capable adversaries who follow logical and effective political strategies designed to help them reach their goals.

But having spent time in a militia group, I realize some psychological issues are in play as well. Many of the terrorists' extremist beliefs require a deliberate willingness to ignore realities that conflict with their beliefs, at the very least. They allow their beliefs to blind them to obvious truths. This enormous vulnerability prevents them from ever being able to objectively assess their political situation.

The arguments terrorists use to justify their violence are inherently hypocritical. Even so many years after the Battle of Algiers, French war crimes and the ultra-colonialist terrorist attacks as the Rue de Thebes bombing still morally outrage Saadi Yacef, but he dismisses his own terrorism as simply a necessary consequence.[1] Terrorist groups often complain that the government's version of events is propaganda, but they almost all have a section in their own training manuals on how important creating persuasive propaganda is to promoting their cause. They claim their lies are necessary to correct the record, but they don't see the irony.

When I was working undercover I referred to this phenomenon as a "suspension of disbelief." Terrorists have a particular worldview and manipulate facts to make them fit into their worldview rather than reshape their worldview to fit the facts. This behavior is not a result of or a symptom of mental illness, rather it reflects the unquestioning acceptance of an unprovable but foundational "truth," akin to a devout religious faith (in fact, in some groups it is a devout religious faith). As with any true believers, no amount of reasoning or empirical evidence will convince them their beliefs are unsound. Their logic is simple: since I know "X" is true, then everything that suggests "not X" is false. I often hear people refer to terrorists as fanatics because they exhibit this mind-set, but unless you are willing to call every person of faith and every ardent patriot a fanatic too, I don't think this description is useful. Calling it "terrorist psycho-logic," as Jerrold Post does,[2] infers mental abnormality or weakness, but we all have beliefs we adhere to without any empirical support: prejudices, superstitions, and distorted images of ourselves and others. It's part of human nature.

As I said in chapter 6, the primary attribute of my identity is my nationality. I let that trait, to the exclusion of others, define me as a person and guide my behavior. If a hostile nation dropped bombs on El Paso, Texas, I would take it personally and prepare to go to war to defend my country; however, if they dropped them a hundred yards away in Juarez, Mexico, I wouldn't feel the same. To a large extent the concept of a nation is just a fiction—lines drawn on a map somewhere that often can't be seen on the ground. Yet we let where we live in relation to these imaginary lines determine who we are as a people.

What I love about America has nothing to do with the land between the borders. It is what the nation stands for—freedom, tolerance, and justice—that makes me willing to fight for it. Because I believe in this intangible concept of justice I have willingly engaged in rather extreme activities, often against my own self-interest, to forward its cause.

Does my willingness to risk my life for my beliefs make me a fanatic? My community didn't think so—they gave me a medal of valor. That someone else might choose to act on a different set of beliefs is no less rational. Belief is simply beyond reason, which is why Wittgenstein didn't want us talking about it.

The problem arises when a group of people becomes convinced their belief is entirely "right" and anyone who disagrees is entirely "wrong." Right is always considered good and wrong is always bad, and thus the world is divided into a good us and an evil them. The danger is, as the Weather Underground's Brian Flanagan said, "when you feel that you have right on your side you can do some horrific things."[3]

As Eco and Paxton have shown, this tendency to divide the world in two is the hallmark of fascist governments. When analyzing fascism in chapter 6 I'm sure you recognized that the characteristics Eco and Paxton described as common to fascist governments were identical in most respects to the features of the terrorist organizations I encountered during my undercover experiences. This similarity was probably not surprising given that the terrorist groups I infiltrated were either overtly neo-Nazi or at least open to recruiting a neo-Nazi. But as we have seen, all terrorist groups operate using similar methods. They use almost identical arguments to justify their violence and identical strategies to accomplish their goals. If we look again at Paxton's mobilizing passions or the fourteen features of Eco's Ur-Fascism we'll see that all terrorist groups share these attributes.

If these attributes indeed define fascism and all terrorist groups share them, then all terrorist groups are fascists, regardless of their ideology. Again we must remember that fascism itself is not an ideology, rather, it is a method of exercising power or, as Eco said, something standing "behind a regime or ideology."[4] Paxton described it similarly as "a form of political behavior."[5]

The only obvious anomaly is Paxton's caveat that fascist leaders, or "natural chiefs" as he calls them, are always male. As we have seen, particularly in the case of Bernardine Dohrn of the Weather Underground, not all terrorist group leaders are men. One possible explanation is that, as Saadi Yacef said about employing women bombers during the Battle of Algiers, sometimes groups mobilize women out of necessity rather than by choice. And it is also important to remember that not all of Paxton's features have to be present for a government (or a terrorist group) to be considered fascist.

But the true explanation for this anomaly is that Paxton described the attributes of fascist governments, not of fascist terrorist groups, and while they share almost identical features there is one fundamental difference between the two: governments hold power and terrorist groups do not. This crucial difference goes to the heart of Paxton's definition of fascism. Paxton's long definition of fascism includes one pivotal phrase in which he describes fascists as "working in uneasy but effective collaboration with traditional elites."[6] Terrorist groups never work with traditional elites, so by Paxton's definition, at least according to this analysis, terrorists are never truly fascist.

The self-described fascists I was working against when I was undercover were not really fascists at all; they were only playacting as fascists. Moreover, they could never be true fascists because traditional elites would never work with them, not even uneasily. Ironically, such a relationship would never form precisely because the neo-fascists identify themselves as fascists.

This reasoning may seem circular at first, but it provides a clue for how we might more appropriately respond to terrorism, and I believe it is what Eco meant when he warned about fascism coming back in "plainclothes."[7] Fascism could never return while calling itself fascism because the traditional elites, whose support is necessary to bring them to power, would never cooperate. The only reason the traditional elites cooperated with the Italian and German fascists was because the movement was brand new. No one knew what fascism was. I'm sure it was exciting to see a vibrant, daring new political movement led by bold men of action who displayed strength, determination, and swagger. Who wouldn't want to experience the excitement of participating in a mass movement? Even if there was some cause for concern about where it might lead, undoubtedly the party was moving forward, and folks wanted to be on board rather than left behind. I can tell you when fascists speak they present a compelling, utopian vision of the future. They are good at hiding what they really are and at convincing their supporters that their nastier behaviors are just temporary necessities.

But now we know where it ends. The traditional elites know where such behavior ends as well, and they would never cooperate with fascism again if they recognized it for what it was. As Eco said, fascism could only come back in an innocent disguise. Harold von Braunhut recognized this truth, which is why he instructed young skinheads to mask their racism and become "trench coat warriors." As did David Duke, who put away his Klan robes when he ran for public office. Even the fascists know they can't regain power if they are identified as fascists.

Fascism is hard to recognize, however. Simply look at the unwieldy definitions learned experts like Eco and Paxton had to create to describe fascism. But its behavior can be described.

The government's goal in responding to terrorism should be to expose as publicly as possible the behavior terrorists engage in, especially behavior that will reveal them for the fascists they are. The truth is no one—certainly not the Sheeple and likely not the sympathizers or the supporters—wants to live under fascist control. Terrorist groups rule their communities through fear and intimidation, just as fascist governments do. Terror occurs inside terrorist groups as well. Focusing our enforcement efforts on these behaviors rather than on the ideologies reduces the risk of offending those supporters and sympathizers who might share the terrorists' ideology but abhor their methodology.

Like fascist governments, fascist terrorist groups have inherent weaknesses. Their worldview rests on a suspension of disbelief, which is why they must enforce their uncompromising ideologies with violence. They can only survive by hiding their weaknesses. Like any bully, they survive through intimidation.

As we have seen, terrorist groups are rigidly dogmatic, both in methodology and ideology, which is a characteristic of any ideologically driven, mission-oriented organization. Just look at the Army as an example. Dogmatic ideologies don't stand up well to real-world experiences or intellectual challenges, though. Indeed, cults and extremist groups often establish compounds (the Army calls them "bases") to isolate themselves from experiences or ideas that might challenge their worldview.

Rigidly dogmatic organizations can't tolerate dissent, so these groups tend to expel dissenters rather than argue with them. As a result these terrorist movements splinter into many different and often competing groups over time. Although the film version of the Battle of Algiers focused on the FLN, many different groups acted within the larger Algerian Independence movement, and the FLN fought them just as brutally as they fought the French. Even after Algeria gained its independence, these rival groups continued to fight and their descendants still do today. This disharmony within terrorist groups is another inherent weakness open to exploitation.

The problem for any terrorist group is that its clandestine environment acts as a pressure chamber; any fissures in the organization quickly become fractures. Turncoats and traitors have to be dealt with quickly and harshly, often before all the evidence has come in, raising the levels of tension and violence within the group. These internecine battles are just as deadly as the armed struggle but are much more difficult for the terrorist groups to justify as necessary to their identity community.

With its COINTELPRO programs, the FBI manipulated these organizational schisms. Perhaps its most effective use of this scheme was its Black Nationalist program, which started in 1967. The first of its five

long-range goals was "to prevent the 'coalition of militant black nationalist groups,' which might be the first step toward a real 'Mau Mau' in
America" (referring to the 1952–60 uprising against British rule in Kenya).[8]
While there was probably little chance of a "real 'Mau Mau' in America"
anyway, the Black Nationalist COINTELPRO did successfully sow enough
discord in and among these groups to prevent them from uniting. In fact
many former Black Panthers credit COINTELPRO for instigating and
fomenting the internal bickering that ultimately destroyed their party.[9]
Oddly, the FBI didn't feel it was as successful. The Church Committee
interviewed one FBI agent, who offered that the Black Panthers might
have fallen apart on their own accord:

> All we know, either through their own ineptitude, maybe it
> emerged through counterintelligence, maybe, I think we like to
> think that that helped to do it, that there was not this develop-
> ment. . . . What part did counterintelligence [play?] We hope that
> it did play a part. Maybe we just gave it a nudge.[10]

Perhaps he was just being modest, because the Black Nationalist
groups were clearly fractured by the early 1970s and all but gone by the
early 1980s. If the FBI's goal was to prevent a coalition of Black Nationalists, they certainly succeeded.

The Black Panthers' fragmentation did not realize the FBI's overriding goal of preventing violence, however. Eldridge Cleaver, one of the
original members of the Black Panther Party, was targeted with a successful COINTELPRO campaign while he was living in exile in Algeria after
a 1968 Black Panther shoot-out with the Oakland Police. Cleaver split
with the Panthers in 1971, which the FBI probably would have considered a success. But Cleaver then went on to found the incredibly violent
Black Liberation Army (BLA). The BLA specifically targeted police officers for assassination to increase the hostility between the police and
the black community, and, it hoped, to foment an uprising. BLA members were believed to be responsible for shooting police officers in New
York, Philadelphia, New Jersey, San Francisco, Atlanta, and Houston.[11]

COINTELPRO later became infamous when it was revealed the
FBI was also using its Black Nationalist program to target peaceful civil
rights activists, such as Dr. Martin Luther King, Jr. In the end, not only
did the program fail to prevent violence, it was exposed as an outrageous
and misguided attempt to repress the legitimate civil rights movement.

Perhaps if we examine what went wrong with COINTELPRO, we
can correct the deficiencies that led to abuse and perhaps salvage any
techniques that were successful in dismantling violent groups. It is not

hard to see what went wrong with COINTELPRO. The approved COINTELPRO techniques included:

> anonymous mailings (reprints, Bureau-authored articles and letters) to group members criticizing a leader or an allied group; using informants to raise controversial issues; forming a "notional"—a Bureau run splinter group—to draw away membership from the target organization; encouraging hostility up to and including gang warfare between rival groups; and the "snitch jacket."[12]

The potential for abuse exists in any police investigation, and some of these techniques are clearly abusive on their face. But one sentence in the FBI memo initiating the Black Nationalist COINTELPRO all but guaranteed that possibility would be realized in these investigations:

> You are also cautioned that the nature of this new endeavor is such that under no circumstances should the existence of the program be made known outside the Bureau and appropriate within-office security should be afforded to sensitive operations and techniques considered under the program.[13]

That no one would ever know what the FBI agents were doing in these investigations removed any outside restraints on FBI power, which opened the door for abuse. Meanwhile a lack of internal controls at the FBI removed any internal constraints that could have prevented it. The lack of internal controls at the FBI was stunning. The FBI Inspection Division assistant director who would have been responsible for reviewing internal investigations during that time made this incredible statement to the Church Committee: "There was no instruction to me, nor do I believe there is any instruction in the Inspector's manual that the Inspector should be on the alert to see that constitutional values are being protected."[14]

This inspector took an oath to support and defend the Constitution when he joined the FBI, but apparently he forgot this small detail as he carried out his duties. The potential for abuse was of course realized, as it always is when government power goes unchecked. Of the five COINTELPRO programs, the Black Nationalist program used the highest number of intelligence operations that involved "serious risk of physical, emotional and economic damage," including "snitch jackets" and techniques that pitted one extremist group against another with the intention of creating violent clashes between the separate organizations.[15]

Secrecy also allowed the FBI to improperly broaden the scope of its Black Nationalist program to include harassing peaceful civil rights organizations. When asked why the FBI targeted the Southern Christian Leadership Conference, which was known for its commitment to nonviolence, one FBI supervisor responded, "I cannot explain it satisfactorily."[16] Perhaps if he knew when he opened the investigation that he would later be required to explain it, the outcomes would have been different, and resources that could have been used to investigate real threats would not have been wasted harassing a peaceful civil rights organization.

It may seem strange that a former undercover agent is so critical of government secrecy; after all, my life depended on operational secrecy. The difference is that I knew from my first day undercover that everything I did would be presented in open court. In fact I even recorded everything so I could provide an unimpeachable accounting of my actions. My incentive was to follow the rules so that all of the evidence I was risking my life to gather would be admissible in court. Could I have abused my power while working undercover? Of course. Could I have gotten away with it? Probably not. The difficulty with keeping the details of covert counterterrorist operations secret is that the terrorists know what's happening to them. If I met with them fifty times but only reported forty meetings, they would know I hadn't reported ten meetings. Could I expect them to keep this discrepancy a secret? If they had evidence indicating I did something improper, they could present that evidence in court. The adversarial process of our criminal justice system ensures that every inconsistency will be addressed, and every fact checked. The transparency of the criminal justice system ensures the accountability of government agents.

Openness and accountability are even more critical in counterterrorism operations, where exposing the terrorists' behavior demonstrates the illegitimacy of their conduct. Rather than retaliate against the black community for the BLA police shootings, as the BLA expected them to, the New York City Police Department (NYPD) simply exposed the BLA's true nature and purpose for the public to see. In an editorial published in Harlem's *Amsterdam News,* NYPD patrolman Ulysses Williams wrote:

There are those who call themselves your brothers. They stand on rhetorical platitudes and shout at the top of their voices that they are fighting for the rights of their black brothers. But how black are they? Black is not only a color as it applies to us. It's a state of mind that stands for courage. And most of all, pride. A pride that would not allow a black man to cravenly shoot down another man when his back is turned, and then condone the act by calling it justice. Especially another black man who has sworn to protect and stand between his people and harm. Cast them out for they are not of you, they have become infected with a poison that could kill us all.[17]

Patrolman Williams was not talking to the BLA, but rather to the community the BLA was trying to persuade. And all he had to do was tell the truth. The government shouldn't need to resort to propaganda to discredit terrorist groups. To most people, reason is preferable to extremism. Exposing the true nature of the BLA helped mute its influence in the black community.

Unfortunately the FBI didn't follow the NYPD's enlightened lead. The extralegal methods the FBI chose to use in COINTELPRO only helped to substantiate the terrorists' propaganda that the FBI was an unjust oppressor. Many criminal prosecutions against terrorists during this period were either lost or abandoned because COINTELPRO techniques could not withstand public scrutiny. Terrorists escaped justice because the government's conduct was just as unsavory as the terrorists'. Some people who were convicted during this era were later released, sometimes decades later, when it was learned that evidence was fabricated and witnesses coerced. Others remain in jail, and we may never know whether their convictions were fairly won.

The agents working on COINTELPRO didn't set out to break the law—quite the opposite. But they never expected to have to defend their conduct so it was too easy to move from aggressive investigations into patently illegal and abusive activities. Worse, because these agents never had to account for their actions, there was never an objective examination of the results of their efforts. Breaking up the Black Panther Party may have seemed a good idea sitting around a conference table, but the resulting violence proved it was counterproductive to COINTELPRO's ultimate mission. The lesson we should have learned from COINTELPRO is that secret counterterrorism programs don't work.

What does work is making counterterrorism agents and their agencies publicly accountable. Presenting evidence in open court will allow the rule of law to prevail over terrorist violence.

Our government should welcome an open comparison of its behavior against that of the terrorists, as even Eldridge Cleaver acknowledged after his travels abroad brought him some perspective:

I'm telling you after I ran into the Egyptian police and the Algerian police and the North Korean police and the Nigerian police and Idie [sic] Amin's police in Uganda, I began to miss the Oak-land police. The last time I saw them suckers, I was shooting at them; and they were shooting at me. But regardless of what our standards are in this country, we do have some laws; we do have some principles that to a certain degree restrain our police.[18]

In the end the FBI's COINTELPRO programs didn't stop the BLA or the other so-called Black Nationalist groups; the civil rights move-ment did. The success of Dr. Martin Luther King's nonviolent campaign for civil rights showed the black community that violence wasn't neces-sary to achieve their political objectives. Some argue that Dr. King could not have achieved such success if the more confrontational groups like the Black Panthers weren't pushing their parallel agendas, and I don't disagree. I would never suggest terrorism isn't effective. But the lesson we should take from this episode is that the peaceful resolution of the politi-cal issue left the terrorists without a sufficient justification to move their entire community to violence. If the FBI's goal was truly to stop the violence, J. Edgar Hoover should have been embracing Martin Luther King rather than trying to discredit him.

10

Terrorism Types

*Nobody can give you freedom. Nobody can give you equality or
justice or anything. If you're a man, you take it.*

—Malcolm X, *Malcolm X Speaks*

After arguing in previous chapters that terrorist groups are essentially
alike in their methodology, I will switch gears in this chapter and
discuss how terrorist groups differ. The most meaningful difference among
terrorist groups is not in their ideology or methodology, but rather in
their end game—that is, the objective the terrorists are trying to accomplish. Some terrorist groups have clear-cut political objectives within a
limited, well-defined, but disputed territory. The FLN, as we've seen,
wanted to end the French colonial occupation of Algeria. The Irish Republican Army wants to end British rule in Northern Ireland and to
reunite it with the Republic of Ireland. Most often the identity communities these terrorists claim to represent are legitimately aggrieved classes
located within, or having a historic claim to, a disputed territory.

The legitimacy of the identity group's grievance does not mean that
the terrorist group legitimately represents that class or that using violence
to redress that grievance is legitimate—far from it. For this discussion's
sake, I will call this kind of terrorist a "legitimately motivated terrorist,"
but this label is not meant to suggest that the terrorist is justified in using
terrorism. While these groups may claim a legitimate motive, if to achieve
those ends they choose illegitimate means—extortion, violence and other
organized criminal activity—they are still terrorists.

Other terrorist groups, such as white supremacists, jihadists, and
animal rights terrorists, have much grander agendas than do the legitimately motivated terrorists. These groups want to fundamentally shift

the paradigms of political power on a global scale and to enforce a rigid adherence to their particular religious, political, or moral philosophy. Their goal is not just to legally protect their community's rights within a specific political system or to take political control of a particular territory, but rather these terrorists are seeking to enforce their ideologies throughout the world. They speak of the utopian regimes they want to establish in broad, generalized terms—a new *Reich* or a new caliphate. When pressed for details on how these regimes will govern, they will typically redirect the discussion to the great war that must be fought to bring the regime into existence. Once the war is won, they reason, the utopian regime will naturally fall into place and its authority will be recognized for its inherent legitimacy. Until the enemy is destroyed, there is no point in discussing the details of how they will rule. An extreme intolerance for those who do not share their ideology drives these groups, so I will call them "extremist terrorists."

A third class of terrorist is the state-sponsored terrorist group. State sponsorship usually includes financial support, logistical support, and a safe harbor—a protected territory in which the terrorist group can train, organize, and operate. State-sponsored terrorist groups can establish a much more formal organization than unsupported terrorist groups, because their safe haven allows them to operate in the open rather than clandestinely. They also benefit from their association with the state's intelligence agencies, which can provide false identity documents, diplomatic support regarding foreign travel, and access to intelligence information. These groups pose the most serious threat because in reality they are not terrorist groups at all; rather they are an arm of the government that sponsors them. States sponsor terrorist groups to act as their proxies so the states can accomplish their hostile purposes without being held responsible.

If a hostile nation harbors, trains, and equips a terrorist group so it can attack the United States, Americans wouldn't expect the government to tolerate this ruse and pretend that the sponsoring hostile state is not responsible any more than they would expect the government to fall for the lone extremist ruse of a domestic terrorist group. We would expect the government to take action against the hostile state with all the power at its disposal—first to expose the relationship between the hostile nation and the terrorist group and then to take whatever diplomatic or military actions necessary to terminate the threat to national security. Thus if a hostile nation sponsors a terrorist group we should not call them terrorists. They are covert intelligence agents of a hostile power. Calling them anything else only confuses everyone and makes it difficult to formulate an appropriate response. Employing counterterrorism efforts in this type of conflict means the government has fallen for the sponsoring state's ruse. The conflict is with the hostile nation, not with the terrorists. I will return to this issue of state-sponsored terrorists in chapter 15.

A government subject to a terrorist attack from a group not sponsored by a hostile nation must determine which kind of terrorist group it is dealing with before developing a rational response. If, after an objective self-analysis using the Government Accountability Scale, the government determines that the community the terrorist is claiming to represent has a legitimate political grievance, the government would conclude that it is dealing with a legitimately motivated terrorist group. Again this label doesn't mean that the terrorists legitimately represent that group or that their resort to terrorism is justified, but it does recognize the terrorists are using a legitimate issue as a motivator. A government threatened by a legitimately motivated terrorist group might respond by working to resolve the underlying political issue to remove the political cause that supports the violence.

Such a response would not be reasonable when facing an extremist terrorist group's violence. If Ku Klux Klan violence erupts after a black family moves into a previously all-white neighborhood, we wouldn't expect the government to negotiate a political settlement with racist Klan sympathizers in the neighborhood. We would expect the government to react quickly, to enforce the law, to remove the threat, and to protect the citizens' rights. But the government can only determine an appropriate counterterrorism response if it knows what type of terrorist it is dealing with.

Imagine another scale, this one called a Terrorist Accountability Scale, with legitimately motivated terrorist groups at one end and extremist terrorists at the other end. The placement of the different types of terrorists on this scale depends to a great degree on the political behavior of the government they are resisting so it is useful to think of the Terrorist Accountability Scale as resting under the Government Accountability Scale. Since fascist governments tend to create legitimate justifications for political resistance, legitimately motivated terrorists would most often be found at the fascist government end of the scale. Likewise, since violence against free governments would be more difficult to justify, extremist terrorists would be found at the free government end of the scale.

Just as with the Government Accountability Scale, no particular terrorist group could be considered completely of one type or the other, and each group's classification would change as its political situation changes. A repressive regime attacked by legitimately motivated terrorists might reform its policies toward the terrorists' identity group. If the legitimately motivated terrorists continue to attack the government after the reforms then they could be considered extremist terrorists. Likewise, an extremist terrorist group that attacks a free government may become legitimately motivated if the free government responds to the violence by repressing the extremist terrorists' identity group. Since a legitimately motivated terrorist group can, by their attachment to a legitimate political issue, draw more supporters and sympathizers than does an extremist terrorist group, the government should always seek to adjust its policies to force the terrorists toward the extremist end of the Terrorist Accountability Scale

In the following chapters we will examine how governments in the past have reacted to the different types of terrorist groups and see how this process has worked. Then we can incorporate the lessons learned into our current counterterrorism strategy. We will determine which government responses have worked to reduce the threat of terrorism and, more important, which have not.

Part III:
How to Win

11

Case Study #2:
The Ku Klux Klan

It may be true that the law cannot make a man love me, but it
can stop him from lynching me, and I think that's pretty important.

—Martin Luther King, Jr.

The Ku Klux Klan is one of the oldest continuously operating terrorist organizations in the world. It presents an interesting case study for examining how the U.S. government responded to the Klan's different types of terrorism over the years and how those counterterrorist responses affected the terrorist organization. This study is not intended to be a definitive history of the Klan by any means, and since the Klan has splintered, reformed, combined with other groups, and then splintered again so often, I will sometimes use the term *the Klan* in a general sense to refer to the white supremacist movement as a whole.

The Ku Klux Klan formed as a fraternal organization of decommissioned Confederate soldiers in Tennessee shortly after the 1865 surrender at Appomattox that ended the Civil War. The Confederates lost the shooting war, but then used the Klan, the White Brotherhood, the Knights of the White Camelia, and similar underground insurgent groups to fight on. They used terror tactics to resist black suffrage and the radical Republicans' Reconstruction policies that disenfranchised white voters who had supported the Confederacy. The Klan even tapped a former Partisan Ranger, Gen. Nathan Bedford Forrest, to be its first Grand Wizard. Their stated goals, like all the terrorist groups we've seen, were noble:

1. To protect the weak, the innocent and the defenseless . . . ; to relieve the injured and oppressed; to succor the suffering and unfortunate . . . ;

2.   To protect and defend the Constitution of the United States . . . ;
3.   To aid and assist in the execution of all constitutional laws, and to
      protect the people from unlawful seizure and from trial except by
      their peers.[1]

While generally remembered as infamous masked "night riders" who
randomly whipped, lynched, and terrorized black citizens under cover of
darkness, Klan-related violence was actually much broader in scope and
operationally focused on influencing elections. Prior to the pivotal 1868
elections Klan violence intended to suppress the Republican vote was
ferocious, with thousands of people killed in election-related violence in
Kansas, Georgia, and Louisiana.[2]

The violence was not successful in reaching its early political aims,
however, and may, in hindsight, have been counterproductive. Republicans took the Congress and the presidency, with dire consequences for
the Klan. In response to the Klan's violence Congress enacted the Enforcement Acts of 1870 (the Force Act) and 1871 (the Ku Klux Klan
Act), giving the U.S. attorney general both the extraordinary power to
enforce the civil rights guaranteed to blacks under the Fourteenth Amendment and federal jurisdiction over acts of Klan violence committed to
infringe those rights. Thousands of Klan members were arrested, and,
with blacks permitted to sit on juries in the federal trials, many were
convicted. President Ulysses S. Grant ordered federal troops into South
Carolina and Louisiana to quell the racial violence and restore order.

Many credit President Grant's aggressiveness in enforcing federal
law through the Enforcement Acts for defeating the Klan of that era. In
fact although he never publicly acknowledged having a role in the Klan,
Forrest had ordered the Klan disbanded a few years earlier, in 1869, after
growing disenchanted with their violent excesses. One sympathetic version of Klan history claims that Forrest actually made a secret deal with
Grant in 1869 in which Forrest agreed to disband the Klan in exchange
for Grant's returning home rule to the South.[3] While this scenario doesn't
fit the timing of events properly, it does fairly well describe how things
turned out.

Because of the clandestine nature of its operations and its dis-
tribution over such a broad territory, whether Forrest—or any other Klan
leader—ever had any real operational control over the Klan is doubtful.
Even if he did, such an order to disband would have done little to reduce
the white supremacist violence. Klan terrorism simply continued in a different guise, and eventually the federal government grew tired of responding to the incessant violence. In 1882 the Supreme Court struck down

the criminal penalties portion of the Enforcement Acts, Reconstruction
was abandoned, and the South was left to the white supremacists for the
next fifty years. They wasted no time in codifying white rule by passing
Jim Crow laws designed to prevent African Americans from exercising
their civil rights. The Supreme Court of the United States validated these
racial segregation policies with their 1896 decision in *Plessy v. Ferguson:*

> Legislation is powerless to eradicate racial instincts or to abolish
> distinctions based upon physical differences, and the attempt to
> do so can only result in accentuating the difficulties of the present
> situation. If the civil and political rights of both races be equal
> one cannot be inferior to the other civilly or politically. If one race
> be inferior to the other socially, the Constitution of the United
> States cannot put them upon the same plane.[4]

The *Plessy* decision gave an air of legitimacy to white supremacy,
but white supremacists could only maintain their control of the government through illegitimate means. Literally thousands of lynchings took
place during the decades after Reconstruction was abandoned, when the
Ku Klux Klan supposedly did not exist.[5] The confusion about how white
supremacist terrorist organizations like the Klan operate—in particular,
the relationship between the aboveground support structure and the underground cells carrying out acts of terrorism—would continue to impede law enforcement efforts to stop organized racial violence for the
next hundred years, and continues to this day.

The Klan as an aboveground organization saw a rebirth in 1915
after the release of D. W. Griffith's *Birth of a Nation.* Col. William
Simmons created a new Ku Klux Klan in Stone Mountain, Georgia, taking traditions from the post–Civil War era Klan and adopting new rites
from the film, including the cross-burning ceremonies. As an FBI analysis of the Klan reports, this new Klan was "an organization of 'pure Americanism' based on a fourfold program of antagonism to Catholics, Jews,
Negroes and persons of foreign birth."[6]

Initially, recruiting was difficult. Whether this new Klan could truly
represent "pure Americanism" was in doubt because of the Klan's history
of racial violence, and indeed violence remained the KKK's hallmark
throughout this period. But after World War I the Klan's racist, nativist,
anti-Semitic, and anti-Catholic platforms found a receptive audience in
a nation coming off a foreign war and facing an influx of European immigration. A Red Scare blamed on alien agitators and composed sub-
stantially of Italian Catholics and Eastern European Jews only intensified

these feelings. In the 1920s the Klan exploded in popularity, driven by a slick, professionally produced public relations campaign. Some suggest this new Klan under Simmons was more a commercial endeavor than a political movement.

In any event it was a successful one. At one point the Klan boasted more than 5 million members, although because the Klan remained a secret organization its true numbers—then and now—are difficult to verify. They did draw an estimated 40,000 Klansmen for a rally and march down Constitution Avenue in Washington, D.C., in 1925.

While the Klan remained a secret—and ostensibly nonpolitical— organization, it had significant influence among the political and social elites. No politician from the South or Midwest would succeed in open opposition to the Klan, and many actively sought its endorsement. The Klan presented itself as a benign, social club, promoting its benevolent public face by raising funds for poor widows and orphans and the like. But Klan terrorism continued and though Klan leaders distanced them-selves from it, everyone understood the Klan's power and influence stemmed from the threat they posed.

In explaining how an organization with such benevolent objectives could be a catalyst for violence, a 1957 FBI report summarizing the Klan's history recounted a reported conversation between two Klan officers, known as "Kleagles":

> One Kleagle, seeking advice as to what new Klans should do upon receiving their charters, was told by his King Kleagle, "Tell them to clean up their towns." It is not surprising that acts of terrorism began to take place.[7]

Robert Paxton identifies the Ku Klux Klan as the earliest example of fascism, though that term was not yet in use.[8] Indeed, Eco's descrip-tion of fascism—detailed in chapter 6 as something "behind a regime and its ideology"—fits how the Klan wielded its influence from behind the scenes, or perhaps behind the mask is more appropriate.[9]

This description may seem to contradict my earlier positions that terrorist groups are not truly fascist and that terrorist groups do not wield political power. To me the mask is the key.

Over time the Klan, in a broad sense as representing the white su-premacy movement's armed vanguard, demonstrates an iteration of ev-ery imaginable type of armed conflict, from the symmetrical warfare of the Civil War to the guerrilla warfare of the Partisan Rangers, from the political terrorism of the first Klan under Forrest to something that's very different, but just as dangerous, today.

Paxton said the Klan "constituted an alternate civic authority, parallel to the legal state."[10] The Klan was actually a shadow government, making it more powerful than a terrorist organization. While not a government itself, the Klan aligned with a government so it could use the legitimate tools of power to wield influence that it could not exercise on its own. When Paxton says the Klan was "parallel to the legal state" it is not clear whether he is referring to the federal government or to the state governments as the legal state. I agree with him if he means the Klan was parallel to the state and local governments because, using Eco's terms, the Klan was standing behind these governments. But the Klan was always at cross-purposes with the federal government, so if anything it ran perpendicular to the federal government. The Klan's position as a shadow to the local governments made it much more influential within its identity community, much more essential to the community at large, and much more dangerous to its enemies.

The Klan ruled the South for almost a hundred years because it was able to transition from a terrorist group to a shadow government. To take a lesson from the Klan experience the key is determining when that transition took place. Ironically, it happened when the Klan was supposedly dead.

To begin operating as a shadow government the Klan needed a mantle of legitimacy. When the federal government abandoned Reconstruction and its efforts to enforce the law—civil rights for all Americans was the law—it left the Klan free to act as it saw fit. The Klan became the law, which meant the Klan became legitimate.

The federal government just got tired of fighting. The Klan and the federal government entered into an uneasy, and ultimately temporary, truce, whether Forrest and Grant ever actually made that agreement or not. What they didn't realize is they weren't solving the problem, they were just pushing it off for later generations to deal with. In the meantime thousands of people died horrible deaths, and more were forced to live in fear and humiliation.

The truth is the Klan never did have real political power. The Klan was never a political party that ran candidates for public office. Klansmen did make it to public office occasionally, even the highest offices. However, they neither ran on a Klan ticket nor proudly announced their connections to this terrorist organization because despite its public relations campaign everyone knew what the Klan was. And despite being a secret organization, the Klan didn't keep its tactics a secret because the public's fear is what gave the Klan power. It ruled through terror and intimidation. If the Klan had been trying to hide its violent side, each new version of the group wouldn't have continued to call itself the Klan. These successive groups all called themselves the Klan—as many new groups still do—to appropriate that violent legacy and reputation to intimidate others. This borrowing of another's reputation was the reason the number of militia groups seemed to explode after the Oklahoma City bombing, when the media publicly connected McVeigh to militia groups. It's also the same reason so many jihadist groups now call themselves al Qaeda.

The reputation for violence is their power. That's why they borrow these familiar names, and that's why they need the masks.

A government fighting terrorism must never cede legitimate authority to the terrorist group. Whether it's law enforcement authority or authority over trash removal services that is being ceded doesn't matter. It can be an attractive lure to let the terrorists police their own community rather than risk the lives of the government's forces when they are not welcomed. But as soon as the government gives over that control, the terrorists are no longer just terrorists; they are the governing authority.

The Klan's heyday was short lived. Political infighting fractured the organization. Scandals over money, sexual improprieties, and a young white woman's murder by a Klan leader in Indiana tarnished the Klan's carefully polished image as a protector of Southern values. Most important, intrepid newspapermen began to unmask Klan members who held influential positions in the community. By the 1930s estimates of the Klan's size were less than 10 percent of what they were only five years earlier. Did the Klan ever really have 5 million members? It depends to a great degree who you're willing to call a Klansman. Were there 5 million lynching murderers? Obviously not. If, however, a Klansman is just someone who goes to a rally, puts his name on a mailing list, or pays a ten dollar membership fee to obtain social status or a political endorsement, then maybe the Klan's numbers were pretty high. The mystery surrounding the membership was another reason the masks were so important. There was no way to know whether the ten masked riders you saw last night on the west side of town the same ten you saw on the east side the week before. When the Klan endorsed a politician did that mean 10,000 votes or ten votes? It's hard to tell with a clandestine organization. There certainly weren't 5 million people willing to align themselves with the Klan publicly, nor were 5 million people willing to kill for the Klan.

The exposure of its violent behavior started killing the Klan. The members still terrorized, but its influence was waning.

After World War II racial attitudes in America started changing and Klan membership dwindled. Part of this shift came from President Harry

Truman's courageous decision to integrate the armed forces. After the war black troops, who proved their worth on battlefields from Europe to the Far East, returned and expected to be treated as full citizens. They should never have had to earn that right, but earn it they did. I believe another reason for the change in attitudes was the exposure of the Nazi death camps, which revealed the horrible but entirely logical result of a racist ideology. After the war the Klan's message grew less acceptable to the majority of Americans. In 1946 a government tax lien put the Klan's commercial enterprises out of business, and the organization splintered once again.

The civil rights movement put the Klan and the U.S. government back at a crossroad. In its 1954 decision in *Brown v. Board of Education of Topeka,* the Supreme Court overturned *Plessy* and ruled that separate was inherently unequal, ending segregation forever.[11] This ruling forced a decision on the Klan, as *Backfire* author David Chalmers explains:

> Not to fight would be to betray the history and meaning of the Klan, but to fight and lose would be to cast it into irrelevancy. If the Klan eschewed violence, it was not the Klan, but when it acted like the Klan, what might be the costs that it would have to pay?[12]

The Klan decided to resist, forcing the federal government to decide whether it would enforce the law in the South. As people beat and abused freedom riders and civil rights marchers in Klan-organized attacks, often with the approval and participation of the local police, the federal government hesitated. According to David Cunningham, author of *There's Something Happening Here,* the FBI was not enthusiastic about having federal agents serve as anything more than observers in the civil rights struggle:

> Hoover himself claimed that more active intervention in such conflicts was beyond the jurisdiction of a federal agency—insisting that the FBI "was strictly an investigative agency, and not a police force with peace-keeping responsibilities"—and Bureau agents took a purely investigative role. Incredibly, this led to several instances of civil rights workers being badly beaten while representatives of the FBI stood to the side taking notes on the illegal events they were doing nothing to prevent.[footnotes in original text omitted][13]

When Birmingham, Alabama, police commissioner "Bull" Connor turned dogs and fire hoses on black demonstrators the whole world watched on television. Horrified by the violence, citizens pressured the federal government to act. Ironically it would be the Klan that finally forced the government's hand. On June 22, 1964, three civil rights workers—James Chaney, Michael Schwerner, and Andrew Goodman—disappeared near Philadelphia, Mississippi, shortly after being released from the Neshoba County jail. The resulting political pressure forced Hoover to send agents to Mississippi and investigate the disappearances. Before long they discovered the workers' bodies and identified the Klan members responsible. When a local grand jury failed to indict the Klansmen, the federal government dusted off the old Enforcement Acts and brought civil rights charges in federal court that finally resulted in convictions. Just as almost a hundred years earlier, enforcing federal law began to diminish the Klan's power.

These Mississippi murders also led the FBI to start its White Hate COINTELPRO. As with other COINTELPRO programs, the White Hate program was secret. Its agents did not seek criminal convictions of violent Klansmen. Instead, they intended to "expose, disrupt and neutralize" the Klan through covert action.[14] This point is where the effort went horribly wrong. Cunningham suggests the secrecy of the White Hate COINTELPRO had advantages for the bureau: "By covertly attacking White Hate groups, the FBI could still maintain positive relationships with local police forces in the South, which were sometimes sympathetic to (and in communities like Birmingham, actively supported) the Klan."[15]

But the problem with an intelligence-gathering focus is that the mission of actually preventing violence can be lost. On March 25, 1965, a carload full of Klansman, including FBI informant Gary Thomas Rowe, chased down and shot into the car of civil rights worker Viola Liuzzo, killing her instantly. Rowe's involvement in the murder was quite controversial, as might be expected, with some making allegations that he may have actually instigated the violence. When it was later revealed that Rowe, who had been an FBI informant for more than a year, had engaged in earlier acts of Klan violence against civil rights workers with the FBI's approval, critics raised questions about the FBI's methods.[16] Having a well-placed source is crucial to intelligence work, and the bureau probably thought having an informant like Rowe inside a Klan "action group" was quite a coup. I'm sure the agents took great efforts to protect Rowe's identity and to avoid revealing the "sources and methods" of their Klan intelligence. Unfortunately, the FBI protected its source instead of protecting Viola Liuzzo. This mistake, protecting sources and methods to the detriment of the overall security mission, would be repeated during the events leading up to September 11, 2001.

The FBI considered the White Hate COINTELPRO a great success, as did the leader of the largest Klan organization of that time, Robert Shelton, who credited COINTELPRO for reductions in Klan membership. But membership, again, is meaningless to the Klan (that is, except to the leaders, like Shelton, who profit from membership fees). Despite COINTELPRO Klan violence would continue to rage into the 1980s and the 1990s, sometimes in different guises, and some of the Klansmen responsible for civil rights–era murders wouldn't be brought to justice until the early twenty-first century.

The racial violence of the civil rights era was a product of the federal government's failure to live up to its responsibility to enforce the law over the previous decades. The Klan wasn't defeated during the civil rights era and will never be entirely defeated, but it was finally exposed. Once the law was enforced the mask could be taken off the Klan.

The federal government's successful prosecutions of Klan murderers and the scenes of racial violence broadcast on television exposed the Klan as the extremists they always were—an ugly image no reasonable person wanted to be affiliated with. Ironically, one of the methods the covert White Hate COINTELPRO used to disrupt the Klan was to expose a target's Klan affiliations by sending anonymous postcards and letters to his or her friends and family. If the FBI had exposed these Klan affiliations in open court rather than through surreptitious and unverifiable means, this tactic probably would have been a lot more effective. In any event, exposing Klan violence ensured that only the most extremist members would remain actively involved. As the Klan moved down the scale from a quasi-legitimate shadow government to an extremist group, its capacity to recruit was much reduced.

Unfortunately, the federal government continued to treat Klan violence as a series of individual crimes rather than as an organized conspiracy, enabling the organization to continue spawning new terrorists. Luckily in 1971 a private attorney named Morris Dees of the Southern Poverty Law Center (SPLC) filled the void. Dees and the SPLC began filing civil lawsuits against white supremacist organizations, such as the Klan, the White Aryan Resistance, and the Aryan Nations. They brought the suits on behalf of victims of racial violence perpetrated by individuals affiliated with these groups, many of whom were already convicted of their crimes. But the lawsuits focused on the white supremacist organizations, exposing their role in recruiting, educating, and training members to carry out violence, and held them responsible in courts of law.[17]

For a Klansman, to be brought into criminal court is one matter. The Klansman can consider himself a "prisoner of war," captured in battle against the oppressor government. The shackles and armed deputies necessary to restrain the prisoner only prove his dangerousness. But to be dragged into civil court by a skinny lawyer in a pressed suit is a disgrace for someone who calls himself a warrior. All of the Klansman's tools of intimidation are gone in a civil court, where the law's supremacy over violence is crystal clear. These civil cases did more to demolish and discredit the white supremacist movement than any criminal investigation ever did.

Calling oneself a Klansman today is to risk almost universal opprobrium and even ridicule. Even within the white supremacist movement the Klan is considered a bit of an anachronism. But the Klan isn't dead. Law enforcement must maintain a proactive approach to prevent a resurgence of its violence, but Klan violence can be managed as a crime problem rather than as a matter of national security.

The history of the federal government's struggle against the Klan demonstrates the importance of maintaining the rule of law. Ceding any legitimate authority to a terrorist group will not solve the government's problem. While returning the rule of law will bring a violent response, that violence will ultimately work against the terrorist group because it will reveal them for the extremists they are. Only by enforcing the rule of law and exposing the illegitimacy of the terrorist group's behavior will a government succeed at forcing the terrorists to society's margins. The most important thing to learn from our conflict with the Klan is that society's victories against the Klan have all been legal victories.

12

A Winning Strategy Against Extremist Terrorists

Force is all-conquering, but its victories are short-lived.

—Abraham Lincoln

The proper response to a violent terrorist attack will vary depending upon which type of terrorist group is responsible. The victim government's immediate goal should be to avoid taking any action—by words or by deeds—that will inadvertently play into the terrorists' hands and allow them to expand their influence among their supporters and sympathizers.

The first thing to determine, obviously, is who is responsible for the act. Fortunately, law enforcement agencies are good at uncovering the facts, and in most cases they can answer this "who" question reasonably quickly.

An act of terrorism committed by an individual without a well-articulated political goal, such as the D.C.–area snipers or the Unabomber, is much more difficult to solve quickly because of the lack of a logical motive. Police reacting to bombings or assassinations initially treat them as criminal matters, because that's what they are. They don't call for military action or secret new government powers to deal with one individual's criminal act simply because it mimics an act of terrorism. And because bombings and assassinations are ultimately treated as criminal matters, the investigations of these terrorist incidents must be conducted in a manner that will preserve the evidence's admissibility in future legal proceedings. Using techniques that identify a suspect but do not produce admissible evidence against him or her is counterproductive in the long run.

Similarly, dealing with extremist terrorists requires a legal approach. In chapter 7, I noted that terrorists are politically weak for one of three possible reasons: they lack political skills, they lack a popular cause, or they have political skills and a popular cause but are politically repressed by their government. They would all argue they fit in the last category, of course, and that without the unjust oppression their cause would naturally gain acceptance.

We have already discussed the government's options when it objectively assesses its own policies and finds them repressive: alter the repressive policies, explain to the public why the policy is necessary, or accept the consequences. But as we said, establishing a transparent and accountable system of government doesn't stop terrorism. How is a free country to react when it is targeted by extremist terrorists who aren't being repressed by an unjust policy?

The Unabomber Ted Kaczynski and D.C.–area snipers John Muhammad and Lee Boyd Malvo are often called terrorists. Indeed if terrorism is defined primarily as a tactic, the tactics they used certainly appear to be acts of terrorism. But most of us would describe these murderers as serial killers rather than terrorists. They certainly didn't claim to represent any particular community. For the D.C.–area snipers, their motives appeared to be completely personal. Thus they are no more examples of terrorists than are other "thrill killers," who might terrorize a community until they are captured but would not be considered terrorists in the sense in which most people use the word. These individuals are criminals and are appropriately dealt with through the criminal justice system.

Ted Kaczynski was slightly different. He confounded the law enforcement community for the better part of two decades as investigators tried to figure out the motive behind his nationwide string of bombings that left three dead and dozens wounded. Eventually Kaczynski published a manifesto that led directly to his identification and arrest, but it also confirmed that there was indeed a political motive behind his attacks.[1] Kaczynski is a Luddite, concerned that scientific, industrial, and technological advancements are damaging society and the environment. Some share his ideology and perhaps he could have recruited people to join his cause, but Kaczynski was an extremely poor politician. He had no followers. He didn't even bother to mention his political motive throughout most of his bombing campaign; therefore, people who would have supported or sympathized with his cause had no way of even knowing Kaczynski was acting on their behalf. Once he did finally write his manifesto, his message was so incoherent that even if his cause had been wildly popular, he never could have inspired a mass movement.

The question is whether the government should treat Kaczynski any differently from such thrill killers as Muhammad and Malvo. Probably not. The government successfully prosecuted Kaczynski for his criminal conduct just as it did with Muhammad and Malvo. Kaczynski's political motivation for the bombings might have been considered as evidence of his premeditation, which must be proved in a first-degree murder prosecution, but other aspects of his behavior in planning and committing bombings over a twenty-year period were probably more than sufficient evidence of his premeditation. The prosecutor didn't need to focus on the political motivation behind the Unabomber's crimes.

Prosecutors should neither ignore nor hide the defendant's political motivation, but emphasizing it in the courtroom, or anywhere within the legal system for that matter, could be counterproductive.

Imagine another serial bomber who, as Kaczynski did, sends out mail bombs that kill several individuals over a long period of time without any explanation. When investigators ultimately identify and arrest the bomber, they discover a long manifesto explaining his motivation was to stop the sexual exploitation of children, which is a truly noble cause. It turns out that all of his intended victims were somehow involved in distributing child pornography. The bomber had written letters advocating for stronger penalties against child pornographers, protested when convicted child molesters were paroled from prison, and finally grew so frustrated with the legal system that he became a vigilante. The bomber's failure to make his manifesto public meant that despite his popular cause, he had no political following.

Next imagine that this bomber, just as Kaczynski, was not precise in his targeting. He sometimes misspelled names and sent bombs to the wrong people or to the wrong addresses. And with bombs being inherently indiscriminate weapons, sometimes innocent people, such as family members or employees of the intended target and even mail carriers, were injured. At the bomber's trial the defense attorney would certainly want to emphasize the bomber's noble purpose, but the prosecutor wouldn't. The prosecutor would argue his motivation was irrelevant and would instead focus on his violations of laws against making bombs and murdering people. The defense attorney would want to bring in evidence of the victims' involvement in child pornography, but the prosecutor would object to its irrelevance and emphasize the importance of the rule of law. The prosecutor would focus on the innocent victims and argue these crimes should be treated just as any other crimes against innocent people. After the bomber is convicted the prosecutor certainly wouldn't ask the judge to increase the sentence because the bomber's intended targets were child molesters.

The prosecutor would de-emphasize the bomber's political motivation because he wouldn't want the trial to become a platform for the bomber's political message, thus inadvertently turning an ineffective politician into an effective one. Perhaps cadres of people similarly frustrated by lax child pornography laws would adopt this bomber's cause and organize their own vigilante groups. Any perceived injustice in the bomber's treatment by the prosecutor or the court could inevitably become a recruiting tool for a larger vigilante movement.

Likewise the legislature might get involved in a case like this one. It might strengthen laws restricting access to bomb-making materials perhaps or increase penalties for sending explosives through the mail. Those efforts would be fine because they focus on the criminal conduct and not the political motivation behind the conduct. Legislators wouldn't, however, pass a Child Pornographer Protection Act to increase criminal penalties for assaults when vigilantes target a child pornographer. To do so would inevitably bring a backlash from the majority of people who don't like child pornographers and don't believe they need special protection. They would find the legislature's move completely illegitimate and difficult to understand. Some might hypothesize that the child pornography industry must be corruptly buying influence in the legislature to get such laws passed. They might fear that these child pornographers, under these corrupt government officials' protection, might come after people who speak out against child molesters. Anti-pornography activists might conclude that the whole legal system is illegitimate and decide it needs to be changed by any means necessary. This hypothetical situation may seem commonsensical, yet when a government prosecutes a terrorist whose cause is unpopular they do the exact opposite: they emphasize the unpopular belief in the prosecution, they ask for stiffer sentences in an attempt to dissuade followers of this unpopular cause, and they ask their legislators to address the particular group's political goals with legislation.

When terrorists resort to violence under a free system of government, they aren't acting against oppression but rather out of frustration that their political message is not gaining the mass audience they expect nor bringing about the social change they favor. Under a free government everyone has the right to speak, to vote, and to petition the government through the legal system, but nobody has the right to force people to listen to them. These terrorists use violence to force people to listen. These are what I call extremist terrorists.

All terrorists are motivated by the perception of persecution, and extremist terrorists are no exception. Absent real persecution, extremist terrorists create conspiracy theories to explain how their identity group is victimized. Again, this reaction isn't delusional; it's based on their sincere beliefs, albeit supported by carefully selected facts and the refusal to accept contraindications. These terrorists are so convinced of the correctness of their beliefs that their lack of a mass following becomes even greater evidence of their repression.

I'll use a white supremacist terrorist as an example of how the legal system handles terrorists who harbor unpopular ideas differently. Unlike with the anti-pornography bomber case, when law enforcement officers arrest the white supremacist terrorist his beliefs are featured prominently in the media and in his subsequent prosecution. The prosecutor takes advantage of the community's disdain for his beliefs to paint him as an evil person. After his conviction the prosecutor asks the judge to sentence the white supremacist more harshly because of his beliefs. The legislature will step in as well, passing hate crime laws to enhance penalties for such race-motivated crimes. What these prosecutors and legislators forget is that while this political cause is unpopular, it does have a following. Their reaction is going to be exactly the same as if their cause was popular. When the prosecutors and legislators emphasize the politics rather than the crime, that small following will begin to feel they are being oppressed for their political beliefs, and rightfully so. They would now have a more legitimate reason to resist the government, and a more effective recruiting campaign.

There are some compelling reasons to pass hate crime laws. I abhor racism and I believe people convicted of racially motivated violence should receive as harsh a penalty as possible under the law. Passing a hate crime law is an important reflection of community standards. It says racist crimes will not be tolerated and will be punished severely. It also makes an important statement to the minority community, letting people know that violence directed against them will be taken seriously.

These efforts are all important. But if the goal of passing hate crime legislation is to suppress hate groups, it will fail. It will actually have the opposite effect. The government will just give racist groups that only imagined they were persecuted a real reason to suggest they are. White supremacist groups use hate crime laws to recruit new members, citing them as evidence of a bias against whites in the legal system.

There's no way of knowing whether hate crime laws have any effect on racial violence because we don't even have an accurate count of hate crimes. As I discussed in chapter 4, a Department of Justice Bureau of Justice Statistics report released in November 2005 revealed that since 1992 the annual number of hate crimes in the United States was actually more than fifteen times greater than the numbers the FBI had previously reported.[2] The problem is determining what to classify as a hate crime. If two high school kids of different races get in a fight over a girl, a missing watch, or spilled milk at the lunch counter and in the heat of the battle one of them utters a racial epithet, in some jurisdictions that might be treated as a hate crime. In other jurisdictions just the variance in race between victim and perpetrator might be enough. How is a police officer to determine what motivated the crime? Do we not charge someone, even if we know he is a racist, with a hate crime if he was smart enough not to yell a racial insult during the attack? How are hate crime laws going to be effective if we don't even know what crimes are hate crimes? What is it we're trying to stop? The confused reporting and lack of prosecutions make clear this is not an effective approach.

If the purpose of passing hate crime laws is to reduce organized hate crime there's a better way. Instead of focusing on the hate, focus on the organized crime.

As I said, there are many good reasons for hate crime legislation, and perhaps these reasons outweigh the possibility that such laws may actually increase organized racial violence. But this dynamic becomes more important as we respond to terrorist attacks from groups whose ideologies are not so universally despised and even more essential when responding to a legitimately motivated terrorist whose cause is politically popular. By making the terrorists' cause the enemy we can end up making more enemies than we started with.

Take the Animal Enterprise Protection Act (AEPA), as an example.[3] Seven activists from Stop Huntington Animal Cruelty (SHAC), an extremist animal rights group, were convicted under the AEPA on March 2, 2006, for an international campaign of threats and harassment against companies affiliated with Huntington Life Sciences (HLS), a pharmaceutical testing company that uses animals for research.[4] This harassment campaign involved numerous criminal violations—including stalking, threats of violence, acts of vandalism, and telephone harassment—conducted over a long period in a well-organized campaign to prevent HLS from exercising its rights to engage in a lawful business enterprise. I am glad these extremists were convicted. My only regret is that it that they were allowed to harass these companies for so long before the FBI took action. But to create a law that protects one particular industry smacks of undue influence and seems to selectively target individuals with one particular political ideology for prosecution. Why does an "animal enterprise" deserve more legal protection than another business? Why protect a butcher but not a baker?

In the activist community, they aren't discussing SHAC's criminal acts but rather the injustice of the Animal Enterprise Protection Act. The "SHAC 7," as they're now called, have become poster children for the First Amendment. It's ironic that people who violated criminal laws and infringed on the rights of the owners and employees of Huntington Life Sciences are now lauded as the martyred champions of civil rights.

Again, I abhor the behavior of extremists who use violence and the threat of violence to achieve their goals. I understand the frustration their victims must feel when the extremists' crimes are not met with just punishment. But the only question that is important is, is the AEPA effective? Consider that it was originally passed in 1992, and by 2004 the FBI called "eco-terrorists"—special interest terror groups such as the Earth Liberation Front and the Animal Liberation Front—the number one domestic terror threat facing the United States.[5] The government could have easily and effectively prosecuted SHAC's criminal activity using criminal statutes already on the books without creating a cause for other environmental extremists.

It's important that we do not to give extremist groups ammunition for their political arguments as we prosecute them for their crimes. The militia movement's decline in the United States resulted when its doomsday prophesies of government repression failed to come true. Militia leaders railed against the concentration camps that were being built to house militia members after the government crackdown, but when militia members were actually arrested they were afforded all their rights, free attorneys, and fair trials. There were no "star chambers," no concentration camps, no military courts. Their open, public trials were heavily attended by militia supporters who could see the militia ideology exposed as a lie. Militia leaders soon lost influence except among the most extreme true believers.

Undoubtedly sending an undercover agent to infiltrate the group is an intrusive investigative technique, but by exposing the militia members' criminal activities in court, the government demonstrated that its approach was necessary and appropriate. These investigations also proved that proactive criminal law enforcement can be effective in preventing terrorism.

But one particularly effective criminal statute that could be used to stop terrorist groups was recently taken out of our counterterrorism arsenal by the U.S. Supreme Court, with little public notice or complaint by the FBI. Terrorist groups by definition are organized criminal enterprises, just as the Italian Mafia, La Cosa Nostra, is an organized criminal enterprise. LCN was a difficult problem for law enforcement because the crime bosses who led the organization and benefited from the "racketeering activities" of their underlings often were not themselves directly involved in criminal activity. While the police could arrest the "soldiers" on the bottom rung of the organization, the Mafia "omerta," or code of silence, ensured that the bosses at the top of the organization remained free to continue pursuing their criminal goals—a system very similar to the leaderless resistance strategy now being used by terrorist groups.

When the government finally recognized the Mafia as a serious problem in the 1950s, Congress passed an extremely useful anti-organized crime statute called the Hobbs Act.[6] The Hobbs Act is a federal anti-extortion statute that prohibits the obstruction of interstate commerce by robbery, extortion, or threats of violence. It is a great anti-Mafia statute because it prohibits exactly the behavior the Mafia engages in: using violence and the threat of violence to get whatever they want. Congress added an even more effective statute, the Racketeer Influenced Corrupt Organizations Act (RICO),[7] in 1970. The RICO Act allows the government to hold the leaders of corrupt organizations responsible for the criminal acts of their members. It provides stiff penalties designed to break the code of silence and financially bankrupt the organizations themselves. All the government has to prove is the existence of a corrupt organization and two criminal "predicate acts" within a ten-year period. The FBI used these statutes effectively over the following years to all but dismantle the Italian Mafia.

RICO could be used just as effectively against terrorist groups. It would allow law enforcement to pierce the "leaderless resistance" veil and hold terrorist leaders responsible for the "lone wolf" acts of terrorism they inspire. The Hobbs Act, which is one of the "predicate acts" under RICO, seems to have been written to prevent exactly the type of organized criminal behavior terrorists engage in: economic sabotage, physical violence, and the threat of violence. What is a terrorist, after all, but an extortionist—someone who uses the threat of violence to get his way? But the FBI's ability to use the Hobbs Act against terrorists was crippled by a 2003 Supreme Court decision in *Scheidler v. National Organization for Women*.[8] This case is a civil suit (RICO has a provision allowing victims to sue for damages) brought in response to the violent abortion clinic protests of the 1980s that has bounced through the court system for over two decades. NOW sued anti-abortion protest groups under RICO, alleging these groups were involved in an organized national conspiracy to shut down abortion clinics through threats of violence, in violation of the Hobbs Act. In District Court NOW won money damages and an injunction that all but put an end to the aggressive, and often violent, anti-abortion protests of that era, but the case was appealed to the Supreme Court, which reversed it.

The Supreme Court's decision in *Scheidler* rested on a distinction between the definition of "extortion"—the threatened use of violence to force someone to give you something you want—and "coercion"—the threatened use of violence to force someone to do something you want them to do. The Supreme Court ruled that extortion under the Hobbs Act requires not just that something of value is taken away from the victim, but also that something of value is obtained by the extorter. In other words, if a Mafia soldier threatens to burn down your restaurant unless you pay a weekly tax to the Mafia, this act is extortion because the Mafia will receive something of value from the threat of violence. But if an animal rights terrorist threatens to burn down your restaurant unless you quit selling sausages, this act is not extortion, according to the Supreme Court, because the animal rights extremist doesn't get anything "of value" as a result of his threat—even though the court acknowledges the victim loses something of value. Needless to say this distinction makes little difference for the victim of these threats.

The Supreme Court said that because coercion is not specifically proscribed in the Hobbs Act, it is not illegal under federal law. Now to be fair, the court did make it very clear that Congress could easily clear up this confusion simply adding the word "coercion" to the Hobbs Act prohibitions. You would think that a government so focused on using all of its counterterrorism tools would quickly add the missing word. But Congress has taken no action. This tool, which has been proved effective against organized crime, sits idly on the shelf in our "War on Terrorism."

The advantage to prosecuting terrorists under the Hobbs Act, as opposed to legislation like the Animal Enterprise Protection Act, is that the Hobbs Act is politically neutral. It proscribes the violent and threatening behavior regardless of whether the victim is a furrier or a woman going to an abortion clinic or a minority who moved into an all-white neighborhood. By focusing on the criminal behavior, the extremist is denied the argument that he is being persecuted for his political views.

13
Case Study #3:
Lessons of the IRA

We wish to be treated "not as ordinary prisoners" for we are not criminals. We admit no crime unless, that is, the love of one's people and country is a crime.

—BOBBY SANDS

Just like the Ku Klux Klan, the Irish Republican Army has been around for a long time. It has fought under different guises over the years while the struggle between Irish Republicans and Britain changed from a war of rebellion in the south to a terrorist campaign in Northern Ireland and then across the Irish Sea. In this chapter I will concentrate on one particularly violent period that began in the late 1960s and became known, in the British tradition of understatement, as "the Troubles." The purpose of this evaluation is not to assess blame. I will put political and moral questions aside to objectively examine each side's methods. I will evaluate the techniques Britain used to counter IRA terrorism to determine which efforts worked to reduce the violence and which did not.

The Anglo-Irish Treaty of 1921 ended the Irish War of Independence but left the Emerald Isle partitioned, giving Irish Republicans, who were sometimes called "Nationalists," only a partial victory in their quest for an independent Ireland. The twenty-six predominantly Catholic counties to the south became the Irish Free State and later the Republic of Ireland. The six "Unionist" counties making up the mostly Protestant province of Ulster in Northern Ireland chose to remain part of the United Kingdom, and its people were therefore sometimes called "Loyalists." Some Republicans refused to accept this compromise and broke from the nascent Irish government, declaring their group the rightful government of the Republic of Ireland. Under the name of the IRA they began a short-lived civil war. Outmanned and outgunned by an Irish government now supported by Britain and even ex-communicated from the Catholic Church, the IRA members found themselves outlawed both north and south before they finally acknowledged defeat in 1923.

Defeated but never dead, the IRA continued a campaign of anti-British, anti-Unionist violence during the prewar years with negligible progress. Demonstrating the political acumen for which it would become legendary, the IRA sided with Germany during World War II under the theory that "England's enemy is Ireland's ally," which of course only further alienated it from the larger Irish population.[1] In 1956 the IRA attempted to revive the Republican struggle by focusing its attention on the "foreign occupation" of Northern Ireland. The IRA began guerrilla-style operations against Unionist targets, primarily Loyalist police and military units stationed along the frontier between the Republic of Ireland and Northern Ireland. This so-called border war was not a military or political success. Catholics to the north or the south never gave it significant support, and the IRA finally just abandoned the campaign in 1962. The IRA found itself at a crossroads with neither its violent tactics nor its radical socialist ideology gaining any traction among Irish Catholics. The era of the armed struggle seemed to be over. By the mid-1960s the heralded Irish Republican Army that resisted British colonialism during World War I was a dispirited, aimless organization.

The IRA's failure to draw political support was not a result of a warming of relations between Catholics and Protestants in Northern Ireland, however. The Unionist Protestant community long regarded the minority Catholic population with distrust, owing largely to its supposed Republican leanings and assumed support for the IRA. Anti-Catholic discrimination was real and officially sanctioned by the outwardly democratic Stormont government of Northern Ireland. The Protestant Unionists had the power in Northern Ireland and intended to keep it. Widespread gerrymandering of electoral districts prevented Catholics from having meaningful representation in local government, so their ability to affect change through proper legal channels was extremely limited. Lest you think my Irish Catholic heritage skews my analysis of these events I will quote from a 1969 report issued by a board of inquiry chaired by Lord Cameron, which the government of Northern Ireland commissioned to investigate the growing sectarian violence:

> Northern Ireland has a population of about one-and-a-half million people and of these about two-thirds may be described as Protestant and one-third as Roman Catholic. Not only has the Government of Northern Ireland since it was established been a Unionist (and therefore Protestant) Government, but at the local

level Councils have tended to reflect the particular religious majority in their areas, except that in certain areas . . . the arrangement of ward boundaries for local government purposes has produced in the local authority a permanent Unionist majority which
bears little or no resemblance to the relative numerical strength of
Unionists and non-Unionists in the area. . . . [W]e have to record
that there is very good reason to believe the allegation that these
arrangements were deliberately made, and maintained, with the
consequence that the Unionists used and have continued to use
the electoral majority thus created to favour Protestant or Unionist supporters in making public appointments—particularly those
of senior officials—and in manipulating housing allocations for
political and sectarian ends.[2]

A European Court of Human Rights decision later described the
situation in more diplomatically modest terms: "The abolition of propor-
tional representation in the early 1920's and the geographical arrangement
of constituencies effected a great increase in the size of the Parliamentary
majority. This situation understandably disenchanted the Catholic community."[3] As a disenfranchised minority, the "disenchanted" Catholics of
Northern Ireland routinely suffered discrimination in employment, housing, and security, with security being perhaps the most troubling of the
three. The IRA would willingly fill this vacuum.

The mid-1960s saw the birth of Protestant paramilitaries, specifically the Ulster Volunteer Force (UVF), which became a serious security
threat to Ulster Catholics. While the UVF was never as sophisticated or
as heavily armed as the IRA, it could be equally deadly. The lack of serious law enforcement action taken against these forces added to their
menace and led some to believe they acted with the government of Northern Ireland's tacit approval or, at the very least, with that of the security
forces. The Northern Ireland police forces—the Royal Ulster Constabulary (RUC) and the auxiliary Ulster Special Constabulary—were overwhelmingly Protestant. As the IRA specifically targeted both forces for
assassination, they were generally less than sympathetic, and many times
openly antagonistic, to their Catholic neighbors' security needs.

The police had at their disposal extraordinary powers to arrest and
detain suspected Republicans under the Special Powers Act of 1922, powers the Cameron Commission later said violated the Universal Declaration of Human Rights and were "in their nature at variance to the common law right of the citizen."[4] The government bestowed these extraordinary powers on the RUC specifically to address the IRA problem, thus
they were exercised almost exclusively against the Catholic community

of Northern Ireland. Neither the Stormont government of Northern Ireland nor the British government made much of an effort to address these imbalances, primarily because of the lingering security issues with the IRA and the lingering distrust of Catholic loyalty to the crown.

In the late-1960s a nonviolent Catholic civil rights movement, modeled on the American civil rights movement, began protest marches to bring public attention to the anti-Catholic discrimination. The civil rights movement, though primarily Catholic, differed from the IRA in that it was not intent on overthrowing the government of Northern Ireland. It merely sought political reform within the existing system.[5] The civil rights associations requested modest reforms, especially in comparison to those sought by the IRA:

+ One person, one vote;
+ An end to the gerrymandered local government boundaries;
+ An end to discrimination in the allocation of housing;
+ An end to discrimination in employment;
+ The repeal of the repressive Special Powers Act.[6]

These are hardly unreasonable demands. Indeed the civil rights movement's leftist politics might have even been effective at uniting the Catholic and Protestant working-classes into one socialist movement had not sectarian hostilities run so deep, particularly in the working-class communities.

Regardless, clearly a legitimate political issue regarding Catholic civil rights did exist, and a nascent nonviolent movement was trying to get those grievances addressed. Unfortunately, the government did not address them in time, and as the security situation deteriorated, the arguable legitimacy of an armed struggle increased.

On October 5, 1968, civil rights activists marcing in defiance of an order banning their route through Londonderry (called "Derry" by Republicans) were met by baton-wielding RUC men. Television news cameras captured images of the police brutally attacking defenseless marchers and even innocent bystanders trapped by the police barriers. As Lord Cameron reported, again in that understated British manner, "The confrontation between marchers and police received worldwide publicity, much of which was unfavourable to the Government of Northern Ireland, [and] to the police."[7] The government of Northern Ireland responded with a civil rights reform package but did not immediately offer universal adult suffrage in local elections; therefore, the activists deemed the concessions inadequate.[8]

The level of violence that followed this recalcitrance was staggering. Historian Paul Arthur observed:

> Those who benefited most from the collapse of the civil rights movement were the militants on both sides. It meant that, in fact, politics as a process, which had never been strong in Northern Ireland, disappeared. It meant that the most strident voices and those who could command weaponry were the people who set the agenda.[9]

More radical elements within the civil rights movement began to take control. During the following year the increasing levels of sectarian violence and rioting resulted in several Catholics killed and wounded in police shootings, further alienating the Catholic community from its government. Richard English, author of *Armed Struggle: The History of the IRA,* described the situation: "Many Catholics unsurprisingly saw police killings as evidence of the hostility of the northern state towards their community: not only were the police offering inadequate protection, they were, on occasion, the attackers from whom protection was so urgently required."[10]

On August 14, 1969, British troops were finally called in to quell the violence, and they quickly became targets of IRA assassins. While considerable evidence suggests an IRA presence in the civil rights movement and in the street violence that resulted from the sectarian rioting, the IRA as an organization, based in the south, still eschewed violence in favor of building a leftist political movement. Indeed a European Court of Human Rights decision would later declare, "The IRA carried out no major acts of violence in 1969."[11] Not everyone was happy with the decision to forgo the armed struggle, however, as IRA men in the north grew frustrated by their inability to protect their community. On December 18, 1969, a splinter group broke from what would then on be called the "Original IRA" to form the Provisional Irish Republican Army (PIRA). Otherwise defenseless, the Catholic community could only welcome them. The PIRA began a campaign of ferocious violence that lasted for the next three decades.

The PIRA's immediate targets were the British troops, who ostensibly had been brought in to protect the Catholics but clearly presented a threat to the PIRA's self-appointed role as the Catholic community's legitimate guardians. PIRA violence directed against the British Army had the specific purpose of antagonizing the soldiers into an inefficient response that would further alienate the Catholic population. Understandably upset by their losses at the PIRA's hands and determined to root out the insurgency, British troops engaged in heavy-handed raids into Catholic neighborhoods to search for weapons. More and more it appeared as if the British were not the neutral peacekeepers they claimed to be. Richard English quotes IRA man Tommy Gorman:

> We were creating this idea that the British state is not your friend
> . . . and at every twist in the road they were compounding what
> we were saying, they were doing what we were saying, fulfilling all
> the propaganda . . . the British Army, the British government,
> were our best recruiting agents.[12]

The PIRA exploited the natural lines of division. British troops felt more comfortable in a "Loyalist" community that favored strong ties with Britain rather than among the Irish Catholics, who had been fighting for 300 years under a war cry of "Brits out!" The PIRA used violence to intentionally provoke the British troops, as Gorman indicates, and it worked. The British responded indiscriminately, and fell into the terrorists' trap. The Black Liberation Army was employing this identical strategy in the United States without success, so the different reactions of the British authorities and the NYPD are instructive to the result.

Political events taking place in London deepened the lines of division. Paul Arthur describes how a new government brought a change of attitude:

> There was a change in government in the United Kingdom in
> 1970. Harold Wilson's Labor government had implemented the
> civil rights reforms. A new conservative government led by Ed-
> ward Heath came into office in May of 1970, which had very
> close links with the unionist government in Northern Ireland. It
> decided that the answer to the Northern Ireland problem was not
> more reforms, but a more punitive military action. It was deter-
> mined to crush any signs of rebellion. So, it resorted to coercion
> rather than conciliation. As a result, it became, in the long view, a
> very powerful recruiting agent for the IRA.[13]

The IRA also began cementing its position of authority within Catholic neighborhoods by barricading Catholic neighborhoods and creating "no-go" zones in which the police and military couldn't enter. Inside the barricades the IRA was the police.

Increasing violence against British Army personnel finally brought a call for stronger action. On August 9, 1971, Prime Minister of Northern Ireland Brian Faulkner announced the initiation of an internment program under the Special Powers Act:

> Every means has been tried to make terrorists amenable to the law. Nor have such methods been without success, because a substantial number of the most prominent leaders of the I.R.A. are now serving ordinary prison sentences. But the terrorist campaign continues at an unacceptable level, and I have had to conclude that the ordinary law cannot deal comprehensively or quickly enough with such ruthless viciousness.[14]

In a British operation code-named "Demetrius," troops conducted mass arrests and picked up almost 350 Catholics without charge, less than a third of whom were actually IRA members.[15] In subsequent inquiries a court determined that "Operation Demetrius . . . was not a selective manoeuvre aimed at individuals but a 'sweeping-up' exercise directed against the IRA organisation as a whole."[16] The internments sparked a wave of Catholic rioting that left twenty-one dead. This effect obviously was not what the government of Northern Ireland was hoping for. As Richard English explains, it would get worse:

> During the pre-internment period of 1971 (up to 9 August) the Provisionals killed ten British soldiers; during the remaining months of the year they killed thirty. For many Catholics, internment confirmed what their experiences had up until then been suggesting. One Belfast woman, explaining why she joined the IRA, referred to having experienced loyalist intimidation, then British Army raids—and then to having witnessed internment: "I felt I'd no other option but to join after that. That's when it became crystal clear to me that the Brits were here to suppress the Catholic minority, and for no other reason."[17]

The British quickly released a large number of those arrested, but what little concession that may have brought was eclipsed by word that they were torturing the internees. English describes the British "special interrogation techniques":

> Among the methods used on the internees were the "five techniques": placing a hood over the head; forcing the internee to stand spreadeagled against a wall for long periods; denying regular sleep patterns; providing irregular and limited food and water; and subjecting people to white noise in the form of a constant humming sound.[18]

Remarkably this internment and torture of suspected IRA terrorists (called highly coercive interrogation [HCI] techniques today) happened just a few years after the release of *The Battle of Algiers* and more than ten years after the French lost the Algerian War. But the British didn't learn from the French troops' mistakes. Tom Parker, a former British counter-terrorism investigator, summarized the effect of these techniques on terrorist operations:

> The deaths of "just" 27 people in the first eight months of 1971 as a result of terrorist violence prompted this more muscular British approach. In the four remaining months of the year after the introduction of internment and HCI, 147 people were killed. Four hundred and sixty seven were killed in 1972 as a result of terrorist action. The number of terrorist bombings in the province increased dramatically from around 150 in 1970 to 1,382 in 1972. The British Army estimated that up to 70 percent of the long-term internees became re-involved in terrorist acts after their release, so the measure clearly did little to deter committed activists.[19]

Whether the British achieved anything for their trouble is still debated. Britain officially claimed some modest success resulting from the HCI use when hauled before the European Court of Human Rights. Parker quotes a former British intelligence officer, however, as saying these techniques were "damned stupid as well as morally wrong. . . . In practical terms, the additional usable intelligence they produced was, I understand, minimal."[20] And of course several innocent people who were convicted in British criminal courts through the use of coerced confessions later had to be released when their innocence was verified, amid much embarrassment for the British government and much unnecessary suffering for the victims. "Damned stupid" and "morally wrong" are exactly right.

By the end of March 1972, the British had interned 900 IRA men. But the violence didn't stop.[21]

In 1972 Britain instituted direct rule to take control of the situation. Internment under the Special Powers Act was phased out and replaced with the "Temporary Provisions Act of 1973," which allowed authorities to detain anyone for up to twenty-eight days for interrogation purposes and indefinitely if a "commissioner" determined the defendant was involved in terrorism. The commissioner could base his determination on evidence reviewed in closed hearings in which the defendant could be required to answer questions. The British later replaced these provisions with the "Emergency Provisions Act of 1973," which established a new criminal court system to try terrorist suspects using relaxed rules of evidence and no juries. "Preventative detention" replaced internment, but the result that Catholics could be rounded up, interned, and interrogated on scant evidence didn't change.

What the British never seemed to realize is that the heavy-handed policies designed to "get tough" with the IRA were exactly what the IRA needed to make their claims of persecution valid. The British defended their policies as necessary derogations from the criminal justice system because the climate of intimidation made witnesses reluctant to come forward. Actually IRA terrorists were tried and convicted in criminal courts during this time, but the British only exercised this option when they had enough evidence to convict. The inherent injustice of this system played into the IRA's strategy. The Provos wanted to be seen as martyrs.

The most dramatic example of the "winning by losing" approach was an incident that took place on January 30, 1972, known as "Bloody Sunday." A regiment of British paratroopers met a civil rights march in Londonderry, opened fire, and killed fourteen civilians, none of whom, apparently, was IRA. While official inquiries immediately followed, people still passionately disagree over whether the paratroopers were actually fired upon first, and this ongoing dispute only highlights that these inquiries lacked the transparency necessary to engender public confidence. At least some evidence indicates that an Official IRA man fired one shot.[22] If this assertion is true, he got exactly what he wanted when the paratroopers responded with indiscriminate fire. Bloody Sunday was the biggest political victory the PIRA had seen to date. Richard English explains:

> understandable rage among northern Catholics led hundreds to join the Provisionals; indeed, the organization seems to have had more potential recruits than they could easily absorb. Not for the first or last time in Ireland, British military violence, intended to quell subversion, had produced a major boost for subversive republican militants.[23]

The IRA's success on Bloody Sunday came from a deliberate attempt to draw the British troops into committing a massacre against its Catholic-identity community. In its terrorism manual, the *Green Book,* the IRA crowed about its victories during the armed struggle:

> We exploit the enemy's mistakes by propagating the facts. So it was with their murderous mistakes of the Falls Road curfew, Bloody Sunday and internment, which were exploited to our advantage support-wise as was the murder of John Boyle in Dunloy.[24]

Notice it doesn't talk about a successful assassination or a well-placed bomb. Only when its community suffers a grievous loss at the hands of government forces does the IRA win. Such a strategy should be a hard sell to any identity community.

As I said, terrorists make bad politicians, and rather than leverage the worldwide sympathy Bloody Sunday engendered for its cause, the PIRA responded with "Bloody Friday." On July 21, 1972, the IRA detonated twenty-two bombs in the city of Belfast, killing nine people. The political backlash to this violence was so severe the IRA documented it in the *Green Book* as an example of what not to do:

> Even the given situations of adequate bomb warnings are exploited which is again our mistake in not having sufficiently considered our defensive before going on the offensive: the so-called Bloody Friday being the prime example. Either we did not stop to consider that the enemy would 'Dirty Joe' us on the warnings or we overestimated the Brits' ability to handle so many operations. But regardless of which is the case we made the mistake and the enemy exploited it.[25]

Bloody Friday has to be considered an incredible operational success, with twenty-two separate bombings in a single day, but it was a political disaster. The terrorist's conundrum is no different than that of the government: the more successful the operation is in terms of inflicting damage on the enemy, the worse it is from a political standpoint. The key to fighting terrorism is realizing that the terrorist is at his weakest immediately following a terrorist attack, because in that moment he has revealed himself for what he is—a violent criminal. It's hard to prove you're the good guy when your only tool is terror.

But the British finally did find one thing that really got to the IRA, precisely because it revealed them for what they were. In 1972 imprisoned IRA terrorists in Northern Ireland were afforded "special category status" in which they were given political privileges somewhat similar to those afforded prisoners of war. The IRA prisoners could wear their own clothes, freely associate with each other within the prison, and even train together. In 1975 the government announced it would end special category status for IRA members convicted after March 1, 1976, as part of a new policy called "criminalization." The IRA vowed to resist.

Imprisoned IRA members had clung to their political status for decades, whether held under internment, detention, or after conviction for politically motivated crimes. In one sense they had a pretty good argument, as Sinn Fein member Tom Hartley explained to Richard English:

"And one of the responses [to IRA terrorism] was to intern republicans. But by its nature internment means that it makes political prisoners out of those who are interned."[26] The British certainly would have had a more legitimate case if they had tried and convicted the IRA members for criminal offenses in open court, but criminalization was a step in the right direction. The IRA hated it.

When instructed to don prison clothing, the IRA prisoners refused, choosing instead to wrap themselves in blankets. Over time these "blanket men" ratcheted up their protest, refusing to leave their cells and beginning what was called "the dirty protest." The IRA prisoners refused to bathe or shave and smeared their prison cell walls with their own excrement. Finally they began a hunger strike, putting their lives on the line for a principle they knew was critical to their cause.

The reasons for the hunger strike reveal much about the IRA and about terrorists in general. They didn't strike over the anti-Catholic discrimination that led to the civil rights movement. They didn't strike over the RUC's police abuse or the stationing of British troops in Northern Ireland. They didn't strike over being arrested without charges, interned, and tortured. They didn't strike over indefinite detentions or even over Bloody Sunday. They knew all those things helped their cause. They went on hunger strike because the British government was going to make them look like criminals.

The strikers' five demands are also telling:

◆ the right to wear their own clothes
◆ the right not to do prison work
◆ free association with fellow prisoners
◆ 50 percent reduction of sentences
◆ normal visiting, mail, educational, and recreational privileges[27]

Notice that none of the demands have anything to do with helping Northern Ireland's Catholic population or with changing its political condition. Their entire focus was on IRA members not being treated like criminals, and ten men were willing to starve themselves to death over it. Hunger striker Bobby Sands wrote in his diary:

> I am a political prisoner. I am a political prisoner because I am a casualty of a perennial war that is being fought between the oppressed Irish people and an alien, oppressive, unwanted regime that refuses to withdraw from our land.
> I believe and stand by the God-given right of the Irish nation to sovereign independence, and the right of any Irishman or woman

to assert this right in armed revolution. That is why I am incarcerated, naked and tortured . . .

They will not criminalise us, rob us of our true identity, steal our individualism, depoliticise us, churn us out as systemised, institutionalised, decent law-abiding robots. Never will they label our liberation struggle as criminal.[28]

I do not doubt Sands's sincerity or that of any of the hunger strikers. The hunger strike brought the Republicans worldwide sympathy and support. Bobby Sands was even elected to Parliament before he died. But the fact that ten terrorists were willing to starve themselves to death rather than dress in prison clothes is, in FBI agent lingo, a clue. They fought so hard over this issue because the IRA knew criminalization threatened its survival as a legitimate army of resistance. Law enforcement should fight just as hard to ensure the members of a terrorist group are always treated as criminals.

There is a lesson in this experience for terrorist groups as well. The IRA was one of the most technically skilled, equipped, and operationally effective terrorist groups ever, but for all of its ferocity, its greatest political success came from a nonviolent protest. IRA members argue the armed struggle was necessary to get them where they are today, but after forty years of brutality they have little more than what the civil rights movement of 1968 achieved.

Ultimately criminalization worked, and it would have worked faster if the British had tried IRA members in regular criminal courts under normal rules of evidence. In fact, the end of the IRA's armed struggle is in sight precisely because the IRA exposed themselves as criminals. A bar fight in Belfast in 2005 ended the IRA's pretense of being a legitimate army of the Catholic community. IRA members stabbed to death a Catholic man, Robert McCartney, in a fight over a barroom insult. His death was originally treated as other IRA murders; everyone cleaned up and shut up. But McCartney's family, tired of living under the fascist rule of a terrorist group, spoke out. And it turned out the community was tired of it, too. When the IRA offered to execute the men responsible for McCartney's death it only reinforced its brutal, lawless image.

The IRA is similar to all other terrorist groups: it is an organized crime syndicate, a group of gangsters, a mafia. Author Ed Moloney recently wrote in the *New York Times* about the true IRA:

The criminality linked to groups like the I.R.A. is staggering. One recent British government report estimated that there were 140 paramiltary-associated criminal gangs, many with international connections, operating in an area that in terms of population is about the size of the Bronx. In 2002, the police confiscated more counterfeit currency and goods—CD's, DVDs, watches, clothes, software—in Northern Ireland than in all of Britain. Cigarette and gasoline smuggling, protection rackets, armed robberies and hijackings are rife.

The I.R.A.'s involvement in this illegal activity has produced a leadership cadre that has combined ruthless paramilitary activism with lucrative criminal sidelines. Figures with no visible means of support have in the last few years suddenly become property moguls and business owners with luxury vacation houses in Ireland and in foreign resorts.[29]

But IRA sympathizers can't stand even a newspaper article calling its members criminals. Rita O'Hare, the Sinn Fein representative to the United States, criticized Moloney: "This media myth that IRA members who for 30 years fought the might of the British Army suddenly became a mere bunch of criminals will fail."[30]

The IRA is to a great extent exactly where it was almost forty years ago. Secret negotiations with the PIRA that began in 1972 finally began to bear fruit with the 1998 Good Friday Accords, and after the McCartney murder the IRA finally agreed to decommission its weapons. The PIRA has given up the armed struggle and is now seeking solutions through the political system, choosing the ballot over the bullet, just as the Original IRA did in 1962. But just as forty years ago, as the older generation seeks peace, a younger one looks for war. A radical splinter group calling itself the Real IRA broke off in 1997 in response to the peace negotiations and vowed to continue the armed campaign. In 1998 a Real IRA bombing in Omagh killed twenty-nine people. Because a terrorist leader has no legitimate method to control other group members, the leader cannot stop the radicals from continuing their violence. The terrorist's only method of control is violence, and if he has renounced violence he is without recourse. The peace has been negotiated with a party whose members have no control over their own terrorists.

As is always the case when a government negotiates a peace with a terrorist group, one man with one bomb or one bullet can scuttle the peace and start the conflict all over again.

14

A Winning Strategy Against Legitimately Motivated Terrorists

Victory attained by violence is tantamount to a defeat,
for it is momentary.

—MAHATMA GANDHI

The British experience with the Irish Republican Army has much to teach us about how to respond to legitimately motivated terrorism. By my definition, legitimately motivated terrorists have some objective validity to their grievances, as the disenfranchised Catholics of Northern Ireland obviously did—but not to the violent methods they use to have their grievances heard. Legitimately motivated terrorists create much more difficult problems for a victim government than do extremist terrorists because their grievances' validity gives the legitimately motivated terrorist group a more powerful mechanism for recruiting support in and beyond its identity community. At different times, for example, the IRA received support from such disparate sources as the United States (through NORAID, the Irish Northern Aid Committee); from Libya's Muammar Gadhafi, and from the Colombia narco-terrorist group, Revolutionary Armed Forces of Colombia (FARC).

Legitimately motivated terrorists also tend to be more active than extremist terrorists because its repressed identity community demands action be taken on its behalf. Its real problems need to be addressed, and if a terrorist group claiming to represent it does not take the necessary action, it will quickly switch its loyalty to another group who will. This pressure to act often causes legitimately motivated terrorist groups to produce extremist splinter groups, as more radical members of the community seek to satisfy community demands. In Northern Ireland the Provisional Irish Republican Army formed when the Original IRA proved

173

unwilling to defend the Catholic community during the unrest surrounding the 1968 civil rights movement, just as the Real IRA formed when the Provos sought peace.

For the victim government two separate problems must be addressed when dealing with legitimately motivated terrorism—a political problem and a security problem. Unfortunately, most governments confronted with this type of terrorism combine the two problems, which serves only to establish the terrorist group as a legitimate representative of the repressed community. When the PIRA formed in 1969 it had no legitimate claim to speak for the IRA, much less the Catholic community of Northern Ireland, but by 1972 the British government was engaged in secret talks with the PIRA leadership. This government recognition brought the PIRA into the political process.

When a government attempts to negotiate the solution of a political issue with a terrorist group, it overtly acknowledges the terrorist group is a legitimate representative of its identity community. Terrorists cannot establish this legitimacy on their own. These negotiations hand the terrorist group complete control over the political process and put the government in a no-win position. If a government refuses to concede to the terrorists' political demands, it only justifies the terrorists' use of violence as a "last resort." They are then able to represent themselves to their community as reasonable actors who tried to resolve the issue short of violence, to no avail.

Conversely, if the terrorists wrest political concessions from the government, their identity group will reward them with even greater support. Their success will reinforce the legitimacy of violence as a tool for achieving political goals, and they will escalate their demands under the threat of a return to violence. The only persuasive methods the terrorists know are violence and the threat of violence, and they will continue to use those methods. Terrorists are extortionists, plain and simple.

Governments that try to control legitimately motivated terrorists by tying political reforms to their cessation of terrorism again hand control of the political situation over to the terrorists and usually to their most extreme members at that. When a government makes such an ultimatum, one person with access to a half pound of black powder has complete control over the political fortunes of thousands or even millions of people. Israel often finds itself in this position, where extremists on both sides scuttle opportunities for peace. While Israel's situation is unique and complicated because it is under constant threat from many different enemies, the repeated failure to find peaceful solutions to political problems has certainly empowered terrorists of varying political and religious motivations (a far-right Israeli extremist assassinated Prime Minister Yitzhak Rabin after the Oslo Accords).[1] Once violence is regarded as a legitimate means to political ends, it becomes a tactic for everyone to use equally. Just as with the British and the IRA, the extremists on both sides of the conflict benefit from the breakdown of the political process.

A victim government needs to keep in mind it has total control over the political situation and does not need to tie the political issue and security issue together. If the government recognizes the political issue's validity, it can resolve that issue unilaterally and thereby remove the terrorists' justification—its legitimate motivation—for violence. The government can turn a legitimately motivated terrorist into an extremist terrorist overnight, and once the terrorist's identity group sees his violence as extremist in nature, the violence can be handled appropriately through the legal system.

At the end of 1969, when the PIRA was just forming, the Cameron Commission had already documented the official discrimination against Northern Ireland's Catholics and thus established the political issue's legitimacy. Moreover, nonviolent civil rights organizations represented the Catholic community, so the British government could have negotiated with these legitimate organizations to resolve their political issues. Such an initiative would have empowered the Catholic community's more moderate voices and further reduced the PIRA's justifications for its use of violence. The British government might even have negotiated with the Original IRA, thus rewarding its unilateral renunciation of violence. If the government had created a nonviolent path to immediately address and resolve the political issues with transparency, the PIRA's legitimate motivation would have evaporated.

To be fair, the British government did begin to institute political reforms in Northern Ireland during the Troubles, but with security issues taking precedence over political issues, it allowed the two issues to be tied into one. The British government's failure to protect the Catholic community from unionist violence enabled the PIRA to establish its legitimate authority as the community's defenders. After the Provos established control, the government's ability to reassert its authority through the legal process became much more difficult. But such efforts would have been worthwhile because the majority of Northern Ireland's Catholics never supported the PIRA violence, which the British didn't seem to recognize. This crucial factor is why the PIRA so often resorted to violence within the Catholic community, using terror to maintain its claim of authority, and why the PIRA so feared criminalization. It knew if the community focused on its conduct as opposed to its politics, it would lose what little support it had. Using violence to enforce authority is the hallmark of a criminal syndicate and a fascist regime, and it represented the true face of the PIRA.

The PIRA's tactic of targeting British troops was extremely effective in turning the British against the entire Catholic population, and while the Catholic community did resist the repressive British antiterrorism measures, its reaction should not have been confused with support for terrorism. During the Troubles, the Catholic community overwhelmingly voted for the more moderate and nonviolent Social Democratic and Labour Party candidates over the IRA-linked Sinn Fein. Sinn Fein only gained electoral prominence through nonviolent protest (the hunger strikes) and ultimately through its commitment to the peace process. The British government would have been far better off dealing directly with the Catholic community's more moderate voices than dealing with the PIRA.

Even as the peace process moves forward, negotiating political solutions with terrorist groups is still risky because the government is essentially asking the terrorist group to negotiate itself out of existence. Resolving the conflict means ending the armed struggle, which is not in the terrorist group's survival interests. Dr. Jerrold Post talked about the "cybernetic balance" terrorist groups need to achieve in order to survive: "It must be successful enough in its terrorist acts and rhetoric of legitimation to attract members and perpetuate itself, but it must not be so successful that it will succeed itself out of business."[2] This observation is true on an organizational as well as on an individual basis. For the terrorist, the political conflict is his reason for being. He sees himself as a warrior in a righteous struggle, a David fighting nobly against Goliath. If the armed struggle ends he has to go back to his previous occupation, which is likely to be much less exciting. During a prolonged conflict many in the terrorist group may have actually made their living from the clandestine organization's illegal activities, so they wouldn't even have a job to go back to. They would go from being criminals with a cause to just plain criminals. As a result the terrorist group, or at least elements within the terrorist group, will resist the conflict's final resolution. Extremists on both sides will benefit from the peace process's collapse, again putting the fortunes of many into the hands of the extremist few.

If legitimately motivated terrorists attack a government, that government's goal should be to immediately establish a peaceful avenue for resolving the political issues while keeping its response to the violence completely apolitical. The only way to ensure an apolitical government response to terrorist violence is to rely on established legal procedures when enforcing the law. When I say "enforcing the law" I do not preclude a military role in counterterrorism. A military response could be entirely appropriate and would be perceived as legitimate so long as it is conducted within the law and with public oversight and accountability. If the British military had been able to properly protect Northern Ireland's Catholic communities from unionist violence the communities would not have had a reason to form the Provisional IRA in the first place.

Just as when dealing with extremist terrorist groups, the government's first goal when dealing with legitimately motivated terrorist groups should be to avoid taking any action that will inadvertently aid the terrorist. We know from reading the terrorists' strategy manuals their operational goal is to compel the government to react inefficiently. With legitimately motivated terrorists the political issues in play complicate the government's response. The government's goal should remain to simply not fall into the terrorists' trap by reacting with unnecessary force or by acting in any manner that gives the terrorist group a legitimacy it doesn't deserve. The legitimately motivated terrorists' success depends entirely on the government's mistakes.

15

Analysis of the Global
War on Terrorism

In preparing for battle I have always found that plans are useless,
but planning is indispensable.

—DWIGHT D. EISENHOWER

A small, stateless band of organized criminals called for an international "holy war" against America, and the U.S. government responded with the "Global War on Terrorism." Does this response make
sense?

Contrary to popular opinion, from the terrorist's viewpoint 9/11
was a political disaster. Its scale was so horrible the world united in solidarity with the United States to denounce terrorism. Terrorism expert
Brian Jenkins used to argue that terrorists wouldn't engage in mass casu-
alty terrorist attacks because high body counts would be counterproductive to gaining community support.[1] His prediction was wrong, of course,
as 9/11 showed us, but his rationale was right. Terrorist attacks are despicable, and the more destruction they cause the more decent people will
be repulsed by them. The terrorist's identity community always includes
more decent people than terrorists, so the more destructive the attack the
more the terrorists will alienate their own community.

After the 9/11 attacks, even many jihadist movement supporters
couldn't accept that fellow Muslims had committed such a hideous crime.
They instead conjured up conspiracy theories suggesting that Israel
planned the attack to frame Muslims.[2] In Tehran, the heart of possibly
the world's most anti-American Muslim nation, there was a spontaneous
candlelight vigil in sympathy for 9/11's victims. Other Muslim countries
with histories of antagonism toward the United States, such as Pakistan
and Syria, agreed to assist U.S. counterterrorism efforts and followed

through on their promises. The United Nations condemned the Taliban for supporting terrorism, and when diplomatic efforts failed to convince the Taliban to arrest and extradite the al Qaeda criminals, the international community supported a multinational military intervention to remove the Taliban from power. Solidarity and cooperation in the international community are poison to transnational terrorist groups. Osama bin Laden and al Qaeda had wildly overestimated their ability to wage a guerrilla campaign against the United States in Afghanistan, and the Taliban, al Qaeda's sponsoring government, fell within just a few short months. Al Qaeda, within its literal meaning as "the base" of the jihadist movement, was destroyed.

This loss was so profound that some al Qaeda strategists even suggested that this defeat was intentional and that al Qaeda purposefully sacrificed itself in order to further the jihadist cause, sort of like an organizational martyrdom operation.[3] But as we've seen, all terrorist groups benefit from a beating. They win by losing. It was no different with al Qaeda, which was destroyed as an organization but became an inspiration. Now every home-grown jihadist terror cell calls itself al Qaeda.

Unfortunately, the U.S. government's failure to understand al Qaeda's strategy, or to even recognize that it had a strategy, led it to make critical mistakes that allowed the terrorists to escape defeat. Language is crucial to a terrorist movement, so when the U.S. government declared a "Global War on Terrorism" it gave jihadists the warrior status they craved. When in executing that war we departed from the established rule of law—from both the Constitution and our obligations under international conventions—we undercut our legitimacy. When we antagonized and alienated the international community, we helped divide the world just as the jihadists wanted it divided. The terrorists didn't do these things to us; we did them to ourselves. We handed these victories to the terrorists. The results—an exponential increase in terrorist attacks worldwide—demonstrate the failure of the "Global War on Terrorism."

Some commentators point to the fact al Qaeda has not attacked the U.S. homeland again since 9/11 as evidence that we're winning the war on terror. This observation again ignores the terrorists' strategy. The 9/11 attack was not intended to be the first step in a jihadist invasion of the United States. The well-documented strategic goal of the 9/11 attack was to provoke the United States into invading the Middle East, where jihadist forces could then wage a war of attrition.[4] They wanted us on their territory so they could kill Americans with less effort and at higher economic costs to America. They also hoped a U.S. invasion would help them draw more supporters to the jihad because, as the al Qaeda strategists know, they have a much stronger argument to justify killing Americans in the Middle

East than killing Americans in New York. We gave them exactly what they wanted.

Journalist Alan Cullison got a rare inside look at this strategy when he purchased a secondhand al Qaeda desktop computer from an Afghan merchant shortly after the Taliban abandoned Kabul to coalition forces in November 2001. His analysis of the material he found appeared in a September 2004 article in *The Atlantic Monthly*:

> Perhaps one of the most important insights to emerge from the computer is that 9/11 sprang not so much from al-Qaeda's strengths as from its weaknesses. The computer did not reveal any links to Iraq or any other deep-pocketed government; amid the group's penury the members fell to bitter infighting. The blow against the United States was meant to put an end to the internal rivalries, which are manifest in vitriolic memos between Kabul and cells abroad. Al-Qaeda's leaders worried about a military response from the United States, but in such a response they spied opportunity: they had fought the Soviet Union in Afghanistan, and they fondly remembered that war as a galvanizing experience, an event that roused the indifference of the Arab world to fight and win against a technologically superior Western infidel. The *jihadis* expected the United States, like the Soviet Union, to be a clumsy opponent. Afghanistan would again become a slowly filling graveyard for the imperial ambitions of a superpower.[5]

Al Qaeda overestimated its strength in Afghanistan and underestimated the U.S. military, but it got its war of attrition against the United States in Iraq. Because of our post–9/11 mistakes, al Qaeda ended up accomplishing all its strategic goals with the 9/11 attacks, and they have no reason to attack the United States again, at least not right away. But this will not necessarily remain the case.

We have to remember that terrorism is economic warfare, not military warfare. Al Qaeda got the response it wanted. In addition to two foreign wars, the United States is also spending billions to improve homeland security. But if government strategists had read Carlos Marighella, they would have realized that money spent on protective security is largely wasted. A defensive security response is exactly what the terrorists want, because they know it is both inefficient and ineffective. Terrorism is too easy, and the targets are too plentiful. Nothing demonstrates this fact better than al Qaeda's attacks on the London subway system in the summer of 2005.

Britain spent hundreds of millions of dollars installing a comprehensive video surveillance system throughout downtown London, designed to protect against just the sort of attacks that occurred in 2005.[6] The security cameras took beautiful pictures of four jihadist terrorists entering and blowing up the London Underground on July 7, 2005, but the cameras didn't prevent the terrorists from accomplishing their mission. Nor did they stop four more jihadist terrorists from executing a copycat bombing in the same subway system using the exact same method of operation just two weeks later. All the jihadists needed to carry out these operations and defeat the multimillion-dollar security system were an Internet connection and a bathtub full of household chemicals. The whole terrorist operation probably cost less than one of the security cameras that took their pictures that day.

Was there a better way to stop the subway bombers? It turned out the British Security Services connected three of the four July 7 bombers to previous antiterrorist investigations.[7] A British parliamentary investigation of the bombings determined that a phone number belonging to July 7 bomber Germaine Lindsay had come up in a previous counterterrorism investigation as well, but it was never traced.

More significant, the Security Services had investigated both Mohammed Sidique Khan, the ringleader of the July 7 plot, and Shehzad Tanweer for their connections to other persons under investigation in 2003 and 2004. They judged Khan and Tanweer to be only peripherally involved in the earlier inquiries and chose not to investigate them further. An unnamed British government official later defended the Security Services' decision not to pursue investigations of Khan and Tanweer as a matter of economics: "We've only got finite resources."[8] But it was not a lack of resources that hampered the Security Services, it was their misallocation of resources. They spent hundreds of millions on video surveillance systems instead of on traditional investigations of individuals who were in direct contact with known extremists. Perhaps if the Security Services' finite resources had been better spent the outcome would have been different.

And similar misallocations of funds are being made here in the United States. After the July 7 bombings demonstrated the ineffectiveness of video surveillance, New York City entered into a $212 million contract with Lockheed Martin to install security cameras in the New York subways.[9] Hiring 2,000 new investigators would have been a far wiser investment. And we also learned that the National Security Agency (NSA) initiated a program to collect telephone toll records of tens of millions of innocent Americans, at what has to be an enormous expense.[10]

But for what benefit? What could the phone records of all these innocent people possibly tell the government about terrorism? Absolutely nothing. Ten million times nothing is still nothing.

Al Qaeda strategists read Marighella, and it shows in their writing. In "Stealing Al-Qa'ida's Playbook" Jarret M. Brachman and William F. McCants explain the al Qaeda strategy that Abu Bakr Naji set forth in *The Management of Barbarism:*

> Naji does not suffer under the illusion that the jihadis can defeat the United States in a direct military confrontation; rather, the clash with the United States is more important for propaganda victories in the short term, and the political defeat of the United States in the long term, as its society fractures and its economy is further strained.[11]

This conflict is an economic-based struggle, and every misspent dollar represents a victory for the jihadists. Indeed, if we had paid better attention to al Qaeda's strategy we would have realized that our homeland security resources could have been better spent protecting our allies.

For example, the Norwegian Defense Research Establishment (FFI) discovered a forty-two-page al Qaeda strategy document called "Jihadi Iraq, Hopes and Dangers" published on a Global Islamic Media Internet forum in December 2004.[12] According to the researchers who analyzed this document, the anonymous author reiterated the theme of the jihadists' struggle as a war of attrition against the United States and suggested they could better isolate U.S. forces in Iraq, and therefore increase the economic burdens of the war, by committing terrorist attacks against U.S. coalition partners.

The document analyzes the relative merits of attacking Britain, Poland, or Spain. The author decided finally that Spain would be the most likely to abandon the coalition if attacked, particularly because of its then-upcoming elections:

> *Therefore we say that in order to force the Spanish government to withdraw from Iraq the resistance should deal painful blows to its forces. . . . We think that the Spanish government could not tolerate more than two, maximum three blows, after which it will have to withdraw as a result of popular pressure* (emphasis in original).[13]

The Norwegian researchers who discovered this document did not realize its importance until after the March 11, 2004, Madrid train bombings, so their March 19, 2004, analysis of this document was unfortunately too late to help prevent the loss of innocent life. But Britain was also mentioned in the text:

> *Lastly, we emphasize that a withdrawal of the Spanish or Italian forces from Iraq would put huge pressure on the British presence (in Iraq), a pressure that Toni Blair might not be able to withstand, and hence the domino tiles would fall quickly* (emphasis in original).[14]

The FFI article was published more than a year before the July 7 and July 21, 2005, London Underground bombings. The U.S. and U.K. Security Services had no excuse for not recognizing England was the jihadists' next likely target.

The problem is that we are still trying to figure out what happened in the last phase of this war while al Qaeda has moved on to the next phase. Again from Brachman and McCants's analysis of Naji's strategy in *The Management of Barbarism* (a section that even more obviously cribs from Marighella):

> First, jihadis should bomb sensitive local targets, such as tourist sites and oil facilities. These "vexation and exhaustion" operations will force the local regime to enhance security around these crucial industries. This drawing in of security forces will then open up security vacuums in remote regions or cities.[15]

Thus, the 2005 al Qaeda hotel bombings in Amman, Jordan, and *Sharm el-Sheikh*, Egypt, should not have surprised anyone.

The problem isn't just that we don't read al Qaeda's strategy; we don't even know who or what al Qaeda is. How can you fight a war if you don't know who you're fighting? President George W. Bush described the enemy as *Islamo-fascists*, and as I've discussed, Islamo-fascist is an accurate description of the jihadist terrorist groups.[16] But Islam is a religious belief and fascism is a form of behavior. It's impossible to fight beliefs or behaviors. We have to figure out whom we're fighting against if we're going to win.

As I mentioned in chapter 7, former White House counterterrorism adviser Richard A. Clarke described the jihadist movement with a series of concentric circles, which was the model I used to describe the identity communities for all terrorist movements. Clarke's analysis of the militant jihadist movement is particularly revealing with respect to his estimates of the size of the different populations within each circle. At the center circle Clarke places "the terrorists of the al Qaeda organization, those who have been allowed the 'privilege' of pledging their loyalty to the group and its leader."[17] Clarke estimates the number of people included in this inner al Qaeda circle is "probably in the hundreds." (Later in the same publication Clark estimates al Qaeda's strength at 400 to 2,000.) The United States has spent hundreds of billions of dollars and invaded two countries in a war against a terrorist group that numbered less than two thousand.

To be fair, Clarke's circles differ from mine in that he includes some terrorists in his second circle. In Clarke's analysis of the jihadist movement he populates the second circle with al Qaeda–related jihadist groups. Clarke estimates this circle contains "several tens of thousands" of people, but not all of them would actually engage in terrorism ("many, but probably not most," in his words).[18]

That only a small number of terrorists make up the jihadist movement is borne out by other evidence as well. The United States has been engaged in a global war for longer than five years, yet U.S. forces have captured less than 1,000 prisoners considered dangerous enough to detain. In early 2006 the Pentagon released the names of 558 "illegal combatants" being held in U.S. custody at a detention facility at Guantanamo Bay, Cuba.[19] Not all of these men, apparently, are al Qaeda, and at least twenty-two have already been found innocent of having been enemies of the United States—at least before U.S. forces incarcerated them for three years.[20] The "high-value" al Qaeda detainees the CIA once held in secret prisons numbered only fourteen.[21] CIA Director Michael Hayden finally confirmed the small size of the enemy forces in a September 11, 2006, statement to CIA employees highlighting their successes in the Global War on Terrorism: "In five years, more than 5,000 terrorists have been captured or killed."[22] To date, the Global War on Terrorism is estimated to have cost over half a trillion dollars, meaning the United States has spent about one hundred million dollars per terrorist captured or killed.

How could such a tiny terrorist force become such a grave security threat to the United States of America, the world's only superpower? Putting aside for the moment the issue of the intelligence agencies' incompetent management of information that could have been used to prevent the attacks, on 9/11 al Qaeda clearly demonstrated it could inflict heavy blows against its enemies. A complex operation involving twenty terrorists over an extended period of time half a world away from its base is quite a feat for a clandestine terrorist organization. As we've already discussed, clandestine organizations face myriad difficulties just in trying to survive in a hostile climate, much less in carrying out an operation of this magnitude.

As Marighella said, engaging in terrorism is easy. What's hard about being a terrorist is living the life of a fugitive. The IRA's *Green Book* provides a glimpse of that life:

Again all people wishing to join the Army must fully realise that when life is being taken, that very well could mean their own. If you go out to shoot soldiers or police you must fully realise that they too can shoot you. Life in an underground army is extremely harsh and hard, cruel and disillusioning at times. So before any person decides to join the Army he should think seriously about the whole thing.[23]

Of course the truth is al Qaeda was not a clandestine organization. Al Qaeda enjoyed the support of the Taliban government in Afghanistan, which provided a safe harbor within which it could organize, train, and equip its operatives. As discussed in chapter 10, when a terrorist group receives state support it is transformed into a proxy of its sponsoring state. So unlike the poorly selected, trained, equipped, and organized armies most terrorist groups field, state-sponsored terrorist groups are professional armies. Terrorism is too easy to allow professional armies to participate. With all the concern over what damage terrorists might do if they get their hands on weapons of mass destruction, we have to remember that 9/11, the most catastrophic terrorist attack in U.S. history, was accomplished with three-inch knives and a few flight lessons.

States typically don't engage in terrorism, or at least they go to great lengths so they aren't caught engaging in terrorism. They don't want to get caught because the consequences are too high: economic sanctions or military intervention. So rogue states use terrorist groups to do their dirty work while they feign a lack of control over the groups to avoid responsibility. State-sponsored terrorism is leaderless resistance on an international scale. The victims of state-sponsored terrorism have no reason to play along with this charade, however. Publicly exposing the state's support for terrorism in an appropriate forum will force the state to either end its assistance or face the consequences. This exposure will put the rogue state in a difficult position because just as the IRA leaders have no means to control the more radical elements within their organization, the rogue nation is not able to control the radical elements within the terrorist group it sponsors. One man with one bomb or one bullet could end the regime. The risks would be too high to allow the terrorist group to remain under the state's protection.

An attack from a state-sponsored terrorist group is an act of war by the sponsoring state, and the victim nation can legitimately treat it as such. A victim nation is within its rights under international law to respond militarily against the sponsoring nation to defend itself and its allies and to neutralize the threat. The United Nations Charter unequivocally states:

> Nothing in the present Charter shall impair the inherent right of individual or collective self-defence if an armed attack occurs against a Member of the United Nations, until the Security Council has taken measures necessary to maintain international peace and security.[24]

Attacking the terrorist group alone in this situation would be counter-productive because the sponsoring state would simply produce more terrorists to fill the ranks.

The victim nation can demonstrate the legitimacy of a military retaliation against the state that sponsored the terrorists by first going before the United Nations, presenting its evidence to the Security Council, and obtaining the support of the international community, both legally through resolutions and operationally through a militarily coalition. With unity comes legitimacy. Once an evidentiary showing is made in an appropriate forum, the victim nation would be entirely justified in directing its military action against the government supporting the terrorist group, rather than at the terrorist group itself. By removing the veil that hides its responsibility, the sponsoring state can be held to account for its actions.

The complexity comes in dealing with the terrorist group itself. The terrorist group has to be treated as either a separate criminal entity or as an enemy combatant. In either situation the victim government must follow an established legal process for any action taken against the terrorist group to be judged legitimate. If the terrorists are determined to be criminals, they should be processed through the normal criminal courts. If they are considered enemy combatants, they should be afforded their rights under the Geneva Convention and treated as other enemy prisoners of war. If these terrorists committed war crimes, they could be tried in military courts-martial or in international tribunals. There is a process in place for each of these options.

Making these determinations, of course, is where the wheels came off the Global War on Terrorism. Anger, fear, and ignorance of the enemy led the U.S. government to make bad choices in how it waged the Global War on Terrorism. Reacting out of anger, the United States declared war against terrorism, as if terrorism was an enemy that could be defeated. Fear led policymakers to believe terrorists were stronger than the U.S. legal system, and they instituted extrajudicial detention, rendition, and torture abroad and secret police powers and warrantless wiretapping at home. Each is anathema to a free and open society, an insult to the rule of law, and a violation of the Constitution of the United States. Ignorance of the historic precedents for this conflict meant the

United States did not learn from the mistakes of the past. Interning terrorists didn't work against the IRA. Torturing terrorists didn't work against the FLN. Domestic spying didn't help catch the Weather Underground, the Klan, or the BLA. U.S. decision makers failed to realize that the terrorists wanted the government to use these illegitimate methods. The terrorists watched *The Battle of Algiers*. They read *The Mini-manual* and the *Green Book*. They learned from others' successes.

Once al Qaeda lost its Taliban sponsor it began to act like a true terrorist movement once again. As with groups from the past, its apparent losses were actually gains. Despite losing their organization, their training camps, and their financial support, the terrorists undoubtedly feel they are winning the Global War on Terrorism. Brachman and McCants agree:

> Thus far, direct engagement with the United States has been good for the jihadi movement. As Naji argues, it rallies the locals behind the movement, drains the United States of resources, and puts pressure on the regimes that are allied with the U.S.[25]

So where do we go from here? How do we turn this around? Brachman and McCants have some ideas in their report. They recognize that the U.S. military intervention in the Middle East has thus far worked to the jihadists' favor so they recommend a reduction in U.S. military troops in the region. They suggest instead that the United States use clandestine military operations and co-opt local militias or indigenous forces to fight when combat is necessary. Such cooperation is fine if these local forces fight our enemies for the right reasons and in a just manner. If they don't, this plan will be disastrous. And we also have to remember that clandestine military action is secret only from the U.S. public. The enemy certainly knows when it's being attacked, and they wouldn't likely be fooled by the use of a proxy force.

When a local force acts as our proxy the U.S. government is responsible for its behavior, just as the state sponsors of terrorism are responsible for the conduct of the terrorists they support. The United States can't claim to stand for justice and then hire a band of thugs to do its dirty work. That's called hypocrisy, and terrorist movements thrive on government hypocrisy. And they look for these discrepancies in more than just military matters. Americans can't claim to be bringing democracy to the Middle East when we actively support autocratic regimes in the same region. Propaganda will not convince people what they see with their own eyes isn't true. We don't need better propaganda campaigns; we need to behave better. Our actions speak louder than our words.

What Brachman and McCants miss is the issue is not about whether our military is involved in combating terrorism, rather it's about how our military is involved. Terrorism is about legitimacy. Our military intervention in Afghanistan was entirely legitimate. It was obviously justified by self-defense, legal under international law, and supported by the international community. The intervention in Iraq was less so. Not that we didn't have a case to depose Saddam Hussein; we just didn't make it. Instead the U.S. government tried to link Iraq to al Qaeda and 9/11, a case that couldn't be made. The American public may not have realized the purported links between Iraq and al Qaeda weren't true, but Iraqis and al Qaeda certainly did. We also should have anticipated that the jihadists would use an American invasion of Iraq to rally their supporters because bin Laden twice cited U.S. sanctions against Iraq as evidence of American hostility to the Muslim world in his declarations of war against the United States. He mentioned U.S. hostility toward Iraq because he knew the Muslim community was sensitive to the issue. He knew a second Iraq war would serve his interests well.

Lost credibility is hard to win back. Regaining it is crucial in our fight against terrorism. We have come to see al Qaeda for what it always said it was—that is, a base for training, for proselytizing, and for planning, financing, and staging operations. Now it has grown into something more. It has become an inspiration any teenager anywhere in the world can follow. I'm sure Richard Clarke's estimate of al Qaeda's membership wouldn't have included a nineteen-year-old Jamaican-born husband and father living in England who had never been to the Middle East. But when Germaine Lindsay strapped a ten-pound bomb on his back and walked into the London Underground he instantly became a "member" of al Qaeda.[26]

For terrorists this struggle isn't about how many terrorists exist today; it's about how many will be created tomorrow. Their recruitment efforts entirely depend on how we act. If our military rescues people from barbarism and anarchy, it will be welcome anywhere. If our military participates in barbarism we will create new terrorists everywhere. If our intelligence and law enforcement agencies bring criminals to justice, justice will prevail. If they act with impunity at home and abroad, we cannot expect anyone else to respect the rule of law. No government that acts in secrecy can honestly call itself a government of the people.

16

Our Constitutional Shield
Against Terrorism

*Since wars begin in the minds of men, it is in the minds of
men that the defenses of peace must be constructed.*

—UNESCO Constitution

Luckily enough, the United States has the most practical counterterrorism strategy ever written, and its record of effectiveness has lasted
over 200 years. All we have to do now is take it off the shelf where it has
been languishing since 9/11 and implement it. The counterterrorism strategy I'm referring to is called the Constitution of the United States of
America.

The Constitution is a workable counterterrorism strategy because
its authors were themselves terrorists—or freedom fighters, if you pre-
fer—fresh from a successful asymmetrical war of attrition waged against
the superpower of their day. The colonists knew what compelled them to
fight and what enabled them to succeed. When they sat down to create
their new government, they wanted to inoculate it against the abuses of
power that drove their just rebellion. In his first inaugural address Thomas Jefferson, whose eloquence justified the Revolution, summed up the
foundational principles of the free nation he helped establish:

> Equal and exact justice to all men, of whatever state or persuasion,
> religious or political; peace, commerce, and honest friendship with
> all nations, entangling alliances with none; the support of the State
> governments in all their rights, as the most competent administra-
> tions for our domestic concerns and the surest bulwarks against
> antirepublican tendencies; the preservation of the General Gov-
> ernment in its whole constitutional vigor, as the sheet anchor of

our peace at home and safety abroad; a jealous care of the right of election by the people—a mild and safe corrective of abuses which are lopped by the sword of revolution where peaceable remedies are unprovided; absolute acquiescence in the decisions of the majority, the vital principle of republics, from which is no appeal but to force, the vital principle and immediate parent of despotism; a well-disciplined militia, our best reliance in peace and for the first moments of war till regulars may relieve them; the supremacy of the civil over the military authority; economy in the public expense, that labor may be lightly burthened; the honest payment of our debts and sacred preservation of the public faith; encouragement of agriculture, and of commerce as its handmaid; the diffusion of information and arraignment of all abuses at the bar of the public reason; freedom of religion; freedom of the press, and freedom of person under the protection of the habeas corpus, and trial by juries impartially selected. These principles form the bright constellation which has gone before us and guided our steps through an age of revolution and reformation.[1]

A nation guided by these principles could not produce a legitimately motivated terrorist group, especially after the Thirteenth, Fourteenth, Fifteenth, and Nineteenth Amendments guaranteed these rights to all men and women. And while extremist terrorist groups can rise from time to time to threaten the peace, the efficient enforcement of the law through the strict observance of constitutional rights ensures these groups will not grow into a movement that can threaten national security.

Unfortunately, the decision makers who set U.S. counterterrorism policies somehow got the idea the Constitution was an impediment to counterterrorism operations rather than an effective strategy to fight terrorism. They said the Bill of Rights unnecessarily handcuffed our law enforcement and intelligence agencies, and they could only effectively counter terrorism if they were freed from constitutional restraints. Further, the al Qaeda threat was so new and so grave it was beyond the capacity of traditional legal solutions. They even rendered the Geneva Conventions "quaint" in this new type of war. They told the American people and their allies we needed to go on the "dark side" if we wanted to fight this threat and win. Even worse, since the Global War on Terrorism began they have led us to believe our own rights threaten our survival. They have lured us into the false belief that we can only ensure our security by sacrificing our civil liberties.

These reactions are not unusual in times of crisis, as we've seen, nor is the United States alone in making the mistake of believing security can be maintained only by restraining liberty. It seems every generation faces threats it then uses to justify taking extraordinary actions. The U.S. government trampled civil liberties here at home during the Red Scare and again during the 1960s and 1970s with COINTELPRO and other domestic spying programs. Different governments have abandoned international standards of human rights in Germany, Algeria, Northern Ireland, and elsewhere when they have felt threatened. The U.S. government abandoned the law altogether in the late 1800s, when it allowed the Klan to rule the South through violence and intimidation. We need to learn from these mistakes.

Thomas Jefferson recognized that some of his fellow revolutionaries worried that a nation based on individual liberty would not be strong enough to survive in a hostile world. But Jefferson disagreed. He saw unconquerable strength in a free nation:

> I know, indeed, that some honest men fear that a republican government can not be strong, that this Government is not strong enough; but would the honest patriot, in the full tide of successful experiment, abandon a government which has so far kept us free and firm on the theoretic and visionary fear that this Government, the world's best hope, may by possibility want energy to preserve itself? I trust not. I believe this, on the contrary, the strongest Government on earth. The wisdom of our sages and blood of our heroes have been devoted to their attainment. They should be the creed of our political faith, the text of civic instruction, the touchstone by which to try the services of those we trust; and should we wander from them in moments of error or of alarm, let us hasten to retrace our steps and to regain the road which alone leads to peace, liberty, and safety.[2]

Over 200 years later the Constitution still protects us, and ours is still the strongest government on earth. Liberty is not a weakness, it is our strength. If we look at the Constitution from the terrorists' perspective, we can see Jefferson is right.

As we learned from reading the various terrorists' strategies, they use tactics specifically designed to provoke an inefficient response. Terrorists want the victimized government to blame an entire community for the acts of a few and punish the innocent as well as the guilty. An effective counterterrorism strategy, then, requires efficiency, both in using allocated resources wisely and in focusing all the counterterrorism efforts squarely on the terrorists. The Constitution is the perfect counterterrorism strategy because it is designed to compel efficiency in the way government power is exercised.

In teaching terrorism courses I often ask law enforcement officers if the Fourth Amendment's warrant requirement makes them more efficient or less efficient at their job, and they immediately say less efficient. This answer seems to make sense, because it would obviously be easier and less time consuming for the police to conduct a search or make an arrest on their own authority without first having to gather the necessary evidence, write a warrant, and bring it to a judge to sign. But when I ask them what they would do all day if they had this unregulated authority, their response is always the same: kick down doors. As the words come out of their mouths they realize they would end up wasting too much time searching places that don't have contraband or criminals, and even when contraband was present, without having conducted a proper investigation they would not know where to look or what to look for. Moreover, the police department would spend more time dealing with the legitimate complaints of the many innocent people whose homes were searched than investigating crimes. Failure to respond to these complaints might lead to a more forceful resistance.

Requiring the police to present evidence of probable cause to a neutral arbitrator before a search or arrest simply ensures the police will not waste time searching for nonexistent evidence and bothering innocent people. The Fourth Amendment forces law enforcement officers to focus their efforts where criminal activity is probably taking place. This probable cause standard is not so difficult a burden to meet that it could harm counterterrorism efforts.

On the contrary, the Supreme Court defined probable cause as *just the amount of information necessary, under the totality of the circumstances, to convince a reasonable person of the fair probability that a crime occurred and that the evidence sought is in a particular place.*[3] It doesn't have to be more probable than not, just fairly probable. The Fourth Amendment simply requires all law enforcement officers to rely on evidence rather than on hunches. Evidence is reliable and objective; hunches are not.

But the Fourth Amendment isn't the only part of the Bill of Rights that forces law enforcement officers to be efficient counterterrorists. The First Amendment's guarantee of freedom of expression ensures the police will not investigate people just for expressing unpopular ideas, or holding unusual political or religious beliefs. Persecuting people for their beliefs doesn't quell violence, it inspires it. Reasonable people don't choose a violent path if a peaceful means to have their concerns heard is available. The First Amendment requires the police to focus on criminal behavior, and therefore on the terrorists themselves, rather than on the groups and ideas they claim to represent. We don't blame Christians and white people for Eric Rudolph's and Timothy McVeigh's crimes, and we can't hold 1.3 billion Muslims responsible for the crimes of a few thousand al Qaeda terrorists. Blaming the innocent will only create new enemies.

The freedom of the press guaranteed in the First Amendment ensures government incompetence and inefficiency are exposed, so the people can demand a new and better government when necessary to protect their security and preserve their rights and liberties. An informed population is an empowered population.

The Second Amendment's right to bear arms ensures people can defend themselves and be free from unwarranted fear. The Fifth Amendment's right against self-incrimination ensures police won't be tempted to coerce confessions through torture or abuse because everyone knows coerced confessions are unreliable. The Fifth, Sixth, Seventh, and Eighth Amendments guarantee accused terrorists fair and public hearings with competent legal representation before independent juries. These rights aren't designed to protect criminals and terrorists; they're designed to protect us by forcing our law enforcement and intelligence agencies to demonstrate their effectiveness. Putting innocent people in prison doesn't protect us from terrorists. Putting innocent people in prison will lead to terrorism. Transparency promotes accountability.

Taken together, these counterterrorism policies make it all but impossible for terrorists to convince anyone that they need to use violence to have their voices heard in the United States. If this strategy is followed, a terrorist group can never turn into a movement, and terrorism can be treated for what it is—a crime.

Proactive law enforcement techniques can be extremely effective in preventing terrorism. I know because I used them repeatedly to prevent acts of terrorism. The FBI has successfully prosecuted other terrorists as well: the blind Sheik Omar Abdel Rahman, Ramzi Yosef, Mir Amal Kansi, Tim McVeigh, Eric Rudolph, and El Sayyid Nosair, to name just a few. The public prosecution of terrorists allows the world to see their behavior for the criminal actions they are and allows the government to demonstrate the legitimacy and effectiveness of its counterterrorism methods. Terrorists can't survive this exposure, which is why they work so hard to convince people they aren't criminals.

Despite repeated success using criminal prosecutions to counter terrorism, the idea that using the legal system against terrorists is somehow going "soft" on them has taken root. I think the terrorists I helped put in jail would disagree, as would Bobby Sands and his nine IRA comrades who starved themselves to death rather than be called criminals. But still some believe "getting tough" with terrorists and fighting dirty are necessary because violence is all the terrorists understand. But their tough techniques in the Global War on Terrorism—secret prisons, extrajudicial detention, extraordinary rendition, and torture—are all propaganda victories for al Qaeda.[4]

First let me say there is nothing "tough" about mistreating a helpless prisoner. It is "damned stupid and morally wrong," as one British intelligence officer put it when discussing the special interrogation procedures they used against the IRA (see chapter 13). I promised to stay away from moral questions, but as to the damned stupid part, Defense Secretary Donald Rumsfeld once complained about news stories reporting the U.S. military's abuse of suspected terrorists, arguing al Qaeda taught its operatives to lie about being tortured.[5] The way I read the *Al Qaeda Training Manual* the authors seem to expect their captured al Qaeda "brothers" to be tortured, and they appear to recommend only that they report the torture rather than lie about it.[6] But even if this instruction could be interpreted as teaching al Qaeda members to lie about being tortured, we must ask ourselves why they would think it was a good idea to complain of abuse. The obvious reason is al Qaeda recognizes that torture is universally despised and prohibited by international law. They know nothing more clearly demonstrates the illegitimate exercise of government power than torture. This reason alone, it seems to me, would suffice to convince a government never to use any interrogation technique that even remotely resembles torture. *The Battle of Algiers,* with its horrendous torture scenes, came out forty years ago, and we know how that story ended. Moreover, the U.S. government knows from its own experience that coerced confessions produce unreliable information. The State of Illinois sent innocent people to death row on evidence derived from coerced confessions that later proved to be false.[7] If someone can be coerced into falsely confessing to a capital crime, we can be sure these techniques produce other unreliable information as well.

Second, as we have seen repeatedly, mistreatment is exactly the response the terrorists want from the government they attack. To gain support they need to show they are victims of a great injustice. They want to be martyrs. What they don't want is their criminal behavior exposed. The government's duty is not to persecute, but to prosecute.

In chapter 3 I said I could understand the terrorists I investigated might feel victimized by the techniques I used to gather evidence against them. I accepted that they might think what I did was evil. But the difference between us is I presented everything I did in open court for all to judge. Throughout the investigations I recorded each meeting, documented each transaction, and preserved each piece of evidence, whether it helped the case or hurt it. In court I submitted to cross-examination for days on end. Where I made mistakes I acknowledged them. My techniques survived the public scrutiny and the legal challenges of each defense attorney. The juries' verdicts and the full public disclosure made my work legitimate. The terrorists, however, hid their operations behind a cloak of secrecy because they knew their actions were illegitimate.

Our largest problem now is the government is keeping much of its counterterrorism effort secret. The National Security Agency began a secret wiretapping program, which James Risen and Eric Lichtblau exposed in a December 2005 *New York Times* article,[8] and the Patriot Act vastly expanded the FBI's power to use secret surveillance powers under the Foreign Intelligence Surveillance Act. The Justice Department likes to point out that some Patriot Act powers, such as roving wiretaps and sneak-and-peek warrants, have previously been authorized in drug investigations. The difference is the Patriot Act allows the FBI to exercise these powers in complete secrecy. People injured as a result of these secret programs are increasingly being denied their day in court because the government uses the State's Secrets privilege to prevent legitimate cases from moving forward. When there's no accountability, abuse and inefficiency always follow, as we saw with the FBI's COINTELPRO programs. The excessive secrecy in the Global War on Terrorism is completely unnecessary and detrimental to our counterterrorism mission.

We have been down this road before. Inexplicably, after 9/11, the greatest security failure in U.S. history, the intelligence agencies that performed so poorly received more money, more power, and less oversight. We need to bring transparency and accountability back into the Global War on Terrorism. We need to show the world who we are and who the terrorists are. We should not shy away from this comparison.

We have overestimated our enemy. Terrorists are not stronger than the rule of law. Why are we letting a few thousand extremists fundamentally change who we are as a people in a nation guided by the rule of law? They know they are not as strong as we are, and they are frank about their weaknesses. Al Qaeda strategists openly express their concerns about their lack of control over their followers, their inability to communicate, the ease at which they can be infiltrated, and the negative consequences of their excessive violence.[9] The only way they can be successful is for us to forget our values. To defeat them we only have to stand by the Constitution.

But maybe I'm wrong. Maybe the Constitution does have flaws that impede our counterterrorism efforts. Here again is where the genius of our founding Fathers shows through, for we can amend the Constitution when the need arises. So which of the amendments in the Bill of Rights do we need to change? Perhaps if we didn't allow freedom of religion in this country our problems would go away. We could ban the religious fundamentalism that so often leads to violence, whether directed by Christian extremists, Jewish extremists, or Islamic extremists. Certainly banning such abhorrent political ideologies as Nazism should be considered. Would these bans work to reduce terrorism? Or perhaps we could establish special terrorist courts and do away with jury trials, as the British did during the Troubles. Would that move help us? Did it help them?

When we turned our backs on the rule of law in the Global War on Terrorism, we threw ourselves back into Hobbes's nasty, brutal state of nature and did just what the terrorists wanted us to do. We're still the "strongest man," but as Hobbes said, even the strong man can fall victim to the secret machinations of a confederacy of enemies. Jefferson predicted in troubled times we might depart from the Constitution, but he provided the solution: "Let us hasten to retrace our steps and to regain the road which alone leads to peace, liberty, and safety."[10] We must return to the rule of law.

It will take admitting our mistakes, and that process could be painful. But the international community recognizes the terrorists committed horrible wrongs against us. No matter what our mistakes or excesses have been in this Global War on Terrorism, the world knows democracy offers a future of peace and prosperity that the terrorists' fascism never could. Admitting our errors will not demonstrate weakness; instead, it will demonstrate our strength.

A foundation exists on which we can build an international rule of law to combat terrorism without infringing on human rights. In 1948 the international community, much as the American Founding Fathers did almost two centuries before, acknowledged the existence of unalienable human rights with the "Universal Declaration of Human Rights."[11] And while the United Nations continues to struggle with its definition of terrorism, it has written at least a dozen international counterterrorism conventions and called for international cooperation to outlaw the methods terrorists use: taking hostages, seizing aircraft, killing diplomats, committing bombings. This work is a start.

The problem is the means to enforce the rule of law in the international community are not yet in place. The International Criminal Court (ICC), established in 1998, has the jurisdiction to "promote the rule of law and ensure that the gravest international crimes do not go unpunished."[12] The United States should bring the criminals of al Qaeda before the ICC for the entire world to see. Exposing the terrorists in such a forum is how we will break the back of transnational terrorist groups as al Qaeda.

We should cooperate with the international community in building a legitimate forum such as this ICC to bring international criminals like Osama bin Laden to justice. It is true the United Nations has so far insufficiently responded to international terrorism. But if we want to defeat transnational terrorism we need to build an international system of justice because Hobbes was right: without a rule of law life will consist of perpetual war. Some international body needs to act as the policeman, intervening when necessary both to protect the innocent and to punish the wrongdoers. This use of force is not legitimate when individuals or individual nations exercise it. Only a "proper authority," established through an international consensus, can exercise this power. But to hold others accountable, we must be willing to be judged ourselves. Transparency, accountability, and unity will confer legitimacy and, ultimately, will ensure victory in the war on terrorism.

We can continue fighting the way we have been fighting. Ours is a rich nation with brave young men and women who will answer their country's call to duty under any circumstances. In return, we owe it to them to fight smart, and fighting smart means understanding the terrorists' strategy, not falling into their traps. We must understand our weaknesses as well. James Madison, the father of the Constitution, warned the most dangerous risk to democracy is a vice "sown into the nature of man"—that is, the tendency to divide the world into factions of "us" and "them."

> A zeal for different opinions concerning religion, concerning government, and many other points, as well of speculation as of practice; an attachment to different leaders ambitiously contending for pre-eminence and power; or to persons of other descriptions whose fortunes have been interesting to the human passions, have, in turn, divided mankind into parties, inflamed them with mutual animosity, and rendered them much more disposed to vex and oppress each other than to co-operate for their common good. So strong is this propensity of mankind to fall into mutual animosities, that where no substantial occasion presents itself, the most frivolous and fanciful distinctions have been sufficient to kindle their unfriendly passions and excite their most violent conflicts.[13]

We can't survive as a nation committed to the rule of law if we divide the world into "us" and "them." We know what that kind of thinking is. That's thinking like a terrorist.

Notes

Preface

1. Warren P. Strobel, "Report Documents Major Increase in Terrorist Incidents," Knight Ridder Newspapers, April 20, 2006, http://www.realcities.com/mld/krwashington/14390584.htm.
2. CNN, "Terror Threat to U.S. Called 'Significant,'" April 28, 2005, http://www.cnn.com/2005/US/04/27/terror.report/.
3. Donald Rumsfeld, Memo to Gen. Dick Myers et al., dated October 16, 2003, reprinted in *USA Today,* "Rumsfeld War-on-Terror Memo," May 20, 2005, http://www.usatoday.com/news/washington/executive/rumsfeld-memo.htm.
4. Dana Priest and Josh White, "War Helps Recruit Terrorists, Hill Told," *Washington Post,* February 17, 2005, http://www.washingtonpost.com/wp-dyn/articles/A28876-2005Feb16.html.
5. Thom Shanker, "Pentagon Hones Its Strategy on Terrorism," *New York Times,* February 5, 2006, http://www.nytimes.com/2006/02/05/politics/05strategy.html?ex=1140498000&en=47304eb91807bd8c&ei=5070.
6. Dan Eggen, "Justice Dept. Investigating Leak of NSA Wiretapping," *Washington Post,* December 31, 2005, http://www.washingtonpost.com/wp-dyn/content/article/2005/12/30/AR2005123000538.html.
7. Rick Klein, "Democrats Say Rove Exploiting 9/11," *Boston Globe,* June 24, 2005, http://www.boston.com/news/nation/washington/articles/2005/06/24/democrats_say_rove_exploiting_911/.
8. Brian Flanagan, interview, in Sam Green and Bill Siegel, *The Weather Underground: The Explosive Story of America's Most Notorious Revolutionaries,* DVD (Berkeley, CA: Free History Project, 2003).

1. Prologue: An Unusual Education in Terrorism

1. The registered trademark Church of the Creator®, now firmly established by case law, is the intellectual property of TE-TA-MA Truth Foundation, a nonprofit religious organization that encourages universal love and respect for all people. It is not to be confused with Matt Hale or his white supremacist beliefs.
2. Creativity Movement website, "Creativity: An Idea Whose Times Has Come," http://www.rahowa.com/creativity12.html.
3 Ben Klassen, *The White Man's Bible* (Otto, NC: Creativity Book Publishers, 1981), www.overthrow.com/creator/wmb/wmb.asp.
4. David Lane, "88 Precepts of Natural Law," http://www.resist.com/Articles/literature/88PreceptsByDavidLane.htm.
5. Louis Beam, "Leaderless Resistance," *The Seditionist* 12 (February 1992), originally published 1988, http://www.louisbeam.com/leaderless.htm.
6. Ibid.
7. Anti-Defamation League Law Enforcement Resource Center, "Hate Symbols," http://www.adl.org/hate_symbols/numbers_14words.asp.
8. Klassen, *The White Man's Bible*.
9. Robert Jay Mathews, "Robert Jay Mathews: Last Letter," Church of the True Israel, the Order, 1984, http://www.churchoftrueisrael.com/the-order/rjm-letter.html.
10. MSNBC, "FBI, You've Got Mail—Not! FBI Official Says Budget Doesn't Cover Accounts for All Agents," March 21, 2006, www.msnbc.msn.com/id/11933204/.
11. Osama bin Laden, interview by John Miller, "Hunting Bin Laden," *Frontline,* May 1998, *http://www.pbs.org/wgbh/pages/frontline/shows/binladen/who/interview.html.*
12. Tzu, Sun. *Art of War,* trans. Lionel Giles (Mineola, NY: Dover Publications, 2002), http://www.chinapage.com/sunzi-e.html.

2. The Difficult Definition

1. Ludwig Wittgenstein, *Tractatus Logico-Philosophicus,* trans. C. K. Ogden (London: 1922), http://www.kfs.org/~jonathan/witt/tlph.html, 3.23–3.24: "In the language of everyday life it very often happens that the same word signifies in two different ways—and therefore belongs to two different symbols—or that two words, which signify in different ways, are apparently applied in the same way in the proposition. . . . Thus there easily arise the most fundamental confusions (of which the whole of philosophy is full)."

2. Zydowska Organizacja Bojowa (Jewish Fighting Organization), a resistance group formed to resist German Nazis in the Warsaw ghetto uprising. See Holocaust Survivors website, "Encyclopedia: Warsaw Ghetto Uprising," http://www.holocaustsurvivors.org/cgi-bin/data.show.pl?di=record&da=encyclopedia&ke=118.

3. Declaration of Independence of the United States of America, July 4, 1776, http://www.archives.gov/national-archives-experience/charters/declaration.html.

4. Carlos Marighella, *The Mini-manual of the Urban Guerrilla* (1969), as appeared at Marighella Internet Archive (marxists.org), 2002, http://www.marxists.org/archive/marighella-carlos/1969/06/minimanual-urban-guerrilla/index.htm.

5. A. P. Schmid, "Academic Consensus Definition," United Nations Office on Drugs and Crime (1988), http://www.unodc.org/unodc/terrorism_definitions.html.

6. A. P. Schmid, "Short Legal Definition Proposed by A. P. Schmid to United Nations Crime Branch (1992)," Definitions of Terrorism, United Nations Office on Drugs and Crime, http://www.unodc.org/unodc/terrorism_definitions.html.

7. Title 28 CFR Part 0.85 (k)(1), Organization of the Department of Justice (2003), http://www.dtra.mil/press_resources/publications/deskbook/full_text/Code_of_Federal_Regulations/28 CFR 0_85.doc.

3. Getting Beyond Good and Evil

1. Dick Cheney, "The Vice President Appears on *Meet the Press with Tim Russert*," September 16, 2001, http://www.whitehouse.gov/vicepresident/news-speeches/speeches/vp20010916.html.

2. Bin Laden, interview with Miller.

3. Bernardine Dohrn, "Declaration of a State of War," May 31, 1970, as it appears in Federal Bureau of Investigation, "Summary of Foreign Influences on the Weather Underground Organization," August 20, 1976, http://foia.fbi.gov/weather/weath1c.pdf.

4. Klassen, *The White Man's Bible*.

5. Osama Bin Laden, "Jihad Against Jews and Crusaders, World Islamic Front Statement," February 23, 1998, as it appeared in *Voices of Terror*, ed. Walter Laqueur (New York: Reed Press, 2004), 410.

6. Dohrn, "Declaration of a State of War."

7. Ben Klassen, *The Little White Book: RAHOWA! This Planet Is Ours* (Otto, NC: Creativity Book Publishers, 1987), http://www.wcotr.com/holybooks/lwb-24.html.

8. Osama bin Laden, "Declaration of War Against the Americans

Occupying the Land of the Two Holy Places," August 23, 1996, Hindukush Mountains, Khurasan, Afghanistan. Text supplied by Muhammad A. S. Al-Mass'ari, Committee for the Defence of Civil Rights in Saudi Arabia, http://www.mideastweb.org/osamabin laden1.htm.

9. Osama bin Laden, "World Islamic Front Statement," *Al-Quds al-'Arabi,* Febuary 23, 1998, http://www.mideastweb.org/osama binladen1.htm.

10. Tom Metzger, *Mini-Manual on Survival,* April 2003, http://www.resist.com/Articles/literature/MiniManualOnSurvival ByTomMetzger.htm.

11. John Brown's last letter, written on the day he was hanged in Charlestown, Virginia, December 2, 1859. Oswald Garrison Villard, *John Brown: A Biography (1910),* as quoted in WGBH, "John Brown: Holy Warrior," *American Experience,* DVD (Boston: WGBH, 1999), http://www.pbs.org/wgbh/amex/brown/filmmore/reference/primary/index.html.

12. Mahala Doyle, letter to John Brown while in jail. Stephen Oates, "To Purge This Land With Blood," as appeared on WGBH, "John Brown: Holy Warrior."

13. Mark Zwonitzer, "Jesse James," *American Experience,* VHS (Boston: WGBH, 2006). Transcript available at PBS Online http://www.pbs.org/wgbh/amex/james/filmmore/index.html.

14. See the Missouri Partisan Rangers, *Missouri Partisan Ranger Virtual Museum and Archive,* http://www.rulen.com/partisan/index2.htm.

15. Zwonitzer, "Jesse James."

16. Thomas Jefferson, letter to W. S. Smith, Nov. 13, 1787, www.Monticello.org/reports/quotes/liberty.html.

17. Klassen, *The White Man's Bible.*

18. Bin Laden, interview with Miller.

19. Ben Klassen, *Nature's Eternal Religion* (Otto, NC: Creativity Book Publishers, 1973), http://www.wcotr.com/holybooks/ner-1-01.html.

20. Klassen, *The White Man's Bible.*

21. Bin Laden, interview with Miller.

22. Timothy McVeigh, "An Essay on Hypocrisy," March 1998, as appeared on Media Bypass, http://www.outpost-of-freedom.com/mcveigh/okcaug98.htm.

23. Many white supremacist groups officially deny the Holocaust occurred, but my experience inside these groups proved most members recognized this denial as propaganda and celebrated the Nazi genocide of the Jews with such anti-Jewish slogans as "Hitler was right."

24. Rex A. Hudson, "The Sociology and Psychology of Terrorism: Who

Becomes a Terrorist and Why?" (Washington, DC: Federal Research Division, Library of Congress, September 1999).

25. Ibid.

26. Jerrold Post, "Terrorist Psycho-logic: Terrorist Behavior as a Product of Psychological Factors," in *Origins of Terrorism,* ed. Walter Reich (Washington, DC: Woodrow Wilson Center Press, 1990), 25.

27. Ibid., 28.

28. Ibid., 38.

29. Bush, George W. "Address to a Joint Session of Congress and the American People," September 21, 2001, http://www.whitehouse.gov/ news/releases/2001/09/20010920-8.html#.

30. Thomas Strentz, "A Terrorist Psychosocial Profile: Past and Present," *FBI Law Enforcement Bulletin* (April 1988): 13.

31. Ibid., 19.

32. Charles L. Ruby, "Are Terrorists Mentally Deranged?" *Analyses of Social Issues and Public Policy* (2002): 15–26, http://www.asap-spssi.org/ pdf/asap020.pdf.

4. Compounding Confusion

1. R. M. Kempner interrogation of Hermann Goering, Nuremberg, Germany, October 13, 1945, International Military Tribunal, USA Exhibit 712, filed January 16, 1946, http://www.kokhaviv publications.com/kuckuck/archiv/karc0004.html.

2. A. Mitchell Palmer, "The Case Against the Reds," in *World War I at Home: Readings on American Life, 1914–1920* (New York: Wiley, 1969), 185–89, http://chnm.gmu.edu/courses/hist409/palmer.html.

3. See A. Mitchell Palmer's testimony before the U.S. Senate at Constitutional Rights Foundation, "America Responds to Terrorism: The Palmer 'Red Raids,'" http://www.crf-usa.org/terror/PalmerRed Raids.htm.

4. Jerry Schwartz, "Will the Law Be Silent in a Time of Crisis?" Associated Press, September 30, 2001.

5. David Cunningham, *There's Something Happening Here: The New Left, the Klan, and FBI Counterintelligence* (Berkeley, CA: University of California Press, 2004).

6. U.S. Senate, Select Committee to Study Governmental Operations With Respect to Intelligence Activities, *Supplementary Detailed Reports on Intelligence Activities and the Rights of Americans: Book III— Final Report,* April 23, 1976, http://www.icdc.com/~paulwolf/ cointelpro/churchfinalreportIIIa.htm.

7. Ibid.

8. Ibid.
9. Ibid.
10. Ibid.
11 Ibid.
12. Ibid.
13. Ibid.
14. Federal Bureau of Investigation, "Summary of Foreign Influences on the Weather Underground Organization," August 20, 1976, 153, http://foia.fbi.gov/foiaindex/weather.htm.
15. Senate, *Supplementary Detailed Reports.*
16. Ibid.
17. FBI, "Summary of Foreign Influences," 159.
18. Final Report, 197
19. Ibid., 63–185.
20. Andrew Blejwas, Anthony Griggs, and Mark Potok, "Terror from the Right: Almost 60 Terrorist Plots Uncovered in the U.S.," *Southern Poverty Law Center Intelligence Report* (Summer 2005), http://www.splcenter.org/intel/intelreport/article.jsp?aid=549.
21. Southern Poverty Law Center, "Hate Crime—Report: FBI Hate Crime Statistics Vastly Understate Problem," *Intelligence Report* (Winter 2005), http://www.splcenter.org/intel/intelreport/article.jsp?aid=586.
22. For an analysis of racism in the FBI, see Cunningham, *There's Something Happening Here,* 113.
23. National Commission on Terrorist Attacks, *The 9/11 Commission Report: Final Report of the National Commission on Terrorist Attacks Upon the United States* (New York: Norton, 2004), 423.
24. Ibid., 271.
25. Scott Shane and Neil A. Lewis, "At Sept. 11 Trial, Tale of Missteps and Management," *New York Times,* March 31, 2006, http://www.nytimes.com/2006/03/31/us/nationalspecial3/31plot.html?pagewanted=2&ei=5090&en=22111b8b2e65cd5e&ex=1301461200&partner=rssuserland&emc=rss.
26. Cunningham, *There's Something Happening Here,* 66.
27. Ibid., 68.
28. Testimony of FBI director Robert S. Mueller, Senate Select Committee on Intelligence, *War on Terrorism,* 108th Cong., 1st sess., February 11, 2003, http://www.fbi.gov/congress/congress03/mueller021103.htm.
29. See Steven Jones, *Others Unknown: The Oklahoma City Bombing Case and Conspiracy* (New York: Public Affairs, 1998), 61.
30. Hudson, "The Sociology and Psychology of Terrorism."

5. Understanding Political Violence

1. John Milius, *Red Dawn,* VHS (United States: MGM/UA Home Video, 1985).
2. See www.GreatSeal.com.
3. Thomas Hobbes, *The Leviathan* (1660), http://oregonstate.edu/instruct/phl302/texts/hobbes/leviathan-contents.html.
4. Ibid., chapter 13.
5. Ibid., chapter 14.
6. Ibid.
7. Ibid.
8. Constitution of the United States (1789), http://www.archives.gov/national-archives-experience/charters/constitution.html.
9. Hobbes, chapter 14.
10. Merriam-Webster Dictionary Online, s.v. "legitimate," http://www.m-w.com/dictionary/legitimate.
11. Ibid.
12. Sinn Fein/Irish Republican Army, *Green Book* (1979), http://www.residentgroups.fsnet.co.uk/greenbook.htm.
13. Black Panther Party, "Ten Point Platform and Program" (October 1966), http://www.itsabouttimebpp.com/home/bpp_program_platform.html.
14. United Nations, *Charter of the United Nations,* chap. VII, article 51 (1945), http://www.un.org/aboutun/charter/index.html.
15. United Nations, General Assembly Resolution 3314 (XXIX), "Definition of Aggression," article 7 (December 14, 1974), http://jurist.law.pitt.edu/3314.htm.
16. Convention of the Organization of the Islamic Conference on Combating International Terrorism, Ouagadougou, Burkina Faso, July 1, 1999, and Organization of African Unity (OAU), Convention on the Prevention and Combating of Terrorism, Algiers, July 14, 1999, http://untreaty.un.org/English/Terrorism.asp.
17. United Nations, *Universal Declaration of Human Rights,* General Assembly Resolution 217A(III), December 10, 1948, http://www.un.org/Overview/rights.html.

6. Grading the Government

1. Anne Bayefsky, "U.N.derwhelming Response: The U.N.'s Approach to Terrorism," *National Review Online* (September 24, 2004), http://www.nationalreview.com/comment/bayefsky200409240915.asp.
2. Robert Barnes and Matthew Mosk, "Steele Apologizes for Holocaust

Remarks, Compared Stem Cell Research to Nazi Medical Experiments," *Washington Post,* February 11, 2006, http://www.washington post.com/wp-dyn/content/article/2006/02/09/AR20060 20902540.html.

3. Hitler, *Mein Kampf.*
4. See *Brown v. Board of Education of Topeka,* Supreme Court of the United States, 347 U.S. 483 (1954).
5. Umberto Eco, "Ur-Fascism," *New York Review of Books* 42, no. 11 (June 22, 1995), http://www.nybooks.com/articles/1856.
6. Ibid.
7. Condensed from Eco "Ur-Fascism."
8. Robert O. Paxton, *The Anatomy of Fascism* (New York: Knopf, 2004), 218.
9. Ibid., 219–20.
10. Eco, "Ur-Fascism."
11. OAU Convention.
12. CNN, "Saddam Gets Perfect Poll Result," October 16, 2002, www.cnn.com/2002/WORLD/meast/10/16/iraq.vote/.
13. First Amendment to the United States Constitution (1789).
14. See the United Nations, Office of the High Commissioner for Human Rights, "International Human Rights Instruments," http://www.unhchr.ch/html/intlinst.htm.
15. George W. Bush, "Address to a Joint Session of Congress and the American People," September 20, 2001, http://www.whitehouse.gov/news/releases/2001/09/20010920-8.html.
16. Benjamin Schwarz, "Books of the Times; Examining Terrorism's Roots and Taking Aim at Its Myths," *New York Times,* June 14, 2003, http://query.nytimes.com/gst/fullpage.html?res=9C07E6DA16 38F937A25755C0A9659C8B63.

7. Methods and Motives

1. *Prairie Fire* was collectively written and edited by the Weatherman Underground and was published in July 1974.
2. *Al Qaeda Training Manual,* released by the Department of Justice on December 7, 2001, originally accessed at http://www.justice.gov/ag/trainingmanual.htm. Because of pressure from the British government, the Justice Department removed this link. Access is now available at http://www.fas.org/irp/world/para/manualpart1.html.
3. Ayman al-Zawahiri, *Knights Under the Banner of the Prophet* (Fursan Taht Rayah Al-Nabi) (Casablanca: Dar-al-Najaah Al-Jadeedah, 2001).
4. Dohrn, "Declaration of a State of War."

5. *Al Qaeda Training Manual.*
6. Post, "Terrorist Psycho-logic," 25.
7. Gary Crowdus, "Terrorism and Torture in 'The Battle of Algiers': An Interview With Saadi Yacef," *Cineaste Magazine* 29, no. 3 (2004): 30–37.
8. See Green and Siegel, *Weather Underground.*
9. Bernardine Dohrn, "4th Communiqué of the Weatherman Underground," September 15, 1970, as it appears in Federal Bureau of Investigation, "Summary of Foreign Influences," 161, http://foia.fbi.gov/weather/weath1c.pdf.
10. Martha Crenshaw, "The Logic of Terrorism: Terrorist Behavior as a Product of a Strategic Choice," in *Origins of Terrorism,* 7.
11. Jarret M. Brachman and William F. McCants, "Stealing Al-Qa'ida's Playbook," Combating Terrorism Center at West Point (2006), http://www.ctc.usma.edu/Stealing%20Al-Qai%27da%27s%20Playbook%20—%20CTC.pdf.
12. Abu Bakr Naji, *The Management of Barbarism* (2004), translation by William McCants, http://www.ctc.usma.edu/Management_of_Savagery.pdf.
13. Brachman and McCants, "Stealing Al-Qa'ida's Playbook," 7.
14. Sinn Fein/Irish Republican Army, *Green Book.*
15. Ibid.
16. Marighella, *The Minimanual of the Urban Guerrilla.*
17. Richard A. Clarke, et al., *Defeating the Jihadists: A Blueprint for Action* (New York: Century Foundation Press, 2004), 16. http://www.tcf.org/Publications/HomelandSecurity/clarke2_nat%20threat.pdf.
18. "Bin Laden: West Waging a Crusade," Aljazeera.net, April 23, 2006, http://english.aljazeera.net/NR/exeres/FEE6E1E5-DCC0-4E8A-80CF-FFCCA2BC4C2A.htm.
19. "Full Transcript of bin Ladin's Speech," Aljazeera.net, November 1, 2004, http://english.aljazeera.net/NR/exeres/79C6AF22-98FB-4A1C-B21F-2BC36E87F61F.htm.
20. Ibid.
21. Marighella, *The Mini-manual of the Urban Guerrilla.*
22. Ibid.
23. Dohrn, "4th Communiqué."
24. Federal Bureau of Investigation, "Summary of Foreign Influences," ii, http://foia.fbi.gov/weather/weath1a.pdf
25. Robert Daley, *Target Blue: An Insider's Look at the NYPD* (New York: Delacorte Press, 1973), 430.
26. Assata Shakur interviewed by Christian Parenti, October 24, 2000,

Havana, Cuba, and appears in "Assata Shakur Speaks from Exile: Post-modern Maroon in the Ultimate Palenque," *Rap News Network*, October 9, 2003, http://www.rapnews.net/0-202-257463-00.html.

27. Stephen Ulph, "Al Qaeda's 'Bowing Out' Strategy," *The Jamestown Foundation Global Terrorism Analysis, Terrorism Focus* 2, no. 17 (September 19, 2005), http://jamestown.org/terrorism/news/article.php?articleid=2369787.

28. Marighella, *The Mini-manual of the Urban Guerrilla*.

29. Dohrn, "Declaration of a State of War."

30. Kris Kristofferson, "Me and Bobby McGee," Combine Music Corp (1969).

31. Marighella, *The Minimanual of the Urban Guerrilla*.

32. Ibid.

33. Ibid.

8. Case Study #1: A Successful Terror Campaign

1. Gillo Pontecorvo and Franco Solinas, *The Battle of Algiers*, Criterion Collection edition DVD, produced by Saadi Yacef (Italy/Algeria: Igor Film, 1966).

2. See Stuart Klawans, "Lessons of the Pentagon's Favorite Training Film," *New York Times*, January 4, 2004.

3. Saadi Yacef, interview by Liza Bear, "On the Front Lines of 'The Battle of Algiers,'" Indiewire.com, January 12, 2004.

4. See Bruce Hoffman, "A Nasty Business," *Atlantic Monthly*, January 2002; and Bill Ayers, *Fugitive Days: A Memoir* (Boston: Beacon Press, 2001).

5. See J. Hoberman, "Revolution Now (and Then)!" *American Prospect*, January 2004; and "25 and 50 Years Ago," *The Militant* 59, no. 43 (November 20, 1995).

6. Pontecorvo and Solinas, *The Battle of Algiers*.

7. *Pieds-noirs*, literally "black feet," was the name given to European settlers who immigrated to the French colonies of North Africa. No one seems to agree why they were given this name.

8. Yacef, interview with Bear.

9. Pontecorvo and Solinas, *The Battle of Algiers*.

10. Crowdus, "Terrorism and Torture in 'The Battle of Algiers,'" 30–37.

11. Pontecorvo and Solinas, *The Battle of Algiers*.

12. Ibid.

13. Beam, "Leaderless Resistance."

14. Pontecorvo and Solinas, *The Battle of Algiers*.

15. Ibid.

16. Ibid.

17. Henri Alleg, *The Question* (London: John Calder Publishers, 1958).

18. Pontecorvo and Solinas, *The Battle of Algiers.*

19. Paul Aussaresses, *Special Services, Algeria: 1955–1957* (Paris: Perrin, 2001); and Adam Shatz, "The Battle of Algiers," *The Nation*, June 18, 2001, http://www.thenation.com/doc/20010618/shatz.

20. BBC News, "French General on Trial Over Algeria," November 26, 2001, http://news.bbc.co.uk/1/hi/world/europe/1675992.stm.

21. Hoffman, "A Nasty Business."

22. Crowdus, "Terrorism and Torture in 'The Battle of Algiers,'" 30–37.

23. Martha Crenshaw, "The Effectiveness of Terrorism in the Algerian War," in *Terrorism in Context,* ed. Martha Crenshaw (University Park: Pennsylvania State University Press, 1995), 493.

24. Hoffman, "A Nasty Business."

25. Ibid.

26. Paxton, *The Anatomy of Fascism,* 218.

27. Tom Parker, "The Torture Question: Is Torture Ever Justified?" by Michael Kirk for WGBH and *Frontline,* October 18, 2005, http://www.pbs.org/wgbh/pages/frontline/torture/justify/.

28. Pontecorvo and Solinas, *The Battle of Algiers.*

29. See interview of Franco Solinas by Piernico Solinas (1972), contained as liner notes for *The Battle of Algiers,* Criterion Collection edition DVD (2004).

9. Ranking the Resistance

1. Crowdus, "Terrorism and Torture in 'The Battle of Algiers,'" 30–37.

2. Post, "Terrorist Psycho-logic."

3. Flanagan interview.

4. Eco, "Ur-Fascism."

5. Paxton, *The Anatomy of Fascism,* 218.

6. Ibid.

7. Eco, "Ur-Fascism."

8. U.S. Senate, Select Committee, *Final Report,* April 23, 1976.

9. See interviews with Kathleen Cleaver and Angela Davis, "Two Nations of Black America," by Henry Louis Gates, Jr., and WBGH, *Frontline,* 1998, http://www.pbs.org/wgbh/pages/frontline/shows/race/.

10. U.S. Senate Select Committee, *Final Report.*

11. See the Black Liberation Army, "The Freedom Fighters 'on the Black Liberation Army,'" *A Blast From the Past Revolutionary Archives From*

the Black Panther Movement (originally written September 18, 1979), http://thetalkingdrum.com/freedomfighters.html.

12. U.S. Senate Select Committee, *Final Report*.
13. Ibid.
14. Ibid.
15. Ibid.
16. Ibid.
17. Daley, *Target Blue*, 425.
18. Eldridge Cleaver interview in "Two Nations of Black America," by Gates and WGBH.

11. Case Study #2: The Ku Klux Klan

1. Federal Bureau of Investigation, *The Ku Klux Klan: Section I, 1865–1944* (July 1957), a revised prescript of the Klan (1868), p. 7, and available via Freedom of Information Act (FOIA) release at the Memory Hole, http://www.thememoryhole.org/fbi/kkk.htm.
2. See "Ulysses S. Grant," *American Experience,* DVD, directed by Adriana Bosch and Elizabeth Deane (Boston: WGBH, 2002), http://www.pbs.org/wgbh/amex/grant/index.html.
3. The Indiana Historical Research Foundation, "A Brief History of the Original Ku Klux Klan, 1865–1869," http://www.kkklan.com/.
4. *Plessy v. Ferguson,* Supreme Court of the United States, 163 U.S. 537, May 18, 1896.
5. See Douglas Linder, "The Shipp Trial Homepage," *Lynching in America: Statistics, Information, Images* (Kansas City: University of Missouri at Kansas City School of Law, 2000), http://www.law.umkc.edu/faculty/projects/ftrials/shipp/lynchstats.html; and Ronald L. F. Davis, "Creating Jim Crow," *The History of Jim Crow,* http://www.jimcrowhistory.org/history/creating2.htm.
6. FBI, "The Ku Klux Klan," iv.
7. Ibid.
8. Paxton, *The Anatomy of Fascism,* 49.
9. Eco, "Ur-Fascism."
10. Paxton, *The Anatomy of Fascism,* 49.
11. *Brown v. Board of Education*.
12. David Chalmers, *Backfire: How the Ku Klux Klan Helped the Civil Rights Movement* (Lanham, MD: Rowman and Littlefield, 2003), 3.
13. Cunningham, *There's Something Happening Here,* 70.
14. U.S. Senate Select Committee, *Final Report*.
15. Cunningham, *There's Something Happening Here,* 112.
16. Ibid., 75.

17. See Southern Poverty Law Center website, "Legal Action: Battling Hate Groups," *http://www.splcenter.org/legal/landmark/hate.jsp.*

12. A Winning Strategy Against Extremist Terrorists

1. Information on the Unabomber investigation and Ted Kaczynski, including a copy of his manifesto, can be found at the *Sacramento Bee's* website, http://www.unabombertrial.com/.
2. Southern Poverty Law Center, "Hate Crime—Report."
3. U.S. Congress, House, *Animal Enterprise Protection Act of 1992,* Public Law 102-346, Title 18 U.S.C., Section 43, 102d Cong., 2d sess., August 26, 1992.
4. SHAC7, "The SHAC7 Conviction: A Blow to Free Speech and Compassionate Activism," *Support the SHAC7,* March 2006, www.SHAC7.com.
5. Statement of John Lewis, deputy assistant director, Federal Bureau of Investigation, to Senate Committee on Environment and Public Works on Oversight on Eco-terrorism Specifically Examining the Earth Liberation Front (ELF) and the Animal Liberation Front (ALF), 109th Cong., 1st sess., May 18, 2005.
6. Title 18 United States Code, Section 1961, *Racketeer Influenced Corrupt Organizations Act of 1950,* Public Law 91-452 Definitions.
7. Title 18 United States Code, Section 1951, The Hobbs Act: Interference with commerce by threats or violence, October 1970, Public Law 91-452.
8. *Scheidler v. National Organization for Women,* Supreme Court of the United States, 537 U.S. 393 (2003).

13. Case Study #3: Lessons of the IRA

1. "The IRA's War News," November 16, 1940, as appeared in Richard English, *Armed Struggle: The History of the IRA* (Oxford: Oxford University Press, 2003), 53.
2. The Honourable Lord Cameron, *Disturbances in Northern Ireland Report of the Commission Appointed by the Governor of Northern Ireland* (Belfast: Her Majesty's Stationary Office, September 1969), paragraph 10.
3. *Ireland v. the United Kingdom,* 5310/71 European Court of Human Rights (January 18, 1978), http://www.worldlii.org/eu/cases/ECHR/1978/1.html.
4. Cameron, *Disturbances in Northern Ireland Report,* paragraph 9.
5. Ibid., paragraph 12.

6. Sinn Fein, "History of the Conflict," http://sinnfein.ie/history.

7. Cameron, *Disturbances in Northern Ireland Report,* paragraph 15.

8. Ibid.

9. Paul Arthur interview, "Behind the Mask," by WGBH and BBC, *Frontline,* 1988, http://www.pbs.org/wgbh/pages/frontline/shows/ira/conflict/.

10. English, *Armed Struggle,* 103.

11. *Ireland v. the United Kingdom.*

12. Tommy Gorman interview in English, *Armed Struggle*, 122.

13. Arthur interview, "Behind the Mask."

14. Sir Edmund Compton, *Report of the Enquiry into Allegations Against the Security Forces of Physical Brutality in Northern Ireland Arising out of Events on the 9th August 1971* (London: Her Majesty's Stationery Office, November 1971).

15. English, *Armed Struggle,* 141.

16. *Ireland v. the United Kingdom.*

17. English, *Armed Struggle,* 141.

18. Ibid., 142.

19. Parker, "The Torture Question: Is Torture Ever Justified?"

20. Frank Steele, as quoted by Parker, "The Torture Question."

21. *Ireland v. the United Kingdom.*

22. English, *Armed Struggle,* 149.

23. Ibid., 151.

24. Sinn Fein/Irish Republican Army, *Green Book.*

25. Ibid.

26. Tom Hartley interview in English, *Armed Struggle,* 187.

27. See English, *Armed Struggle,* 194.

28. Bobby Sands, "Bobby Sands' Diary," *Irish Hunger Strike 1981* (1981), http://www.irishhungerstrike.com/bobbysdiary.html.

29. Ed Moloney, "The IRA's Gift of Gab," *New York Times,* August 5, 2005, http://www.nytimes.com/2005/08/05/opinion/05moloney.html?ex=1280894400&en=c3e0117119faa324&ei=5088&partner=rssnyt&emc=rss.

30. Rita O'Hare, "The True Face of the IRA," Letter to the Editor, *New York Times,* August 12, 2005.

14. A Winning Strategy Against Legitimately Motivated Terrorists

1. CNN, "'I Have No Regrets': Law Student Confesses to Killing Rabin," November 5, 1995, http://www.cnn.com/WORLD/9511/rabin/amir/index.html.

2. Post, "Terrorist Psycho-logic," 38.

15. Analysis of the Global War on Terrorism

1. See Hudson, "The Sociology and Psychology of Terrorism."
2. See Anti-Defamation League, press release, "Conspiracy Theories About Jews and 9/11 Cause Dangerous Mutations in Global Anti-Semitism," September 2, 2003. It is interesting to note that militia groups did the same thing when Tim McVeigh destroyed the Murrah Federal Building, suggesting he was a "patsy" set up by the government to justify more restrictive antiterrorism and gun control laws.
3. See Ulph, "Al Qaeda's 'Bowing Out' Strategy."
4. See Brachman and McCants, "Stealing Al-Qa'ida's Playbook," 2006, http://www.ctc.usma.edu/Stealing%20AlQai%27da%27s%20Playbook%20—%20CTC.pdf; and Stephen Ulph, "Al Qaeda's Strategy Until 2020," *Jamestown Foundation Terrorism Focus* 2, no. 6 (March 17, 2005), http://jamestown.org/terrorism/news/article.php?articleid=2369441.
5. Alan Cullison, "Inside Al-Qaeda's Hard Drive," *Atlantic Monthly*, September 2004, http://www.theatlantic.com/doc/200409/cullison.
6. Marcus Nieto, Kimberly Johnston-Dodd, and Charlene Wear Simmons, "Public and Private Applications of Video Surveillance and Biometric Technologies" (Sacramento: California Research Bureau, California State Library, March 2002), http://www.library.ca.gov/crb/02/06/02-006.pdf.
7. Intelligence and Security Committee, *Report Into the London Terrorist Attacks on 7 July 2005* (London: Her Majesty's Stationery Office, May 2006).
8. David Leppard, "MI-5 Judged Bomber 'No Threat,'" *Sunday Times,* July 17, 2005, http://www.timesonline.co.uk/article/0,,2087-1697562,00.html.
9. Brendan Coyne, "New York City Gives Lockheed $212 Million Subway Camera Contract," *New Standard,* August 24, 2005, http://newstandardnews.net/content/index.cfm/items/2272.
10. Leslie Cauley, "NSA Has Massive Database of Americans' Phone Calls," *USA Today,* May 11, 2006.
11. Brachman and McCants, "Stealing Al-Qa'ida's Playbook."
12. Brynjar Lia and Thomas Hegghammer, "FFI Explains al-Qaida Document," Norwegian Defence Research Establishment (Forsvarets forskningsinstitutt), March 19, 2004, http://www.mil.no/felles/ffi/start/article.jhtml?articleID=71589.
13. Ibid.
14. Ibid.
15. Brachman and McCants, "Stealing Al-Qa'ida's Playbook."

16. George W. Bush, "President Discusses War on Terror at National Endowment for Democracy," Washington, DC, October 6, 2005, http://www.whitehouse.gov/news/releases/2005/10/20051006-3.html.

17. Clarke, *Defeating the Jihadists,* http://www.tcf.org/list.asp?type=PB&pubid=498.

18. Ibid.

19. CNN, "List of Guantanamo Detainee Names Released," April 19, 2006, http://www.cnn.com/2006/US/04/19/gitmo.detainees.ap/index.html.

20. Uyhghur Human Rights Project, "Uyghurs in Guantanamo," *Issue of Concern,* 2006, http://www.uhrp.org/issues/uyghurs_in_guantanamo.

21. Eggen, Dan and Dafna Linzer, "Secret World of Detainees Grows More Public," *Washington Post,* September 7, 2006, p. A18, *http://www.washingtonpost.com/wp-dyn/content/article/2006/09/06/AR2006090602142.html.*

22. Hayden, CIA Director Michael V Statement to Employees by Central Intelligence Agency Director Gen. Michael V. Hayden on the Fifth Anniversary of 9/11, September 11, 2006, https://www.cia.gov/cia/public_affairs/press_release/2006/pr09112006.htm.

23. Sinn Fein/Irish Republican Army, *Green Book.*

24. United Nations, *Charter.*

25. Brachman and McCants, "Stealing Al-Qa'ida's Playbook."

26. Leppard, "MI-5 Judged Bomber 'No Threat.'"

16. Our Constitutional Shield Against Terrorism

1. Thomas Jefferson, First Inaugural Address, March 4, 1801, Avalon Project, Yale Law School, http://www.yale.edu/lawweb/avalon/presiden/inaug/jefinau1.htm.

2. Ibid.

3. *Illinois v. Gates,* Supreme Court of the United States, 462 U.S. 213 (1983).

4. See Dana Priest, "The CIA Holds Terror Suspects in Secret Prisons," *Washington Post,* November 2, 2005, http://www.washingtonpost.com/wp-dyn/content/article/2005/11/01/AR20051101101644.html; Neil A. Lewis and Eric Schmitt, "Cuba Detentions May Last Years," *New York Times,* February 13, 2004, http://www.nytimes.com/2004/02/13/politics/13GITM.html?ex=1392008400&en=e85cdb61869ffa31&ei=5007&partner=USERLAND; Richard Norton-Taylor, "1,000 Secret CIA Flights Revealed," *Guardian Unlimited,* April 27, 2006, http://www.guardian.

co.uk/usa/story/0,,1762212,00.html; Dana Priest and Bradley Graham, "Guantanamo List Details Approved Interrogation Methods," *Washington Post,* June 10, 2004, http://www.washington post.com/wp-dyn/articles/A29742-2004Jun9.html; and James Sturcke, "General Approved Extreme Interrogation Methods," *Guardian Unlimited,* March 30, 2005, http://www.guardian.co.uk/Iraq/Story/0,2763,1448282,00.html.

5. Donald Rumsfeld, speech to the Council on Foreign Relations, Harold Pratt House, New York, New York, February 17, 2006, http://www.defenselink.mil/speeches/2006/sp20060217-12574.html.

6. See "Bin Laden's Terrorism Bible," *The Smoking Gun,* http://www.thesmokinggun.com/archive/jihadmanual.html.

7. See Northwestern University Law School, Center on Wrongful Convictions, "A Constituency for the Innocent," January 16, 2005, http://www.law.northwestern.edu/depts/clinic/wrongful/History.htm.

8. James Risen and Eric Lichtblau, "Bush Lets U.S. Spy on Callers Without Courts," *New York Times,* December 16, 2005, http://www.nytimes.com/2005/12/16/politics 16program.html?ex=11503 47600&en=f8d5ab00bd0fd8fb&ei=5087&excamp=GGGN wiretaps.

9. See Brachman and McCants, "Stealing Al-Qa'ida's Playbook."

10. Jefferson, First Inaugural Address.

11. United Nations, *Universal Declaration of Human Rights.*

12. *The Rome Statute of the International Criminal Court* (The Hague: Public Information and Documentation Section, ICC, 1998), http://www.icc-cpi.int/library/about/officialjournal/Rome_Statute_120704-EN.pdf.

13. James Madison, "The Same Subject Continued: The Union as a Safeguard Against Domestic Faction and Insurrection," no. 10 of *The Federalist Papers* (New York: J. and A. McLean, 1787).

Bibliography

Primary Sources

Alleg, Henri. *The Question*. London: John Calder Publishers, 1958. Arthur, Paul. Interview. "Behind the Mask." By WGBH/BBC. *Frontline*. Documentary by Taylor, Peter and Will, Lyman, PBS video, Frontline Series, (1997). http://www.pbs.org/wgbh/pages/frontline/shows/ira/conflict/.

Aussaresses, Paul. *Special Services, Algeria: 1955–1957*. Paris: Perrin, 2001.

Ayers, Bill. *Fugitive Days: A Memoir*. Boston: Beacon Press, 2001.

Bakr Naji, Abu. *The Management of Barbarism*. 2004. Translation by William McCants available at *http://www.ctc.usma.edu/Management_of_Savagery.pdf*.

Barnes, Robert, and Matthew Mosk. "Steele Apologizes for Holocaust Remarks, Compared Stem Cell Research to Nazi Medical Experiments." *Washington Post*, February 11, 2006. http://www.washingtonpost.com/wp-dyn/content/article/2006/02/09/AR2006020902540.html.

Bayefsky, Anne. "U.N.derwhelming Response: The U.N.'s Approach to Terrorism." *National Review Online,* September 24, 2004. http://www.nationalreview.com/comment/bayefsky200409240915.asp.

Beam, Louis. "Leaderless Resistance." *The Seditionist* 12 (February 1992) (originally published 1983). http://www.louisbeam.com/leaderless.htm.

bin Laden, Osama. "Declaration of War Against the Americans Occupying the Land of the Two Holy Places," August 23, 1996, Hindukush Mountains, Khurasan, Afghanistan. Text supplied by Muhammad A. S. Al-Mass'ari, Committee for the Defence of Civil Rights in Saudi Arabia. http://www.mideastweb.org/osamabinladen1.htm.

————. "Full Transcript of bin Ladin's Speech." Aljazeera.net, November 1, 2004. http://english.aljazeera.net/NR/exeres/79C6AF22-98FB-4A1C-B21F-2BC36E87F61F.htm.

————. Interview. "Hunting Bin Laden." By John Miller. *Frontline.* May 1988. http://www.pbs.org/wgbh/pages/frontline/shows/binladen/who/interview.html.

————. "Jihad Against Jews and Crusaders, World Islamic Front Statement," February 23, 1998. In *Voices of Terror,* edited by Walter Laqueur, 410. New York: Reed Press, 2004.

————. "World Islamic Front Statement." *Al-Quds al-Arabi,* February 23, 1998. http://www.mideastweb.org/osamabinladen1.htm.

Blejwas, Andrew, Anthony Griggs, and Mark Potok. "Terror from the Right: Almost 60 Terrorist Plots Uncovered in the U.S." *Southern Poverty Law Center Intelligence Report* (Summer 2005). http://www.splcenter.org/intel/intelreport/article.jsp?aid=549.

Brachman, Jarret M., and William F. McCants. "Stealing Al-Qa'ida's Playbook." Combating Terrorism Center at West Point, 2006. http://www.ctc.usma.edu/Stealing%20Al-Qai%27da%27s%20Playbook%20—%20CTC.pdf.

Bush, George W. "Address to a Joint Session of Congress and the American People," September 20, 2001. http://www.whitehouse.gov/news/releases/2001/09/20010920-8.html#.***

————. "President Bush Calls for Action on the Economy and Energy." Office of the Press Secretary, October 26, 2001. http://www.white house.gov/news/releases/2001/10/20011026-9.html.

————. "President Discusses War on Terror at National Endowment for Democracy," October 6, 2005, http://www.whitehouse.gov/news/releases/2005/10/20051006-3.html.

Cauley, Leslie. "NSA Has Massive Database of Americans' Phone Calls." *USA Today,* May 11, 2006.

Chalmers, David. *Backfire: How the Ku Klux Klan Helped the Civil Rights Movement.* Lanham, MD: Rowman and Littlefield, 2003.

Cheney, Dick. Press release. "The Vice President Appears on *Meet the Press with Tim Russert.*" September 16, 2001. http://www.white house.gov/vicepresident/news-speeches/speeches/vp20010916.html.

Clarke, Richard, et al. *Defeating the Jihadists: A Blueprint for Action.* New York: Century Foundation Press, 2004. http://www.tcf.org/Publications/HomelandSecurity/clarke/2_nat%20threat.pdf.

Coyne, Brendan. "New York City Gives Lockheed $212 Million Subway Camera Contract." *New Standard,* August 24, 2005. http://newstandardnews.net/content/index.cfm/items/2272.

Crensha7erviews with Tommy Gorman and Tom Hartley.

Ford, Henry. *The Internation Jew.* Dearborn, MI: Dearborn Publishing, 1920.

Gandhi, Mahatma. Satyagraha Leaflet no. 13, May 3, 1919.

Gates, Henry Louis, Jr. "Two Nations of Black America." VHS. Produced by June Cross Boston: WGBH, 1998. http://www.pbs.org/wgbh/pages/frontline/shows/race/. Includes interviews with Eldridge Cleaver, Kathleen Cleaver, and Angela Davis.

Green, Sam, and Bill Siegel. *The Weather Underground: The Explosive Story of America's Most Notorious Revolutionaries.* DVD. Berkeley, CA: Free History Project, 2003. Includes interview with Brian Flanagan.

Hayden, Michael V. Statement to Employees by Central Intelligence Agency Director Gen. Michael V. Hayden on the Fifth Anniversary of 9/11. September 11, 2006, https://www.cia.gov/cia/public_affairs/press_release/2006/pr09112006.htm.

Hitler, Adolf. *Mein Kampf.* Vol. 2, *The National Socialist Movement.* chapter 1, "Philosophy and Party." 1925. Translated by Ralph Manheim. Boston: Houghton Mifflin, 1971.

Hobbes, Thomas. *The Leviathan,* 1660. http://oregonstate.edu/instruct/phl302/texts/hobbes/leviathan-contents.html.

Hoberman, J. "Revolution Now (and Then)!" *American Prospect,* January 2004.

———. "25 and 50 Years Ago." *The Militant* 59, no. 43 (November 20, 1995).

Hoffman, Bruce. "A Nasty Business." *Atlantic Monthly* January 2002. http://www.theatlantic.com/doc/200201/hoffman.

Hudson, Rex. "The Sociology and Psychology of Terrorism: Who Becomes a Terrorist and Why?" Washington, DC: Federal Research Division, Library of Congress, September 1999.

Jefferson, Thomas. First Inaugural Address, March 4, 1801. Avalon Project, Yale Law School (1996), http://www.yale.edu/lawweb/avalon/presiden/inaug/jefinau1.htm.

———. Letter to W. S. Smith. November 13, 1787. http://www.Montcello.org/reports/quotes/liberty.html.

Jones, Steven. *Others Unknown: The Oklahoma City Bombing Case and Conspiracy.* New York: Public Affairs, 1998.

Kaczynski, Ted, Unabomer Manifesto, Sacramento Bee website, http://www.unabombertrial.com.

Kempner, R. M. Interrogation of Hermann Goering, Nuremberg, Germany, October 13, 1945. International Military Tribunal, USA Exhibit 712, filed January 16, 1946. http://www.kokhavivpublications.com/kuckuck/archiv/karc0004.html.

Klassen, Ben. *The Little White Book: RAHOWA! This Planet is Ours.* Otto, NC: Creativity Book Publishers, 1987.

———. *Nature's Eternal Religion.* Otto, NC: Creativity Book Publishers, 1973.

———. *Salubrious Living.* Otto, NC: Creativity Book Publishers, 1982.

———. *The White Man's Bible.* Otto, NC: Creativity Book Publishers, 1981.

Klawans, Stuart. "Lessons of the Pentagon's Favorite Training Film." *New York Times,* January 4, 2004.

Klein, Rick "Democrats Say Rove Exploiting 9/11," *Boston Globe,* June 24, 2005, http://www.boston.com/news/nation/washington.

King, Martin Luther, Jr., *Wall Street Journal,* November 13, 1962.

Kristofferson, Kris. "Me and Bobby McGee." Combine Music Corp, 1969.

Lane, David. "88 Precepts of Natural Law." http://www.resist.com/Articles/literature/88PreceptsByDavidLane.htm.

Leppard, David. "MI-5 Judged Bomber 'No Threat.'" *Sunday Times,* July 17, 2005. http://www.timesonline.co.uk/article/0,,2087-1697562,00.html.

Lewis, John. Testimony to Senate Committee on Environment and Public Works on Oversight on Eco-terrorism Specifically Examining the Earth Liberation Front (ELF) and the Animal Liberation Front (ALF), 109th Cong., 1st sess., May 18, 2005.

Lewis, Neil A., and Eric Schmitt. "Cuba Detentions May Last Years." *New York Times,* February 13, 2004. http://www.nytimes.com/2004/02/13/politics/13GITM.html?ex=1392008400&en=e85cdb61869ffa31&ei=5007&partner=USERLAND.

Lia, Brynjar, and Thomas Hegghammer. "FFI Explains al-Qaida Document." Norwegian Defence Research Establishment (Forsvarets forskningsinstitutt), March 19, 2004. http://www.mil.no/felles/ffi/start/article.jhtml?articleID=71589.

MacArthur, John D. www.GreatSeal.com, 1998-2006.

MacDonald, Andrew. *Hunter.* Hillsboro, WV: National Vanguard Books, 1998.

———. *The Turner Diaries: A Novel,* 2nd edition. Ft. Lee, NJ: Barricade Books, 1996.

Marighella, Carlos. *The Mini-manual of the Urban Guerrilla.* 1969. Marighella Internet Archive (marxists.org), 2002. http://www.marxists.org/archive/marighella-carlos/1969/06/minimanual-urban-guerrilla/index.htm.

Mathews, Robert Jay. "Robert Jay Matthews: Last Letter." Church of True Israel, the Order, 1984. http://www.churchoftrueisrael.com/the-order/rjm-letter.html.

McVeigh, Timothy. "An Essay on Hypocrisy." Media Bypass, March 1998. http://www.outpost-of-freedom.com/mcveigh/okcaug98.htm.

Metzger, Tom. *Mini-Manual on Survival,* April 2003. http://www. resist.com/Articles/literature/MiniManualOnSurvivalBy TomMetzger.htm.

———. "Our Positions: Government." http://resist.com/.Milius, John. *Red Dawn.* VHS, United States: MGM/UA Home Video, 1984.

Moloney, Ed. "The IRA's Gift of Gab." *New York Times,* August 5, 2005. http://www.nytimes.com/2005/08/05/opinion/ 05moloney.html?ex=1280894400&en=c3e0117119faa324&ei= 5088&partner=rssnyt&emc=rss.

Mueller, Robert S. Testimony. U.S. Congress. Senate. Select Committee on Intelligence. *War on Terrorism.* 108th Cong., 1st sess., February 11, 2003. http://www.fbi.gov/congress/congress03/mueller 021103.htm.

Nieto, Marcus, Kimberly Johnston-Dodd, and Charlene Wear Simmons. "Public and Private Applications of Video Surveillance and Biometric Technologies." Sacramento: California Research Bureau, California State Library, March 2002. http://www.library.ca. gov/crb/02/06/02-006.pdf.

Nietzsche, Friedrich. *Beyond Good and Evil.* Translation by Walter Kaufmann. New York: Random House, 1966.

Norton-Taylor, Richard. "1,000 Secret CIA Flights Revealed." *Guardian Unlimited,* April 27, 2006. http://www.guardian.co.uk/usa/story/ 0,,1762212,00.html.

O'Hare, Rita. "The True Face of the IRA." Letter to the editor. *New York Times,* August 12, 2005.

Orwell, George. *Nineteen Eight-Four.* London: Secker and Warburg, 1955.

Palmer, A. Mitchell. "The Case Against the Reds." In *World War I at Home: Readings on American Life, 1914–1920.* New York: Wiley, 1969. http://chnm.gmu.edu/courses/hist409/palmer.html.

Parker, Tom. Interview "The Torture Question: Is Torture Ever Justified? Six Legal Experts Debate the Necessity of Torture in a Post–9/11 World." By Michael Kirk for WGBH and *Frontline,* October 18, 2005. Includes interview with Frank Steele. http://www.pbs.org/ wgbh/pages/frontline/torture/justify/3.html.

Paxton, Robert O. *The Anatomy of Fascism.* New York: Knopf, 2004.

Pontecorvo, Gillo, and Franco Solinas. *The Battle of Algiers.* Criteron Collection edition DVD, 2004. Produced by Saadi Yacef. Italy/ Algeria: Igor Films, 1966.

Post, Jerrold. "Terrorist Psycho-logic: Terrorist Behavior as a Product of

Psychological Factors." In *Origins of Terrorism,* edited by Walter Reich. Washington, DC: Woodrow Wilson Center Press, 1990.

Priest, Dana. "The CIA Holds Terror Suspects in Secret Prisons." *Washington Post,* November 2, 2005, p. A1. http://www.washington post.com/wp-dyn/content/article/2005/11/01/AR20051101 01644.html.

Priest, Dana, and Bradley Graham. "Guantanamo List Details Approved Interrogation Methods." *Washington Post,* June 10, 2004, http://www.washingtonpost.com/wp-dyn/articles/A29742-2004 Jun9.html.

Priest, Dana, and Josh White. "War Helps Recruit Terrorists, Hill Told." *Washington Post,* February 17, 2005. http://www.washington post.com/wp-dyn/articles/A28876-2005Feb16.html.

Ruby, Charles L. "Are Terrorists Mentally Deranged?" *Analyses of Social Issues and Public Policy* (2002).

Rumsfeld, Donald. Memo to Gen. Dick Meyers et al. (October 16, 2003). Quoted in USA Today.com, May 20, 2005. http://www.usa today.com/news/washington/executive/rumsfeld-memo.htm.

———. Speech to the Council on Foreign Relations. Harold Pratt House, New York, New York, February 17, 2006. http://www.defense link.mil/speeches/2006/sp20060217-12574.html.

Sands, Bobby. "Bobby Sands' Diary." *Irish Hunger Strike 1981,* 1981. http://www.irishhungerstrike.com/bobbysdiary.html.

Schmid, A. P. "Academic Consensus Definition." United Nations Office on Drugs and Crime, 1988. http://www.unodc.org/unodc/ terrorism_definitions.html.

———. "Short Legal Definition Proposed by A. P. Schmid to United Nations Crime Branch (1992)." Definitions of Terrorism, United Nations Office on Drugs and Crime. http://www.unodc.org/unodc/ terrorism_definitions.html.

Schwartz, Jerry. "Will the Law Be Silent in a Time of Crisis?" Associated Press, September 30, 2001.

Schwarz, Benjamin. "Books of the Times; Examining Terrorism's Roots and Taking Aim at Its Myths." *New York Times,* June 14, 2003. http://query.nytimes.com/gst/fullpage.html?res=9C07 E6DA1638F937A25755C0A9659C8B63.

Shakur, Assata. Interview. "Assata Shakur Speaks from Exile, Post-modern Maroon in the Ultimate Palenque" (Havana, Cuba, October 24, 2000). By Christian Parenti. *Rap News Network,* October 9, 2003. http://www.rapnews.net/0-202-257463-00.html.

Shane, Scott, and Neil A. Lewis. "At Sept. 11 Trial, Tale of Missteps and Management." *New York Times,* March 31, 2006. http://www.

nytimes.com/2006/03/31/us/nationalspecial3/31plot.html?
pagewanted=2&ei=5090&en=22111b8b2e65cd5e&ex=13014
61200&partner=rssuserland&emc=rss.

Shanker, Thomas. "Pentagon Hones Its Strategy on Terrorism." *New York Times,* February 5, 2006. http://www.nytimes.com/2006/02/05/
politics/05strategy.html?ex=1140498000&en=
47304eb91807bd8c&ei=5070.

Shatz, Adam. "The Battle of Algiers." *The Nation,* June 18, 2001. http:
//www.thenation.com/doc/20010618/shatz.

Simpson, James B. *Simpson's Contemporary Quotations.* Boston: Houghton Mifflin, 1988.

Solinas, Franco. Interview. Liner notes by Piernico Solinas (1972). *The Battle of Algiers.* Criterion Collection edition DVD, 2004. Italy/
Algeria: Igor Films, 1965.

Strentz, Thomas. "A Terrorist Psychosocial Profile: Past and Present." *FBI Law Enforcement Bulletin*, April 1988.

Strobel, Warren P. "Report Documents Major Increase in Terrorist Incidents." Real Cities, Knight Ridder Newspapers, April 20, 2006.
http://www.realcities.com/mld/krwashington/14390584.htm.

Sturcke, James. "General Approved Extreme Interrogation Methods." *Guardian Unlimited,* March 30, 2005. http://www.guardian.co.uk/
Iraq/Story/0,2763,1448282,00.html.

Tzu, Sun. *Art of War.* Translated by Lionel Giles. Mineola, NY: Dover Publications, 2002. http://www.chinapage.com/sunzi-e.html.

Ulph, Stephen. "Al Qaeda's 'Bowing Out' Strategy." *The Jamestown Foundation Global Terrorism Analysis: Terrorism Focus* 2, no. 17 (September 19, 2005). http://jamestown.org/terrorism/news/article.php?
articleid=2369787.

———. "Al Qaeda's Strategy Until 2020." *The Jamestown Foundation Terrorism Focus* 2, no. 6 (March 17, 2005). http://jamestown.org/
terrorism/news/article.php?articleid=2369441.

Villard, Oswald Garrison. *John Brown: A Biography* (1910). Quoted in WGBH, "John Brown: Holy Warrior," *American Experience,* DVD.
Boston: WGBH, 1999. http://www.pbs.org/wgbh/amex/brown/
filmmore/reference/primary/index.html.

Wittgenstein, Ludwig. *Tractatus Logico-Philosophicus.* Translated by C. K. Ogden. London: 1922.

X, Malcolm. *Malcolm X Speaks.* 1965. New York: Grove/Atlantic, April 1990.

Yacef, Saadi. "On the Frontlines of 'The Battle of Algiers.'" Interview by Liza Bear. Indiewire.com, January 12, 2004.

Zawahiri, Ayman al-. *Knights Under the Banner of the Prophet* (Fursan Taht Rayah Al-Nabi). Casablanca: Dar-al-Najaah Al-Jadeedah, 2001.

Other Sources

Al Qaeda Training Manual. Released by the U.S. Department of Justice, December 7, 2001. Originally accessed in May 2005 at http://www.justice.gov/ag/trainingmanual.htm currently available at http://www.fas.org/irp/world/para/manualpart1.html.

Aljazeera.net. "Bin Laden: West Waging a Crusade," April 23, 2006. http://english.aljazeera.net/NR/exeres/FEE6E1E5-DCC0-4E8A-80CF-FFCCA2BC4C2A.htm.

———. "Full Transcript of bin Ladin's Speech," November 1, 2004. http://english.aljazeera.net/NR/exeres/79C6AF22-98FB-4A1C-B21F-2BC36E87F61F.htm.

Anti-Defamation League. Press release. "Conspiracy Theories About Jews and 9/11 Cause Dangerous Mutations in Global Anti-Semitism," September 2, 2003.

Anti-Defamation League Law Enforcement Resource Center. "Hate Symbols." http://www.adl.org/hate_symbols/numbers_14words.asp (accessed January 15, 2006).

BBC News. "French General on Trial Over Algeria," November 26, 2001. http://news.bbc.co.uk/1/hi/world/europe/1675992.stm.

"Bin Laden's Terrorism Bible." *The Smoking Gun.* http://www.thesmokinggun.com/archive/jihadmanual.html.

Black Liberation Army. "The Freedom Fighters 'on the Black Liberation Army.'" A Blast From the Past: Revolutionary Archives From the Black Panther Movement, originally written September 18, 1979. http://thetalkingdrum.com/freedomfighters.html.

Black Panther Party. "Ten Point Platform and Program," October 1966. http://www.itsabouttimebpp.com/home/bpp_program_platform.html.

Bosch, Adriana, and Elizabeth Deane. "Grant, Ulysses S.," *American Experience*, DVD. Boston: WGBH, 2002. http://www.pbs.org/wgbh/amex/grant/index.html.

Cameron, The Honourable Lord. *Disturbances in Northern Ireland: Report of the Commission Appointed by the Governor of Northern Ireland.* Belfast: Her Majesty's Stationary Office, September 1969, http://cain.ulst.ac.uk/hmso/cameron.htm.

Compton, Sir Edmund. *Report of the Enquiry into Allegations Against the Security Forces of Physical Brutality in Northern Ireland Arising out of Events on the 9th August, 1971.* London: Her Majesty's Stationery Office, November 1971.

Constitutional Rights Foundation. "America Responds to Terrorism: The Palmer 'Red Raids.'" http://www.crf-usa.org/terror/PalmerRedRaids.htm.

CNN. "'I Have No Regrets': Law Student Confesses to Killing Rabin." November 5, 1995. http://www.cnn.com/WORLD/9511/rabin/amir/index.html.

————. "List of Guantanamo Detainee Names Released." April 19, 2006. http://www.cnn.com/2006/US/04/19/gitmo.detainees.ap/index.html.

————. "Saddam Gets Perfect Poll Result." October 16, 2002. http://www.cnn.com/2002/WORLD/meast/10/16/iraq.vote/.

————. "Terror Threat to U.S. Called 'Significant.'" April 28, 2005. http://www.cnn.com/2005/US/04/27/terror.report/.

Constitution of the United States, 1789. http://www.archives.gov/national-archives-experience/charters/constitution.html.

Creativity Movement. "Creativity: An Idea Whose Time Has Come." http://www.rahowa.com/creativity12.html.

Declaration of Independence of the United States of America, July 4, 1776. http://www.archives.gov/national-archives-experience/charters/declaration.html.

Federal Bureau of Investigation. *The Ku Klux Klan: Section I, 1865–1944.* July 1957. Available via Freedom of Information Act (FOIA) release at the Memory Hole: http://www.thememoryhole.org/fbi/kkk.htm.

————. "Summary of Foreign Influences on the Weather Underground Organization." August 20, 1976, http://foia.fbi.gov/weather/weath1a.pdf.

First Amendment to the United States Constitution, 1789. http://www.archives.gov/national-archive experience/charters/bill_of_rights.html.

Indiana Historical Research Foundation. "A Brief History of the Original Ku Klux Klan, 1865–1869." http://www.kkklan.com/.

Intelligence and Security Committee. *Report into the London Terrorist Attacks on 7 July 2005.* The Rt. Hon. Paul Murphy, MP, chairman, presented to Parliament by the prime minister by command of Her Majesty. London: Her Majesty's Stationery Office, May 2006. www.cabinetoffice.gov.uk/publications/reports/intelligence/govres_7july.pdf.

Linder, Douglas. "The Shipp Trial Homepage." *Lynching in America: Statistics, Information, Images.* Kansas City: University of Missouri at Kansas City School of Law, 2000. http://www.law.umkc.edu/faculty/projects/ftrials/shipp/lynchstats.html.

Madison, James. "The Same Subject Continued: The Union as a Safeguard Against Domestic Faction and Insurrection," no. 10 of *The Federalist Papers.* New York: J. and A. McLean, 1787.

Merriam-Webster Dictionary Online. www.m-w.com

Missouri Partisan Rangers. *Missouri Partisan Ranger Virtual Museum and Archive.* http://www.rulen.com/partisan/index2.htm.

MSNBC/Associated Press. "FBI, You've Got Mail—Not!" March 21, 2006. http://www.msnbc.msn.com/id/11933204/.

National Commission on Terrorist Attacks. *The 9/11 Commission Report: Final Report of the National Commission on Terrorist Attacks Upon the United States.* New York: Norton, 2004.

Northwestern University Law School, Center on Wrongful Convictions. "A Constituency for the Innocent." January 16, 2005. http:// www.law.northwestern.edu/depts/clinic/wrongful/History.htm.

Organization of African Unity. Convention on the Prevention and Combating of Terrorism. Algiers, July 14, 1999. http://untreaty.un.org/ English/Terrorism.asp.

Organization of the Islamic Conference, Secretary-General. Convention of the Organization of the Islamic Conference on Combating International Terrorism. Ouagadougou, Burkina Faso, July 1, 1999. http://untreaty.un.org/English/Terrorism.asp.

Risen, James and Eric Lichtblau, "Bush Lets U.S. Spy on Callers Without Courts," *New York Times,* December16, 2005, http://www. nytimes.com/2005/12/16/politics/16program.html?ex=1150347 600&en=f8d5ab00bd0fd8fb&ei=5087&excamp=GGGNwiretaps.

The Rome Statute of the International Criminal Court (The Hague: Public Information and Documentation Section, ICC, 1998), http:// www.icc-cpi.int/library/about/officialjournal/Rome_Statute_ 120704-EN.pdf.

SHAC7. "The SHAC7 Conviction: A Blow to Free Speech and Compassionate Activism." *Support the SHAC7,* March 2006. http:// shac7.com.

Sinn Fein/Irish Republican Army. *Green Book.* Belfast, Ireland, 1979. http://www.residentgroups.fsnet.co.uk/greenbook.htm.

———. History of the Conflict. http://sinnfein.ie/history.

Southern Poverty Law Center. "Hate Crime—Report: FBI Hate Crime Statistics Vastly Understate Problem." *Intelligence Report* 120 (Winter 2005). http://www.splcenter.org/intel/intelreport/article.jsp? aid=586

———. "Legal Action: Battling Hate Groups." http://www.splcenter.org/ legal/landmark/hate.jsp

Title 18 U.S.C., Section 1951, The Hobbs Act: Interference with commerce by threats or violence. October 15, 1970.

Title 18 U.S.C., Section 1961. *Racketeer Influenced Corrupt Organizations Act of 1950.*

Title 28 Code of Federal Regulations (CFR), part 0.85 (k)(1). Organiza-
    tion of the Department of Justice, 2003. http://www.dtra.mil/
    press_resources/publications/deskbook/full_text/Code_of_
    Federal_Regulations/28%20CFR%200_85.doc.
United Nations. *Charter of the United Nations.* chap. VII, article 51, 1945.
    http://www.un.org/aboutun/charter/.
————. "Definition of Aggression." General Assembly Resolution 3314
    (XXIX), article 7, December 14, 1974. http://jurist.law.pitt.edu/
    3314.htm.
————. Office of the High Commissioner for Human Rights, "Interna-
    tional Human Rights Instruments." http://www.unhchr.ch/html/
    intlinst.htm.
————. *Universal Declaration of Human Rights.* General Assembly Reso-
    lution 217A(III), December 10, 1948. http://www.un.org/Over-
    view/rights.html.
U.S. Congress. House. *Animal Enterprise Protection Act of 1992,* Public
    Law 102-346. Title 18 U.S.C., Section 43. 102d Cong., 2d sess.
    August 26, 1992.
U.S. Senate, Select Committee to Study Governmental Operations With
    Respect to Intelligence Activities. *Supplementary Detailed Staff Re-
    ports on Intelligence Activities and the Rights of Americans: Book III—
    Final Report.* April 23, 1976. http://www.icdc.com/~paulwolf/
    cointelpro/churchfinalreportIIIa.htm.
Uyghur Human Rights Project. "Uyghurs in Guantanamo." Issues of
    Concern (2006). http://www.uhrp.org/issues/uyghurs_in_
    guantanamo.
Weather Underground (Celia Sojourn, Jeff Jones, Bill Ayers, and
    Bernardine Dohrn). *Prairie Fire: The Politics of Revolutionary Anti-
    Imperialism Political Statement of the Weather Underground.* Oak-
    land, CA: AK Press, 1974.
Zwonitzer, Mark. "Jesse James," *American Experience*, VHS. Boston:
    WGBH, 2006. http://www.pbs.org/wgbh/amex/james/filmmore/
    index.html.

Court Cases

Brown v. Board of Education of Topeka. Supreme Court of the United
    States, 347 U.S. 483 (1954).
Illinois v. Gates. Supreme Court of the United States, 462 U.S. 213 (1983).
Ireland v. the United Kingdom. 5310/71 European Court of Human Rights
    (January 18, 1978), http://www.worldlii.org/eu/cases/ECHR/1978/
    1.html.

Plessy v. Ferguson. Supreme Court of the United States, 163 U.S. 537 (1896).

Scheidler v. National Organization for Women. Supreme Court of the United States, 537 U.S. 393 (2003).

Index

abolitionism, 40–41

abortion clinic protests, 156–157

academic consensus definition of terrorism, 34

accountability: Government Accountability Scale, 89–93; and just government, 91; in law enforcement, 80–81, 130–131; and military response, 177; recommendations for, 199; Terrorist Accountability Scale, 135–136

AEPA. *See* Animal Enterprise Protection Act

affiliation, evolution of, 71

Afghanistan War, 180, 189

ALF. *See* Animal Liberation Front

Algeria, 111–121; splinter groups in, 127

al Hamzi, Nawaf, 67–68

Ali, Muhammad, 104

Allah, Sayf, 107

Alleg, Henri, 117–118

al Mihdhar, Khalid, 67–68

al Qaeda, 188, 196; computer information on, 181; groups affiliated with, vii, 185; organization of, viii–ix, 69; publications by, 38–39; and September 11, 2001, 179–180; training manual of, viii, 95–96

al-Zawahiri, Ayman, 95

American Revolution, 24, 32, 40, 100

anarchists, 56, 58

Anderson, "Bloody Bill," 42

Animal Enterprise Protection Act (AEPA), 154–155

Animal Liberation Front (ALF), 25

anti-Americanism, white supremacist movement and, 11

antiglobalization groups, 25

anti-Semitism: and Nazism, 84; white supremacist movement and, 4, 10, 15–17, 20

armed struggle, versus terrorism, 80

Arthur, Paul, 163–164

Aryan Nations, 6

Asatru, 8

Assassins, viii, 100

Aussaresses, Paul, 118

The Battle of Algiers, 111–112

Beam, Louis, 13–14, 21, 69, 116–117

Berg, Alan, 29

Berkman, Alexander, 56–57

Beyefsky, Anne, 83

big lie, 10–11, 25

Bill of Rights, 80, 90; as counterterrorism tool, 191–199

bin Laden, Osama, 25, 189; characteristics of, 40–41; on terrorism, 38, 44–45; on "them," 101–102

Birth of a Nation, 43, 141

BLA. *See* Black Liberation Army

Black Liberation Army (BLA), 65, 106, 128, 130–131

Black Nationalist COINTELPRO program, 60, 65, 128–130

Black Panther Party, 65, 112, 128; manifesto of, 79

blanket men, 169

Bloody Friday, 168

Bloody Sunday, 167

Booth, John Wilkes, 43

Boston Tea Party, 32

Brachman, Jarret M., 98–99, 183–184, 188

Britain: and IRA, 159–171; London subway attacks, 181–182, 184
Brown, John, 40–41
Brown v. Board of Education of Topeka, 145
Bruders Schweigen, 17–18
Bush, George W., 37, 87, 184
Butler, Richard, 6–7

Cameron Commission, 160–162, 175
case studies: on Irish Republican Army, 159–171; on Ku Klux Klan, 139–148; on National Liberation Front, Algeria, 111–121
Catholic Church, in Ireland, 159–161, 165
Chalmers, David, 145
Chaney, James, 146
Cheney, Dick, 37, 47
Chesimard, Joanne, 106
Christian Identity, 6–7, 20
Church Committee, 60–63, 65, 128–129
civil disobedience, versus crime, 103–104
civilians: just war theory on, 82; terrorism and, 45, 101–102; Yacef on, 115–116
civil liberties: Global War on Terrorism and, 187, 192; in Weimar Germany, 56
civil rights movement: and KKK, 145; and Weather Underground, 105–106
civil suits, as exposure, 147–148
Civil War, and terrorism, 41–43
clandestine lifestyle: difficulties of, 185–186; psychological effects of, 52–53
Clarke, Richard, 101, 184–185
Cleaver, Eldridge, 106, 128, 131–132
coercion, versus extortion, 156–157
COINTELPRO. *See* Counter-intelligence Program
communication, in leaderless resistance strategy, 21–22
communism: COINTELPRO and, 60; Red Scare and, 56–59; and WUO, 64
community purification, 12–13, 15
community service: *The Battle of Algiers* on, 113; KKK and, 143; terrorist groups and, 102–103
Connor, "Bull," 145
conspiracy thinking: government response and, 152–153; militia movement and, 75–76; white supremacist movement and, 4, 10, 15–17
Constitution of United States: Bill of Rights, 80, 90; as counterterrorism

tool, 191–199; on government, 78; KKK and, 140; militia movement and, 24; moral issues and, 40; and torture, 187
cooperating witness (CW), 3–4, 8
counterintelligence methods, 67–68
Counter-intelligence Program (COINTELPRO), ix, 59–60; divisions of, 60; New Left program, 60–64, 66; techniques of, 60, 62–63, 127–130; White Hate program, 65–66, 146–147
counterterrorism: accountability and transparency in, 130–131; *The Battle of Algiers* and, 112; case studies in, 139–148; Constitution and, 191–199; against extremist terrorists, 149–157; against legitimately motivated terrorists, 173–177; techniques of, 117–120
Creativity Movement, 8–9; publications by, 38–39; purification process of, 11–12
Crenshaw, Martha, 97, 119
criminal acts: versus civil disobedience, 103–104; IRA and, 170–171; versus legitimacy, 106; significance of, 103, 114–115; WUO and, 105–106
criminals, treating terrorists as: and definitional issues, 34–35; difficulty with, 37; FBI and, 67; in Ireland, 168–170; versus moral debate, 46–47; terrorist fear of, 19–20, 35, 104–105. *See also* law enforcement
Crowdus, Gary, 115
Cullison, Alan, 181
Cunningham, David, 69–70, 145
CW. *See* cooperating witness
cybernetic balance, 176

Days of Rage, 62
Declaration of Independence, 31–32, 40
Dees, Morris, 147
democracy: and fascism, 87; and social contract, 90
dictatorships, terrorism within, 92–93
dirty protest, 169
disbelief, suspension of, 123–124, 127
dissent, 127
division of labor, white supremacist movement and, 13–15
Dohrn, Bernardine, 64, 96, 105, 125
dollar bill, symbolism of, 76
domestic terrorism, term, 66

dualism, 25, 96; fascism and, 125; Madison on, 199; white supremacist movement and, 20–21
Duffy, Trent, viii
Duke, David, 66

Earth Liberation Front (ELF), 25
Eco, Umberto, 85, 88, 125
economics of terrorism, 109, 181, 183
eco-terror groups, government response to, 65–66
Eisenhower, Dwight D., 179
elections, and just government, 89–90
ELF. *See* Earth Liberation Front
elites, traditional, and fascism, 126
Enforcement Acts, 140, 146
English, Richard, 163–165, 167, 169
environmental issues, white supremacist movement and, 12
European Court of Human Rights, 163, 166
evil. *See* moral debate
exposure: in Algeria, 119; of KKK, 144, 147; NYPD and, 130–131; of state-sponsored terrorists, 134, 186
extortion, versus coercion, 156–157
extremist terrorists: countering, 149–157; definition of, 134; identification of, 135

factionalism, Madison on, 199
FARC. *See* Revolutionary Armed Forces of Colombia
fascism, 84–88; definition of, 84, 86; features of, 85; in governments versus terrorist groups, 125–126; KKK and, 142; as method, 85; mobilizing passions of, 86
Faulkner, Brian, 164
Federal Bureau of Investigation (FBI), 2–3; characteristics of, 51; and civil rights movement, 145–146; critique of, 128–131; on definition of terrorism, 34–35; and Mathews, 17–18; and Palmer raids, 56–59; on WUO, 105. *See also* Counter-intelligence Program
Ferracuti, Franco, 71
Fifth Amendment, 90, 194–195
financial issues: militia movement and, 23; white supremacist movement and, 12
First Amendment, 80, 194–195
Flanagan, Brian, xi, 125
FLN. *See* National Liberation Front

Foch, Ferdinand, 111
followers, characteristics of, 52
force: legitimacy and, 39–40; self-defense and, 77–78
Ford, Henry, 6
Foreign Intelligence Surveillance Act, 197
Forrest, Nathan Bedford, 43, 139–140
Fourteenth Amendment, 90, 140
Fourth Amendment, 90, 194
France, and Algeria, 111–121
Franklin, Benjamin, 40
freedom, Jefferson on, 193
Fricke, Henry Clay, 57
fringe members, 14–15

Gadhafi, Muammar, 173
Gale, William Potter, 6
Gandhi, Mahatma, 173
Geneva Conventions, 192
German, Mike, undercover experiences of, x–xi, 1–26
gerrymandering, in Ireland, 160–161
Global War on Terrorism: analysis of, 179–189; effects of, vii; and legitimacy, 80; precedents of, viii; rationale for, 179; recommendations for, 188–189
Goering, Hermann, 56
Goldman, Emma, 56
good. *See* moral debate
Good Friday Accords, 171
Goodman, Andrew, 146
Gorman, Tommy, 164
Goss, Porter, vii
government: and authority, 143–144; and extremist terrorist groups, 151–154; identity group of, 108–109; legitimacy of, 55, 78; and legitimately motivated terrorist groups, 174–177; responses to terrorism, 55–57, 67–69, 127, 149; terrorist provocation of, 107–110, 119–120, 164
Government Accountability Scale, 89–93, 108
Grant, Ulysses S., 140
Griffith, D. W., 43, 141
groupies, 14
Guantanamo Bay detention facility, 185
guerrilla warfare. *See* terrorism
Gulf War, 45

Hale, Nathan, 75
Hartley, Tom, 168–169
hate crimes: incidence of, 66; laws against, 153–154

Hayden, Michael, 185
Haymarket Square, 57, 62, 103
Heath, Edward, 164
Henry, Patrick, 40
Hitler, Adolf, 1, 7–8, 84; seizure of power by, 55–56
Hobbes, Thomas, 76–77, 90, 198
Hobbs Act, 156
Hoffman, Bruce, 118–119
Holocaust, white supremacist beliefs on, 6
Hoover, J. Edgar, 56, 59, 65, 146
hostile power, covert intelligent agents of, 134–135
House Un-American Activities Hearings, ix
Hudson, Rex, 48, 71; lack of, 48–49
Huntington Life Sciences, 154
Hussein, Saddam, 93, 189

ICC. See International Criminal Court
identity, 87
identity group(s), 109; dynamics of, 100–101; of government, 108–109; identification of, 96–97
ideology: and definitions of terrorism, 31; FBI and, 66; getting beyond, 37–53; law enforcement and, 35; in white supremacist movement, 6–8
immigration: Red Scare and, 56–58; white supremacist movement and, 15
informants, 146; COINTELPRO and, 61; terrorist groups and, 3, 15
innocents: just war theory on, 82; terrorism and, 45, 101–102
intelligence wall, 67–68
International Criminal Court (ICC), 198–199
international law, on legitimacy, 79–80
international terrorism, term, 66
Iraq War, 181, 189; effects of, vii
Irish Republican Army (IRA), 159–171; aid to, 173; splintering of, 173–174
Islamic fundamentalist terrorist groups, 25; in Algeria, 111–121; Global War on Terrorism and, 179–189; on provocation, 107–108; structure of, 101, 184–185
Islamo-fascism, term, ix, 184
Israel, 174–175; and definitions of terrorism, 83

James, Jesse, 42
Jefferson, Thomas, 31, 43, 79, 191–193, 198

Jenkins, Brian, 179
jihadist movement. See Islamic fundamentalist terrorist groups
Jim Crow laws, 141
Joint Terrorism Task Force (JTTF), 3, 22
just government: characteristics of, 89–91; Jefferson on, 193
justice, 124–125
justice system, 130, 195–196; and just government, 90–91; and militia movement, 25; and white supremacist groups, 22–23
just war theory, 81–82

Kaczynski, Ted, 150–151
Kansas, Civil War and, 40–42
Khan, Mohammed Sidique, 182
King, Martin Luther, Jr., 60, 128, 132, 139
Klassen, Ben, 8, 11–12, 17, 43–44
Knights of the White Camelia, 42, 139
Koresh, David, 18
Ku Klux Klan (KKK), 4, 7, 58, 139–148; government response to, 59, 65; history of, 42–43, 139–140; organization of, 70

labor, white supremacist movement and, 12
Lane, David, 12, 16, 29, 32
language: problems with, 47–48, 180; on terrorism, xii, 30–31; of white supremacist movement, 4–5
law. See rule of law
law enforcement: accountability and transparency in, 80–81, 130; and definition of terrorism, 34–35; and legitimately motivated terrorist groups, 176–177; as response to terrorism, 67–69, 72, 149–150, 155, 182, 191–199; and white supremacist groups, 22–23. See also criminals, treating terrorists as
leader(s): characteristics of, 40–41, 51–52; and division of labor, 13
leaderless resistance strategy, viii–ix, 13–15, 69, 117; law enforcement response to, 156; and state-sponsored terrorism, 186
leafleting, 9
Leary, Timothy, 97
left-wing terrorist groups, 25; government response to, 65–66
legitimacy, 55; versus criminality, 106; Global War on Terrorism and, 180,

189; and Government Accountability Scale, 89; term, 78–79; versus torture, 121

legitimately motivated terrorists: countering, 173–177; definition of, 133; identification of, 135

Liberation Tigers of Tamil Eelam (LTTE), 120

Lichtblau, Eric, 197

Lincoln, Abraham, 149

Lindsay, Germaine, 182, 189

Liuzzo, Viola, 146

lone extremist, myth of, 70–72

lone wolf tactics, 69; law enforcement response to, 156

Los Angeles, counterterrorism in, 3, 22

LTTE, 120

Madison, James, 199

Madrid attacks, 183–184

Mafia, government response to, 155–156

Malcolm X, 133

Malvo, Lee Boyd, 150

manifestos, 38–39; and legitimacy, 79; and sympathizers, 103; Unabomber and, 150

Marighella, Carlos, 33, 99–100, 104–105, 109; on provocation, 108, 119–120

Massu, Jacques, 118–119

materialism, white supremacist movement and, 12

Mathews, Robert Jay, 17–18

McCants, William F., 98–99, 183–184, 188

McCartney, Robert, 170

McKinley, William, 57

McVeigh, Timothy, 23, 43, 71; on rationale, 45–46

message of terrorism, viii; audience of, 95–96, 102. See also publications

methods of terrorism, xi, 95–110

Metzger, Tom, 39–40, 55, 69

M'Hidi, Ben, 116–118

Middle East: and definitions of terrorism, 83; September 11, 2001 and, 180–181

militarism, white supremacist movement and, 21

military response, and legitimately motivated terrorist groups, 176–177

militia movement, 23–25, 75, 155

Milius, John, 75

mind-set of terrorists, 76; studies of, 49–51

Mohammed, Khalid Sheikh, 68–69

Moloney, Ed, 170–171

moral debate, getting beyond, 37–53

motives of terrorism, xi, 95–110; and definitions of terrorism, 31; law enforcement and, 35

Moussaoui, Zacarias, 67–68

Mueller, Robert, 70

Muhammad, John, 150

myth of the lone extremist, 70–72

Naji, Abu Bakr, 98–99, 183–184, 188

National Alliance, 7

National Liberation Front (FLN), 96, 111–121

National Security Agency (NSA), 182, 197

National Socialist Movement, 7

Nazi fascism, term, 84

Nazism, definition of, 84

negotations, 174–175

neo-Nazi groups: and moral debate, 46; undercover work in, x–xi, 1–26. See also white supremacist movement

neo-pagan religions, 8

New Left COINTELPRO program, 60–64, 66

Newton, Huey, 106

Nichols, Terry, 71

Nietzsche, Friedrich, 37, 123

9/11 Commission, 67–68

nonidentity group, 101–102

nonviolence, 128, 132, 162, 170

NORAID, 173

Norse mythology, 8

Norwegian Defense Research Establishment (FFI), 183–184

notional, definition of, 129

NSA. See National Security Agency

Odinism, 8

O'Hare, Rita, 171

Oklahoma City bombing, 23

Order, the, 17–18

Organization of African Unity, 80

Organization of Islamic Conference (OIC), 80, 83

organization of terrorist groups, viii–ix, 69–70; The Battle of Algiers on, 113–114, 116

Original IRA, 163

Orwell, George, 85

Palestine, and definitions of terrorism, 83

Palmer, Mitchell, 56–59

Palmer raids, ix, 56, 58
paranoia, in terrorist groups, 15
Parenti, Christian, 106
Parker, Tom, 121, 166
Partisan Rangers, 100
Patriot Act, 68, 197
Paxton, Robert O., 86, 120, 125, 142
phantom cells, 13–14, 117; cooperation among, 21
Pierce, William, 23, 71
PIRA. *See* Provisional Irish Republican Army
Plessy v. Ferguson, 141
political violence, understanding, 75–82
Pontecorvo, Gillo, 111
Post, Jerrold, 49–50, 96, 124, 176
Post, Louis, 57
Pottawatomie Creek massacre, 40–41
powerlessness, and terrorism, 97–98, 126
probable cause, 194
profiling, 114
propaganda, 188
Provisional Irish Republican Army (PIRA), 163–164, 171, 173–176; *Green Book,* 79, 99, 167–168, 185–186; and legitimacy, 106
provocation, 107–110, 119–120, 164; responses to, 177
publications by terrorists, viii, x, 38–39; characteristics of, 39; on leaderless resistance strategy, 13; by white supremacists, 5–6
public face of terrorist groups, problems with, 14–15
punishment, 78
purification process, 11–12; *The Battle of Algiers* on, 113–115; of community, 12–13, 15; WUO and, 96

Quantrill, William, 42

Rabin, Yitzhak, 174
racism, and Nazism, 84
Racketeer Influenced Corrupt Organizations Act (RICO), 156
rationality of terrorists, xi
Real IRA, 171, 174
recruitment: *The Battle of Algiers* on, 112–114; FBI and, 2–3; government responses and, 189; KKK and, 141–142; white supremacist movement and, 9–11
Red Dawn, 75–76
Red Scare, ix, 56–58, 141–142

religious ideology, in white supremacist movement, 6–8
Revolutionary Armed Forces of Colombia (FARC), 173
RICO. *See* Racketeer Influenced Corrupt Organizations Act
right-wing terrorist groups, government response to, 65–66
Risen, James, 197
Rove, Karl, x
Rowe, Gary Thomas, 146
Royal Ulster Constabulary (RUC), 161–162
Ruby, Charles L., 52–53
RUC. *See* Royal Ulster Constabulary
Rudolph, Eric, 72
rule of law, 77, 80, 82, 131, 148; Global War on Terrorism and, 180; recommendations for, 196–199
Rumsfeld, Donald, vii, 196

Sands, Bobby, 159, 169–170
Schiedler v. National Organization for Women, 156
Schmid, A. P., 34
Schwerner, Michael, 146
Second Amendment, 75, 90, 195
secrecy, 130–131; contraindications to, 197
security, issues with, 107–109
self-defense, right of, 77–78
separation phase, 11–12; *The Battle of Algiers* on, 113
September 11, 2001, 179–180; goal of, 180–181; intelligence failures and, 67
serial killers, versus terrorists, 150
SHAC. *See* Stop Huntington Animal Cruelty
Shakur, Assata, 106
Sheeple, 10; definition of, 101; influencing, 106–108; message and, 102
Shelton, Robert, 147
Silent Brotherhood, 17–18
Simmons, William, 141–142
Sinn Fein, 168, 176
Sixth Amendment, 90
skinheads, symbolism of, 11
snitch jacket, 61
social contract, 77, 90, 108
Socialist Worker's Party COINTELPRO program, 60
soldiers, characteristics of, versus terrorists, 52–53
Solinas, Franco, 112, 121

Sons of Liberty, 32, 100
Southern Christian Leadership Conference, 130
Southern Poverty Law Center, 147
Spain, attacks on, 183–184
splinter groups, 127–128, 173–174
state-sponsored terrorist groups: countering, 186–188; definition of, 134
state sponsors of terrorists, 30
Stop Huntington Animal Cruelty (SHAC), 154–155
Strentz, Thomas, 51–52
strikes, in Algeria, 121
student protest groups: COINTELPRO and, 60–64, 66; and Weather Underground, 105–106
Students for a Democratic Society (SDS), 62
suicide terrorists, 104
Sullivan, William, 59
Sun Tzu, 26, 83, 95
supporters, 101; message and, 102
suspension of disbelief, 123–124, 127
Swift, Wesley, 6
sympathizers, 101; influencing, 103; message and, 102

Taliban, 180
Tamil Tigers, 120
Tanweer, Shehzad, 182
terrorism: academic consensus definition of, 34; definitions of, 29–35; domestic versus international, 66–67; effectiveness of, 43–44; history of, viii, ix–x, 40–43; methods of, xi, 95–110; motives of, xi, 31, 35, 95–110; as political problem, 55; strategy in, 98–99; study of, problems in, 48; term, 47–48; types of, 133–136
terrorist(s): characteristics of, xi, 25, 33, 49–53; versus serial killers, 150
Terrorist Accountability Scale, 135–136
terrorist attacks: incidence of, vii; response to, 149
terrorist groups: characteristics of, 19–20; conflict within, 8; splintering of, 127–128, 173–174; structure of, 101–102; violence within, 15
terrorist psycho-logic, 49–51, 96, 124
"them." See nonidentity group; us-and-them mentality
Third Amendment, 90
Thugs, viii, 100
torture, viii; in Algeria, 117–118, 120; effectiveness of, 120–121, 196; in

Global War on Terrorism, 187; in Ireland, 165–166
traditional elites, and fascism, 126
transparency, 155; and just government, 90–91; in law enforcement, 81, 130; recommendations for, 197, 199
trench coat warriors, 22
Troubles, the, 159–171
Truman, Harry S., 144–145

Ulph, Stephen, 107
Ulster Special Constabulary, 161
Ulster Volunteer Force (UVF), 161
Unabomber, 150–151
undercover work, x–xi, 1–26; difficulties of, 3–4; training for, 3–4
understanding: versus dualist thinking, 48; of fascism, 88; FBI and, 66; importance of, viii; of political violence, 75–82; versus sympathy, x, 47
United Kingdom: and IRA, 159–171; London subway attacks, 181–182, 184
United Nations: Charter, 80, 186–187; and criminalization, 35; on definition of terrorism, 33; Educational, Scientific and Cultural Organization, 191; on legitimacy, 79–80; militia movement and, 23; response to September 11, 2001, 180; response to terrorism, 83, 199
United States: and civil rights movement, 145–146; on definition of terrorism, 33; intelligence failures of, 67, 72, 185; and KKK, 139, 143–144; resource allocation by, 182–183; white supremacist movement and, 11
Universal Declaration of Human Rights, 161, 198
urban guerrillas, 33, 100
Ur-fascism, 85, 88
us-and-them mentality, 25, 96; fascism and, 125; Madison on, 199; white supremacist movement and, 20–21
usury, white supremacist movement and, 12
UVF. See Ulster Volunteer Force

van der Lubbe, Marinus, 55
victim bias, and study of terrorism, 48
violence: justifications of, 31–32, 75–82, 124; understanding, 75–82
von Braunhut, Harold, 22, 24
von Hindenburg, Paul, 55

WAR. *See* White Aryan Resistance

War on Terrorism. *See* Global War on Terrorism

Weather Underground Organization (WUO), xi, 63–64, 103, 108; COINTELPRO and, 62; and criminality, 105–106; identity group of, 96–97; organization of, 69; publications by, 38–39, 95

Weaver, Randy, 18

White Aryan Resistance (WAR), 7

White Brotherhood, 42, 139

white supremacist movement, viii–ix; characteristics of, 19–20; civil suits against, 147–148; Civil War and, 42–43; COINTELPRO and, 60, 65–66, 146–147; conflict within, 8; diversity in, 5–8; government response to, 153;

mainstreaming of, 22, 24; and McVeigh, 71; undercover work in, x–xi, 1–26. *See also* Ku Klux Klan

Williams, Ulysses, 130–131

Wilson, Harold, 164

Wittgenstein, Ludwig, 29–30

Wodenism, 8

women and terrorism, in Algeria, 113–114

World Church of the Creator, 8

World War II: IRA and, 160; white supremacist beliefs on, 6

WUO. *See* Weather Underground Organization

Yacef, Saadi, 96–97, 111, 115, 119, 124

Younger, Cole, 42

Zealots, viii, 100

About the Author

MIKE GERMAN served sixteen years as a special agent with the Federal Bureau of Investigation, where he specialized in domestic terrorism and covert operations. His undercover work against white supremacist skinhead groups, and right-wing militias, disrupted planned acts of terrorism and led to multiple criminal convictions. He served as a counterterrorism instructor at the FBI National Academy before leaving the FBI in June of 2004.

German lectures frequently on counterterrorism and intelligence matters, and his commentary has appeared in the *National Law Journal, Washington Post, San Francisco Chronicle,* and *Miami Herald.* German is a contributor to the conference report "Law vs. War: Competing Approaches to Fighting Terrorism," published by the Strategic Studies Institute of the U.S. Army War College. Now living in the Mid-Atlantic region, he is a private consultant, an adjunct professor at the National Defense University, and a Senior Fellow with Globalsecurity.org.

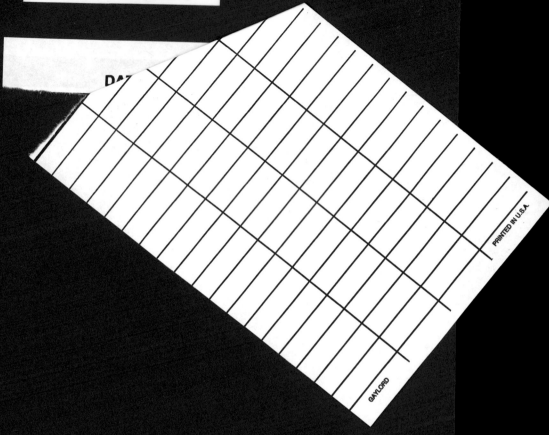